Through Windows of Time

God's Grace in Midst of the Storms

Book 1 of 2   Revised 2023

Charlotte Krigbaum, Tucker, Rowlett

Copyright © 2024

All rights reserved.

All rights reserved. No part of this publication may be reproduced, distributed, or transmitted in any form or by any means, including photocopying, recording, or other electronic or mechanical methods, without the author's prior written permission, except in the case of brief quotations embodied in critical reviews and certain other non-commercial uses permitted by copyright law. For permission requests, please get in touch with the author.

Contents

Dedication i

Acknowledgments ii

Preface 1

Chapter 1 After the Civil War 4

Chapter 2 William and Elmira Krigbaum 6

Chapter 3 The Music Begins 12

Chapter 4 Mattie's Special Day 15

Chapter 5 Typhoid Epidemic 17

Chapter 6 Time for a Change 20

Chapter 7 The Big Move 23

Chapter 8 Finding Shelter for the Winter 26

Chapter 9 An Early Spring 28

Chapter 10 The Krigbaum Farm 31

Chapter 11 Thanksgiving Day 37

Chapter 12 Always Room for One More 40

Chapter 13 Finding Time for Music 42

Chapter 14 Nothing Lasts Forever 46

Chapter 15 The Choctaw Nation 50

Chapter 16 Grandpa's Homestead 54

Chapter 17 The One Room School 56

Chapter 18 Finding a Job 61

Chapter 19 Laura Graham 63

Chapter 20 Wagon Trip to Oklahoma 74

Chapter 21 No Place Like Home 81

Chapter 22 The New Family Life 84

Chapter 23 Papa Talks of War 87

Chapter 24 WW I 90

Chapter 25 The Late Letter 94

Chapter 26 Sharecropping on the Homestead 96

Chapter 27 Snow in the Cabin 100

Chapter 28 Repairing the Roof 107

Chapter 29 Grandpa Becomes Ill 110

Chapter 30 Too Little Room in the Cabin 122

Chapter 31 Precious Memories 126

Chapter 34 Moving the School House 139

Chapter 35 Rose Catherine 143

Chapter 36 Saving for a Home 151

Chapter 37 Redeeming the Homestead 154

Chapter 38 Home at Last 159

Chapter 39 Family Values 163

Chapter 40 The Unforgettable Noon Meal 166

Chapter 41 Pa's Special Mule 168

Chapter 42 The New Horses 170

Chapter 43 Ma and the Horses 173

Chapter 44 War Time Again 175

Chapter 45 The Surprise Wedding 176

Chapter 46 The Little House 179

Chapter 47 Going to Ma's for Breakfast 181

Chapter 48 Learning to Cook with Ma 185

Chapter 49 Precious Years with Ma 188

Chapter 50 Learning as We Grow 191

Chapter 51 The Fire Place 193

Chapter 52 Gathering Wood with Ma 196

Chapter 53 Picking Cotton in Oklahoma 198

Chapter 54 Back to the Little House 200

Chapter 55 Saturday Trip in the Wagon 205

Chapter 56 Ma's Memories of Her Family 212

Chapter 57 The Blacksmith Shop 216

Chapter 59 Daddy's Model T 226

Chapter 60 The Big Change 228

Chapter 61 Life's exciting Moments 230

Chapter 62 Berry Picking with Ma 233

Chapter 63 Quilting Experience 236

Chapter 64 Going to Church in the Snow 239

Chapter 65 Revival at Paint Rock 242

Chapter 66 Summer Evenings with Pa and Ma 245

Chapter 67 Ma's Lessons 249

Chapter 68 The Grandchildren 253

Chapter 69 Thomas Dean 257

Chapter 71 Laura's (Ma's) Birthday 262

Chapter 72 Finding Time for Prayer 265

Chapter 73 The Watch and The Horse 271

Chapter 74 My Little Sister 275

Chapter 75 Dorothea 277

Chapter 76 Nothing Lasts Forever 281

Chapter 77 Growing Up is Hard 283

Chapter 78 Bad Year with The Flu 288

Chapter 79 My Repeated Dream 292

Chapter 80 My First Job 294

Chapter 81 My Unexpected Move 297

Author's Biography Charlotte Krigbaum Tucker Rowlett 304

Dedication

I would like to dedicate this book to the memories of my grandparents, Harley and Laura Krigbaum, who were forever encouraging me to do the best I could with what God had blessed me with, and to my children and grandchildren, my greatest blessings.

Acknowledgments

I would like to add a little note of appreciation to those who helped make this book happen. It took a lot of time and research. Finding dates and pictures was time-consuming but well worth the effort.

I would like to thank artist Donald Smith for allowing me to copy his paintings of my grandparents for the back cover and my son, Christopher, and his wife, Kaleigh, for the use of their cabin for the front cover.

Also, I appreciate my children, grandchildren, and nephews for making the picture possible and for allowing me the time to write.

I would like to thank my cousin, Carolyn, and My cousin's wife, Helen, for helping me find pictures that were of the best quality possible, considering they were old pictures. And, my cousins James Fitzjurls and Louis Whitson and others for sharing their stories.

My Aunt Clossie had allowed me to go through her pictures and take any that I thought would help. I wish she had lived to read the book because she encouraged me a lot.

Last but not least, I want to thank my son, Kevin Tucker, for coming up with a title. He said, "How about Through Windows of Time?" It was perfect.

Preface

This is an expansion of my first book that was based on the lives and stories of my grandparents, Harley and Laura Krigbaum, better known as Pa and Ma by many who knew them, and how they made such a difference in our lives over the years. Much of this is the same, but much is added. It would take several books to expound on the many ways that God has blessed and carried our families through the many trials. One book would not hold what I feel in my heart that I should write. This will be one of two, I hope.

I have decided that I left out too much in what I thought was my only book about my family, the first book, Through Windows of Time. Therefore, I am rewriting it and correcting anything I find incorrect. It seems there is so much more I wanted to write about the great blessings the Lord has given us over the years. He deserves to be praised.

A big part of my desire to publish this book is because I lived during the time change of going from wagons and teams of horses to riding in motor vehicles. It seemed to me there was something lost in that transition.

Harley thought that it seemed like we were becoming a fast-paced world going nowhere sometimes. Time with God and family was cut short in many cases. Going to town or to visit was no longer a leisurely drive enjoying God's creation; it became, hurry up and get there.

Their simple life was a blessing to many. Living most of their lives in and around the backwoods of Logan County, near Paris, Arkansas, Harley and Laura married in 1911 and eventually lived on an eighty-acre tract of land, originally homesteaded by Harley's grandfather, Phylander Storts.

Harley, his siblings, aunts, uncles, and cousins had spent much of their childhood on that farm. Harley and Laura were both born in 1893, about twenty-eight years after the Civil War.

The South especially still felt the effects of the war. Harley's grandparents and his family had come to Arkansas from Ohio and homesteaded the farmland.

They built a house and farmed the land for several years. He was later forced to give up his homestead because he met with extremely hard times and could not pay their taxes.

Phylander and his wife, Lucy, knew they must set an example for their children by teaching them that life is sometimes what you make it. They must take the hard times and make the best of them. God would take care of them, and good times would come again.

Harley hoped to eventually buy back the homestead; meanwhile, they needed a place to live and sharecropped for several years while working wherever he could find work, often in cotton fields or farm work. Occasionally, he worked at a factory. However, he had to travel so far to and from work that it made more sense to make less money.

Harley found that if there was a need or a job opening, he could learn to do about anything. He eventually built a blacksmith shop on his farm that proved to be almost essential, bringing work to him, plus he could repair his own machinery and harnesses. It made money and saved time.

Ma worked right along with Pa in the fields when she could, although, as the years passed, much of her time would be spent caring for their small children.

Home was a special word and a special place. They never seemed to venture far away for any length of time. Traveling to cotton fields and visiting family in Oklahoma was one of their few trips by covered wagon.

After staying for a few weeks, they returned home and tried to make the best life they could for their children, farming the land with mules or horses. Harley preferred them to the oxen he had used a few times as a boy. The oxen were strong but not very smart, as he saw it. The horses seemed to understand what he wanted them to do. He said they had better horse sense. The mules were more stubborn but could handle the pull of a plow or wagon better. Ma and Pa raised a large family and did whatever it took to provide for them. Life was sometimes hard, but they were a family who helped each other and their neighbors.

The children learned early in life that working together made lighter work for everyone; no matter the tragedy or total devastation, Pa and Ma would never give up. I often heard the words, "Where there is a will, there is a way," or "You haven't failed until you have quit trying." One way they learned to cope with the hard times was to enjoy the good times and depend on the Good Lord to supply what they could not.

An afternoon of music was the highlight of many days. Pa played his fiddle as if it was his close companion. Others played guitars or whatever was available; if they didn't have an instrument to play, often they would make one out of anything they could find. Country or gospel music was all we ever heard.

Ma didn't play an instrument; however, she listened to the music and encouraged the children to learn to play or sing if they could. Between the songs, there might be a story that was just as entertaining, funny, or maybe sad. Ma and Pa could keep us spellbound and wanting more by just talking about their lives over the years.

Much of this book is written about the stories they told us as a form of entertainment or education. Most of it is based on only sketches of what I can remember because I didn't write their stories down as I was growing up, thinking I would never forget them.

Maybe because we knew they were true, to the best of their knowledge, or maybe because we didn't have a television.

Either way, I will always be grateful for my many hours and days with them. They lived with the idea that it was their responsibility to teach the young ones from an early age to be productive citizens. It was never noted that we need to make a lot of money. Everyone had their place and should be the best they could be with whatever talents God had given them. He would provide as He saw the need.

I could listen to them for hours, thinking how blessed we were to have a family so rich yet without a lot of money. An evening with Ma and Pa was better than a good movie.

I need to try to get all the actual dates and events as correct as possible. It still has a lot of stories that are just from my own imagination. Actually, I remember lots of stories. Some of the details are a little sketchy, so, when I couldn't remember, I opened my heart and wrote whatever came to my mind, anxious to find what was on the next page. Not all the stories are absolute facts. The fact is that the Good Lord brought them through so many storms that I feel the need to share their stories to the best of my ability, with God's help and guidance.

Because of the times and many changes in lifestyles, I would at least want my children and grandchildren to know that life truly is sometimes what we make it.

Though these are blessings when used correctly, and I am thankful for them, there is still more to life than TV, computers, cell phones, and video games.

We are at God's mercy. Our lives may change daily, but God is the same yesterday, today, and forever.

Chapter 1
After the Civil War

The Civil War was over, yet those who had survived the fighting found that life presented still more challenges. Many had little or no money or the supplies they needed, especially in the south. It would take a long time to rebuild a country that had been so overwhelmed by such grief, pain, and destruction.

Many had family on both sides and were just glad it had come to an end. Others couldn't seem to allow it to end. Some wondered if they could ever bridge the gap between the states.

Phylander Storts, my great-great-grandpa, and his twin brother Leander were born on April 21, 1833, in Ohio, USA. Their parents, John and Isabella Hall Storts, had come to the United States in the early 1800s, where they met and married.

John Storts was born in Germany in 1791 and was 74 years old at the end of the war; Isabella Hall Storts was born in Ireland in 1792 to Mr. and Mrs. Moses Hall.

John and Isabella had eight children; Emily, born in 1816; Jane in 1817; David in 1819; Moses in 1826; Martha in 1827; Margaret in 1830; Leander and Phylander in 1833.

My great-great-grandma, Lucy Place Storts, was also born in Ohio in 1834. Her parents were Joseph Place and Sarah Bridges Place, both lifetime residents of Ohio.

Phylander and Lucy married on July 7, 1851. About a year and a half later, their first child, Elmira, was born in 1852, and then Sara Jane in 1854; Jamie Temperance in 1859; Joseph Phylander, 1860; and Emily (Emeline) in 1863.

Their lives had been changed by a war between the states. Phylander didn't want to fight in a war with his own countrymen but registered for the draft.

He was drafted into the army, 18th regiment, on September 27, 1864, leaving Lucy alone to carry the heavy load of raising their five children while expecting another. He hated to leave his family, who needed him, but more than that, he hated the thought of the war-torn country, praying it would not be divided forever.

After the war ended in 1865, he was discharged as a private, with thoughts of his family and the much obliteration the country had endured in both the North and the South.

Their son, John, was born while he was away in 1865. This was one of many families who lived through a civil war that brought much sadness to many and tore homes apart. It was said that the North won, but it was a bitter victory, as he saw it. It saddened him to know that so many lives were lost on both sides.

Phylander and Lucy later had other children: Isabella in 1868; David (Dave), 1870; Moses Hall was born March 28, 1873; Mattie in 1874; Leander in 1875; and Martha in 1878.

John Storts passed away in 1872 at 81 years, leaving his wife, Isabella, to the care of her children and grandchildren, who assisted her when they saw the need.

Lucy had lots of help with four-year-old Isabella and two-year-old Dave. She would miss Elmira when she married but hoped she would be happy.

Chapter 2
William and Elmira Krigbaum

That same year, 1872, Elmira Storts married William Monroe Krigbaum, a boatman on the Ohio River. Her parents would have a baby boy, Moses, in March of the next year. "I know she needs the help; I really hate to leave her. It seems to take all of us to watch the two boys sometimes," she said to William.

He worked with his father, traveling from port to port. He was glad to be able to work with him, but he would hate to leave his wife alone for so long, so when he and Elmira married, they moved close to her parents because he could be gone for days, maybe even weeks, at any given time. "This will help all of us. We can help each other."

Her little sister, Mattie, was born about a year and a half later, in 1874. Elmira enjoyed helping her mother with Mattie, thinking of the time when she and William would have a baby of their own. She was hoping William would be able to stay home more first.

Then, in July 1875, their first son, Thurman Delson, was born. William was sometimes gone for weeks on the riverboat; however, when it was time for their new baby, he made a point to let someone else go in his place so he could be sure to be home when his baby was born.

He had just finished a new crib because Lucy still needed hers. She and Phylander also had a son born that year; His name was Leander. They could grow up like brothers.

They enjoyed sharing the care of their three young children. Elmira loved Mattie as much as her own. "I hope to have a little girl someday. Maybe our next baby will be just like Mattie with beautiful long hair to braid." Mattie looked up and smiled as Elmira was brushing her long, curly red hair.

"She's a pretty girl. That's for sure, "Grandma Isabella said as she looked up from her knitting, proud of her pretty red hair. It was much like her own when she was young. "Could be, but you better let The Lord decide that. He knows what you really need."

A year later, Elmira gave birth to another son. She was totally pleased with little Gideon and thankful that her mother and grandmother were close by.

Later that year, Grandma Isabella became rather feeble and could not really be left to care for herself for long periods of time, and it seemed she could not regain her strength; soon, she moved in with Phylander and Lucy.

Mattie had always been a good baby, mild-tempered, and was company for her grandma while the others worked. Grandma could call for help if Mattie got into something she shouldn't. But usually, she could just talk to her and get her to obey. The boys were a bit too much for her with her failing health. The family took turns caring for her.

She began to feel as if she was in the way wherever she was; although she knew her children and grandchildren loved her, God had other plans for her. Grandma Isabella Storts passed away a few months after Gideon was born, in 1876, at age 84.

The Storts family's lives seemed somewhat gloomy, with both of them gone. Mattie especially missed Grandma. She was only three and didn't understand why she had gone.

Arkansas became a state in 1836. William had heard lots of talk about it on his riverboat journeys. For many years, it had belonged to Indians; it had been a part of the Louisiana Purchase, Missouri Territory, and Arkansas Territory. Finally, it had become a state.

This piece of land in the middle of the United States was wanted by many, owned by several, and still attracted the attention of many more, having much to offer in natural resources and beauty; many seemed to want a part of it.

William began to think about maybe going there sometime to see what it was like. Working on the Ohio River all the time, he saw no reason why he couldn't go down to Arkansas.

He and his father, Andrew Jackson Krigbaum, talked about Arkansas and wondered what the land and weather might be like. "I might just go check it out someday, Papa. No train goes near there yet. But there is a river that runs through it."

"It may still be a rough country, Son. Remember, the war has left many battle scars. Don't know if I'd want to take the babies yet."

"Well, it's just a thought, but I may check into the ship and maybe train routes. I wonder how close the nearest railroad runs."

He thought of the many adventures and stories of his family that had been passed down through the years and loved to study their history in the back of the family Bible. He would read his family records, trying to remember as much as he could. "Papa, can I take this home with me? I'd like to share this with Elmira. We have a family Bible that I would like to record some of this in."

"Of course, your mama already mentioned it to me just a few weeks ago; I guess she thought I would give it to you." He sat at the table and continued reading for several minutes before leaving.

His grandfather, William Harley Krigbaum, was born in Allegany County, Ohio, in 1802. He was the oldest of eight children of Johann Peter and Mary McBride Krigbaum.

Grandfather William married Barbara Waxler, born on February 29, 1820, in Hampshire County, Virginia. They had five boys and three girls; Johann Peter, born in 1820; Richard in 1822; Conrad in 1826; Andrew Jackson in 1827; Maria in 1829; Eleanor in 1831; Catherine in 1832; and James Bird in 1835.

Barbara's parents were Michael and Sarah Waxler. She had four brothers and three sisters. Barbara died in 1861.

William married Mary Coalman in 1863. They had one child, Isabelle, born in 1864.

He sat thinking about all the generations and where they had come from. The year of their wedding was a bittersweet year for both Elmira and William. She lost her grandpa, John Storts, and his grandfather, William Krigbaum, died at age 69; both died in Muskingum County, Ohio.

As they began their lives together, Elmira joined him in reading the history of his family in the big Bible. They recorded their wedding date and then began to add a history of both families from the information in their parents' Bibles. Elmira was fascinated by the many stories William could tell them about his adventurous family. Some of his family had come to the new country on the May- Flower. Grandfather William's great-great-grandfather, Conrad Krigbaum, had been an immigrant from Holland in the early 1600s.

His father, Andrew Jackson Krigbaum, was born on March 15, 1827, in Cumberland, Maryland, and married Margaret Dickerson, who was born on April 21, 1828. In 1849, he moved to Beverly, Ohio, where he became a riverboat captain and lock tender on the Ohio River. William was thankful to be able to work there with his father.

Their children were Gideon, born July 21, 1849; William Monroe, born December of 1850; Emanuel, born 1855; a sister born in 1857. Sadly, she died in her teens; Conrad was born on January 18, 1862.

When William's father would come to visit, Elmira would listen intently as he told story after story. She noticed that William said very little but loved the time with his father.

The Krigbaum family had been one of many whose lives had been forever changed by the War Between the States. It had claimed the lives of some of their family members and had injured others. William and Gideon had been left to take care of things while their father was away at war as they had prayed earnestly for his return but feared that he would not and for the war to come to an end. It seemed to go on forever!

There was much relief when he came home at the end of the war in 1865, but sadness because not all of their family would be returning. His heart went out to those whose whole world was war-torn.

The war had taken some of them south, and they had seen the splendor in spite of the devastation; the land was beautiful, yet much different from Ohio.

Andrew mentioned that as long as the country remained divided, there would be a chance of another war. "I hope it will eventually be over in the minds of everyone."

William thought about what he had said and wondered if it might help to bridge the gap by combining the lives of their families. As he pondered these things, the more he thought about moving his family south. Of course, it would be years before he could save enough money for a move such as that, so he kept his thoughts to himself.

In 1878, to everyone's amazement, Elmira and Lucy both had babies in the same year again. This time, they were both girls. Elmira was so happy to have a girl that she named her Lucy, after her mother. Lucy named her baby Martha. They would grow up almost like sisters.

Mattie and Isabella were glad to have a little sister and niece. Mattie was almost five years old and thought she was old enough to help care for both of them. "This is almost like the second set of twins," Lucy commented. There were only a few months difference in their ages.

All of their lives were changing, as were the times. In the year 1880, Andrew and Margaret Jackson decided it was time for a change for them. He was ready to get off the river. His wife was not in the best of health, and he didn't like leaving her for so long while he was on the river.

The train went all the way to the west coast. She had family there already. Their children all had lives of their own, so they began to tie up loose ends in Ohio, boarded a train to Oregon, and settled near Estacada, southeast of Portland. Some of their family went with them and maybe would go on to California later. William hated to see his family go but was glad his Mama would not be alone so much.

This brought the thought of moving fresh in William's mind. They could visit by train and post letters. Still, he would miss them, especially he would miss working with his father. By 1884, William and Elmira had four children; Thurman was 9, Gideon was 8, and Lucy was 4. Their third son, John Sheridan, was born on May 19 of that year.

"You know, Elmira, we're not getting any younger, and our family is not getting any smaller. I've been thinking about maybe moving south. What do you think about moving to Arkansas? Your family might even want to go with us."

"I don't see that as a possibility, and I sure would hate to leave them when they have always been right here when we needed them. Besides, we can't travel with a baby so young."

"What if I go alone on one of my voyages and check it out, maybe even find us a place to live, and then come back for you and the children? We don't have to move right away, maybe in a few years, but I would like to at least see what it's like. There is a river that runs through it. We might find a small town south of it.

People there are from everywhere. More people are moving to Arkansas every year. Our forefathers fought to free this country, and we should be thankful for it."

His family had fought with the North. He really hoped the war was over in the minds of the people in the South. He would be just as proud to be from Arkansas!

"You do what you think is best, William. I will stay here and look after Mama and Papa, and we all will watch after the kids. It would devastate them to be separated! They are like siblings, you know! I don't know if I could leave them at all, especially Mattie. Her heart was broken when Grandma died. I could hardly stand to watch her. She is ten now and needs me as much as I need her." They sat silently for a while.

"I love your family, William, but sometimes your sense of adventure is a bit much for me. The mother in me just wants to keep my children at home and safe! You can see what it is like if you wish. You might not even like it." She stormed off to the kitchen and started wiping a table that was already clean.

He let the conversation drop and went on with his work, trying to put the thought of moving out of his mind, knowing Elmira was right about separating the children.

He would be leaving on the riverboat in a few days, so he went out to visit with the boys without mentioning anything about a move, wanting to spend quality time with his family, not argue with them. He wouldn't want to put friction between them.

Chapter 3
The Music Begins

Occasionally, William would find a real treat on his travels. One trip he made was a surprise to him. He normally didn't purchase things for himself, but this was an exception.

He ran into an elderly man from Germany who made and repaired fiddles. William's grandfather had taught him to play several songs years before. He had forgotten about it and wasn't even sure where his grandpa's fiddle had gone. Mr. Storts had shown the boys how to play a little, but he really couldn't tell how interested they were. His heart sort of leaped out at this one, thinking that if they had one of their own, maybe they would play.

The man noticed him looking at it and then walking away. "Sir, I couldn't help but notice. Your eyes tell me that you have the heart of a musician. "Do you play?" He lifted the fiddle in one hand and the bow in the other. "You're welcome to play this one."

William stopped and walked over to the man. "Not really; I was thinking that my children might like to learn. I would just be wasting your time, Sir. I only play a little. My Grandfather played when I was a child. I just remember listening to him. It's been a long time. Besides, I'm not really prepared to purchase one."

"Here, just try this one." He handed him an old fiddle that he had just set up. I don't have much in it. I really have always liked restoring them more than playing. If you play, go ahead; play us a tune. Then we'll talk about it."

William couldn't resist any longer; he played songs that brought back such fond memories of his grandpa and a real desire to play again. He just had to have a fiddle! "How much are you asking for it?"

"Well, now, if you'll play a few more tunes for me, I'll let you have it for twenty dollars, and I'll throw in the case and rosin. I can't play like I used to, but I love to listen. It's old but not bad at all if I know anything about them."

"My wife wouldn't know what to think. But all children need to grow up with music. I have boys old enough to play now. I think I might take you up on that offer, Sir. What would you like to hear? Mind you, I'm sort of limited as to what I can play. It's been years.

William and his shipmates stayed there for a while, and the man picked up a guitar nearby and played with him. That was the first time in his adult life that he had played music with anyone. One of his buddies said, "Willie, this is a lot of fun, but we don't get paid to have fun. Don't you think we had better get back to the ship?"

"Yes, I guess I just lost track of time. I haven't had this much fun in many years. I do want my children to have a chance to play if they want to. Thank you, Mr." he added as he handed him twenty dollars that he had tucked away for expenses. He had tried not to spend it so he could take it back home to his family. "This is about as important as anything I can think of for my children."

"You're welcome. So glad you came along. I just happen to have a guitar that needs a little work; I'll give it to you if you think your kids could use it. Mine have all moved on to better instruments or lost interest. It's served its purpose here. The strings are still playable, maybe, but you will need to replace them soon. Here is a set that I was going to put on when I got it repaired."

"Yes, thank you so much! My boys have rhythm in their bones, always tapping on something! I'm not accustomed to taking charity. But I sure would love to get a guitar for them. I don't know how to repay you with no more money to spare. I am short as it is. My wife has often told me I should carry more cash in case I need it. I hate to take some that they might need. It's my job to provide."

"You don't owe me anything. It is just sitting here; it wasn't worth much when it was new, and I would rather spend my time on fiddles. I just hated to throw it away."

"Ok, thank you again." William took both instruments and was on his way. It just happened that they were on their way home at the time, so he wouldn't have to worry so much about keeping them safe for so long on the boat.

As the boat landed near their home, William grabbed the instruments and started walking toward his house.

The children were always glad to see him. Thurman was outside playing when he arrived. "Papa! What do you have?"

"Well, open one of them up, and let's see what you think. You have a choice: a guitar or fiddle, maybe even both."

Thurman took the guitar, and Papa carried the fiddle into the house and handed it to Gideon. John Sheridan was a little small for either of them, but it wouldn't be long before he would be trying to play.

William began to make a few minor adjustments to the keys and bridge of the guitar. He had to glue the sides and back in one place and then put the new strings on. He began to teach them to play guitar chords so either of them could play along with him on the fiddle.

Thurman learned fast, and from then on, it was music every evening that Papa was home. Phylander was more excited than the boys. "I don't know much about the guitar, but my Irish blood brings out the love for the fiddle, I guess. I'll be glad to work with them when you are gone. Of all things, you brought home a fiddle!"

William replied, "I know they play a little on your instruments, but I thought if they had one of their own, they might be more interested."

Phylander and Lucy often brought their children over to listen or to play with them if they wanted to. Some of the older ones had guitars, and Grandpa had a fiddle. He would help any of them as he could. They practiced every day; Gideon would often take out the fiddle and try to play a tune. Before long, they were playing together when Papa was away.

The instruments were to be treated with care but were never put out of reach, even while Papa was gone. "Let them play any time they have the opportunity, as long as they don't neglect their chores. Music can help them in many ways," he said to Elmira. "If they have the talent, it will soon be visible. I want them to have a chance if they're interested."

From then on, there was no question as to what they would do when Papa came home from his job. In a few years, Sheridan was determined he could play a little on the fiddle; his arms were way too short, but Grandpa Storts said, "Where there is a will, there is a way. I believe he has music in his blood, too."

Chapter 4
Mattie's Special Day

Mattie was eleven years old in 1885. Elmira wanted to do something special for her. She was almost a teenager and would be grown soon, so she made her a pretty new dress and gave her a new ribbon for her hair. "You are growing up too fast, little sister! This is because you help Mama and me so much with the babies. I sure do love you! I don't know what we would do without you!"

"I love you too, Elmira. I'm sure you would manage. See what Mama and Papa gave me?" She had on a new pair of shoes. "I don't know how they knew that my old ones were hurting my feet. I didn't tell them. Honest, I didn't!"

"They are beautiful, Mattie! You know that mothers always know when their children are hurting or have a need. It is our job. And look, they match your new dress." She held it up against Mattie and then hugged her. They both smiled.

"I'm sure glad tomorrow's Sunday so I can wear my new dress. Mama said I could wear my shoes anytime; oh, by the way, she said to tell you she was making supper for you all tonight. I think we have a cake. She wouldn't let me help her."

They ate supper together that evening at the Storts' house. The table was set for the adults at the big table and the smaller one for the children. Mattie usually sat with them to help them.

"Not this time, Mattie, you sit with us. You're too big for that table now." Mama put her arm around her and pointed to her regular seat at the table. "I do appreciate the help you always are with the babies. This is your special day."

Sara Jane brought out a cake and sat it in front of Mattie. Then, reaching into her apron pocket, she handed her a small package wrapped in brown paper. "Happy birthday, little Sister; I made it myself, just for you." It was a new apron with her name embroidered on the pocket. They all sang Happy Birthday to her, and the cake was cut and served.

"Thank you, everyone. This is the best birthday ever!" It was a joyous occasion just being together. William was home, which made the evening seem complete. Mattie loved him also. She was there most of the time when he came home. He treated her as one of his own. If he brought treats of any kind, he made sure they had enough to share with all of them.

The next day, Mattie was up early and ready for church before breakfast. "Mama, thank you for my new shoes! They feel great!"

"You are growing so fast; I'm afraid we let you outgrow your old ones. You took good care of them so we can put them up and save them for Martha. It won't be long before she can wear them."

Life went on as usual for several months. William didn't say anything else about moving, but it was ever on his mind. He watched his wife and children with the Storts family and thought, "How could I ever ask them to separate? I just don't have the heart. Mattie and Elmira are especially close." He resolved himself to the fact that they had a good life there. The war was not even mentioned anymore. He was very thankful for his family and the musical instruments. "What are the chances of finding two instruments at one time?" The boys were getting better all the time.

Changing schools would be a hard thing for them also. Their grades were fairly good. He would not want to cause them to get behind. It was enough that he took the two with him from time to time on the river. They had to study extra hard to catch up then. So, he decided not to mention it again.

Chapter 5
Typhoid Epidemic

One day, when Mattie came home from school, she had a high fever and soon became very ill. William went for the doctor, who informed him that other similar cases had been reported nearby. He said that it appeared to be typhoid.

"I'll do what I can; time will tell. I'll be back in the morning. Just give her this medicine every four hours and do what you can to keep her fever as low as possible, and give as much liquid as you can get her to drink; even if she can't keep it down, it should help cool her fever a little. It is robbing her body of all liquids."

Trying to keep her fever down was hopeless, yet Lucy kept washing her down with cool water and treating her as the doctor had ordered while trying to get her to take a drink of water every few minutes. Between the fever and the vomiting, Mattie was very ill.

Lucy prayed and stayed awake day and night, trying to get the fever to break. She would not leave her side, only taking short naps due to exhaustion, leaning on her bed while Mattie was sleeping. Often, she prayed, but her faith was getting weak. "Why, Lord? Why my baby? Please don't take her from us!"

Elmira and Isabella tried to give Mama a break and sit with her. They were worried about their mother, also. They watched after the other children. Mama didn't want Elmira to get too close for fear it might be dangerous for her unborn baby. "Just try to watch after the little ones and keep a safe distance from the fever."

Elmira was torn between her unborn baby and a sister she loved so dearly. "Mama, she needs me, and you need a break!" At times, Mattie was so sick that she didn't know or care who was there. When she felt a little better, she asked about Elmira and the kids; however, Mama was the one she needed the most, so she never complained.

The sadness and worry in the house were overwhelming. Phylander tried to comfort Lucy, but he was devastated. Fear became a factor. Mattie's fever just seemed to escalate, no matter what anyone did. The doctor had come every morning and evening and had done all that he could do, giving her what medicine he could with instructions to keep cooling her with water. "If she lives, it should run its course in a short while."

A week or so should tell the outcome. If we can keep her alive for that long, the rest will just be recovery time. I wish I could give you more hope. I am afraid it is out of my hands, but God is a loving God. He will have the final say."

"This is not the only case of typhoid in the area. Research is being done to find the cause. Someone will be by soon to ask questions as to where Mattie could have picked it up. It won't help her, but it might prevent others from getting sick."

He left and came back as often as he could. He had more and more patients with the same symptoms. They decided to boil all drinking water, and other precautions were taken by all families nearby. The source of the sickness was unknown.

A few days later, Mattie passed away from typhoid fever at the very young age of eleven years. She was buried next to her grandma and Grandpa Storts in Ohio.

The sadness felt in both houses was like none they had ever experienced. "How do we go on without her? She is the one that gave life to both families," Elmira cried.

About the time she or Lucy would try to deal with the pain of losing her, one of their babies would cry for her, "Mattie! Where is Mattie? I want Mattie to read to me or play with me." Their lives had no more meaning, only despair.

Elmira was not feeling well as the time of her delivery drew nearer. "How can we do this without Mattie? She loved the babies so much! I still can't believe she is gone! I didn't realize how much difference she made in all of our lives."

Some things just will not wait. The Krigbaum baby was ready whether they were or not. It gave them something else to focus on for a little while; on March 31, 1885, baby Sarah was born. Elmira wanted to name her after Mattie, but the pain was too great. No one could take Mattie's place in her heart. It was too soon even for a name. "Mattie would love you, Sarah."

Instead of being comforted by the new baby, Elmira was saddened even more, thinking of how Mattie loved babies and had wanted Elmira to have a little girl. She began to cry again.

William tried to comfort her, but the more he tried, the worse she felt. "It will be ok. I think you and your mother need to focus on the other children more. They love you, too, and it would not hurt if you told the boys that they could play their instruments again. They try so hard not to disturb you."

"I take care of our children, and with you gone for weeks! How could you say otherwise?"

"I know you're taking care of them, but your grieving heart is not fair to them or you. They lost her, too! They try to help, but they don't know what to do! Maybe you and your mother should talk this thing out. It is clear that I'm getting nowhere."

"My little sister is gone. Why was it not me? She was so good to all of us. I can't stand to think about her, yet I can't get her off my mind, even for a minute! Having Sarah just makes me miss her even more. Sometimes, I think I see her looking over into her crib."

"You have to try to get some control of your feelings, Elmira. She's not coming back! Think of your mother. She needs you now more than ever. The children need you both." They sat quietly for a while. She knew he was right.

"I would like to take the two older boys with me this week. It should be a short run. They need to think about something else for a while. Do you think you could manage without them for a few days?"

"They have wanted to go with you more often. We'll manage. It's not fair that they get left behind. They're growing into manhood and need time with their father."

"They have saved every penny they've earned. I think they hope to buy another instrument. They could have worse hobbies." William looked up at her; she almost smiled.

Elmira had gone to check on Baby Sarah when she heard a knock on the kitchen door. As she opened the door, she said, "Sara Jane, it is good to see you! Your namesake's been waiting for you! I'm so glad you came! Have you seen Mama?"

"Not yet; I had to see that baby you called Sarah; she must be special! I thought Mama might be over here."

"She doesn't come as often as she used to. We don't do anything like we used to. I had no idea that Mattie was such a part of everything we did." She paused. "How are you?"

"I'm fine. I know it is hard. I miss her too, and I was away most of the time she was growing up. I can't imagine what you and Mama must be going through. "They talked for a while as Sara Jane played with the baby, and then she went on to visit her mother.

Chapter 6
Time for a Change

In November of the year, Mattie passed away, and William's mother, Margaret Dickerson Krigbaum, also died in Oregon. William hadn't seen her since they moved from Ohio. He had planned a trip in a few weeks; however, Mattie's illness had changed everything.

Elmira tried to comfort him as best that she could. "I'm sorry you didn't get to see her as you had planned. She wasn't alone; several of your family were with her. She knew you loved her."

"I know; I am thankful for that, but I really miss them. I spent most of my life with them, even working with Papa for years. We did everything together! I meant to find a way to go see them this summer! I knew she wasn't well, but I can't believe she's gone!"

The sadness in both homes was more than enough to make them all say things they didn't mean to each other. It was lonely and quiet, or someone was angry about something.

Another year went by as Phylander began to think more about moving, maybe even to Arkansas. William had talked about it. He had to do something to give them a reason to live again. The babies were being loved and cared for, but the joy was gone from every part of their lives. One couldn't help the other, as was their custom.

Phylander thought to himself. "I feel like an empty vessel. How can I help my family? Lord, only you can ease the pain of this kind."

Everywhere they went in either house, Mattie was there. If they went to church, she was there, too. He knew they didn't want to forget her, but they couldn't bring her back, either. The living needed to go on living. The children were too quiet!

Realizing that many from the South had major hard feelings for those in the North, however, they hated the war as much as he did, he agreed with William that someone needed to make an effort to bridge the horrific gap the war had caused.

He had seen the war first-hand, and it wasn't pretty on either side. The pain in his family was just as bad. He felt as if the whole country just needed a new start. Broken hearts don't mend themselves.

In Arkansas, it wasn't just people from the South. They came from many places. The United States was in real need of restoration. He had heard of homestead land available in Arkansas.

Lucy was not interested at first. She was grieving so that he could hardly get her attention. Finally, he told her, "We have to do something, Lucy! We can't go on like this, and grieving is not going to bring her back! God is taking care of Mattie; she doesn't have a fever any longer. She is happy now! We must let go and let God have her! He loves her more than we ever could."

"How are we supposed to do that? I can't and won't!" She began to cry; he put his arms around her and held her as she cried, which felt better than the dead, empty feeling of sadness she had felt for many months.

"Look at the other kids; they don't even play as they used to, music or otherwise! For that matter, I don't feel like playing either. Elmira is in no better shape than we are. William can't do anything to please her. We are all hurting and need to help each other."

"You're right, I know. I just miss her so much! It has been almost two years, and it still seems like yesterday. Maybe we do need a change. I suppose we have been neglecting the other children while wanting the one I can't have."

"William has been talking about moving to Arkansas, but Elmira doesn't want to move off and leave us. Why don't we give that some thought? We could travel together by wagon if you want, then the children won't have to separate. They don't need to lose each other after being raised together."

To separate them now would be cruel. Let me talk to Elmira and Sara; then we can talk about it again later." They went to bed that night with a new feeling of hope and a little comfort.

Elmira was quite surprised to have Mama ask her about moving. She had not mentioned it to her family at all. It had been the furthest thing from her mind. "Mama, do you want to travel so far with all these children?"

"Well, not really, but we have to move on with our lives. If William and your father want to go, I guess it is our place to go along and be the helpmates God intended us to be. Your papa said that William has wanted to go for several years."

"I suppose that is true, but when it is all said and done, we'll be the ones left there while he's away on a ship for weeks, maybe even months at a time! He has talked about it, but I couldn't leave you and the kids, especially after Mattie—-." She couldn't go on. Mattie was like her own baby! She began to cry. "How could we leave her here, Mama?"

"She's not here, Sweetheart; she's in the arms of Jesus, smiling and happy as can be, that is unless she is allowed to look down on us and see all these gloomy, grieving faces. I expect that would make her a little sad. You know Elmira; it has always been heart-rending for her to see you when you were hurting.

Besides that, if we go together, you and the kids would not be alone while William's gone. Your father and I have had a long talk about this. He's right. We have to move on, either here or some other place. We have wasted a lot of time and are not being fair to the other children by just living. We owe it to them to be happy and to give them hope."

This was the first sign of any peace that Elmira had felt in a long time. "Thank you, Mama. I never want to separate our children. They often think they are siblings instead of cousins. It is hard to know which children are going to be at what house. Lucy and Martha would refuse to separate. They do everything together."

Chapter 7
The Big Move

In the months ahead, the families began to make plans for the long journey, not really knowing what could lie ahead for them. Protecting the children would be imperative. It would take a long time by wagon and required careful planning, but as soon as provisions could be made, they would be off on a great adventure.

At least, the children thought so. Lucy wasn't so sure and didn't want to leave Mattie, but she would make the best of the trip. Separation from family and friends would be difficult, but they could write to each other.

Lucy feared that she might never see some of them again. Her family was dear to her, and she didn't want to leave any of them; albeit she would not change her mind. "We do have to do something. Maybe moving is the best thing.

Some might later be able to visit by steamboat or train, but visits would not be often." Keeping her thoughts to herself, she began to pack as they all began to load the wagons, preparing as many beds and seats as possible out of anything that would work.

The dishes and anything breakable were packed with soft padding of towels and carefully placed in a wooden box that was used as a seat up near the front. Only metal dishes would be used for the trip. Some of them would hang onto the outside of the wagon for easy access.

Though William had traveled a lot on the steamboat, he was sure this would be good for all of them. The wagon trip would be a voyage they could share and might take their minds off some of their sorrows.

Several families would be traveling together for a while; among them would be some of the Krigbaum family.

The Storts and Krigbaum families would soon be on their way to Arkansas. The wagon train would not stop there. Some planned to go on to Oklahoma, maybe further west.

Some of William's family would travel with them and then later go on to see family in Oregon. He was glad someone was going to be near his father. Others wouldn't know where they were going until they got there; just searching for a home and traveling together made the trip safer for all.

Elmira and Sara began to get things packed for the move. "We can only take the things we really need, children. Pack carefully; the wagon will only hold so much."

Though William was a steamboat man by trade, they would travel as Phylander had planned. He had respect for him and faith in his judgment. "Mr. Storts, Elmira doesn't want you to make that trip alone. I am more used to the river and steamboats, but it would cost a lot more. It would be better to travel together. If you think wagons are the way to go, then let's do it together."

"I have been hoping to hear just that, William. We might have to do both before we get there. This is new to me, also. My Pa always said, "Where there is a will, there is a way. If we have the will, I figure God has the way."

Phylander and William moved their families southwest, battling many harsh elements and trials of a very long trip. It would take months to travel by wagon, but they could take more of their belongings. The rain was an ongoing problem. More than once, a wheel got stuck in the mud, or a spoke broke and had to be repaired. If that wasn't enough, it seemed someone was getting sick along the way.

The journey was taking much longer than they had hoped. If one broke down, they all stopped. Sometimes, when they came to a river or creek, the women would wash the clothes that needed to be washed or cook a meal while the men tried to find anything that would help conserve their food.

The weather was getting cooler as they got closer to Arkansas, but still not as cold as they had been accustomed to.

There was no way of knowing what they would meet with once they arrived. What would the people be like? Their families had fought on opposite sides of a civil war. Whether they would be accepted or not was yet to be seen. But then, people from many states were moving to Arkansas for one reason or another.

The children were fascinated with the many different kinds of trees and were in awe of the mountains and often got off the wagon to walk and enjoy the scenery. "Stay close to the wagons and stay together," instructed Elmira. "We must be getting closer. It's sure going to be a change for us. The people we have met speak the same language, I guess, but it's hard to understand what they say at times. I had not thought of that. Well, we'll soon understand one another."

Lucy added, "Children, be careful not to offend anyone, and don't take it to heart if others laugh at your speech."

"Yes, Ma'am." They walked off, not thinking too much about what she had said until they met up with two boys fishing. When they got back to the wagon, Gideon asked, "Do you have any idea what they said?

"The reply was, "not really." As they approached the river, William began to feel more at home. It was, however, a different story finding a place to cross in the wagons. There were trails that led into the river in three different places. Deciding to take the one that seemed traveled the most, they finally found a place to cross that was not too wide, and the current seemed mild. He and two other men took horses across first, walking part of the way, choosing the best place to cross with the wagons.

"Can we not just find a place on this side of the river?" one of the children questioned. Lucy and Elmira were not sure either but knew it was no use asking. William had something in mind and would know it when he saw it.

After they had found a safe crossing and William and Phylander and their families were on the other side of the river, some of them continued on westward toward Oklahoma without crossing the river and to the jobs that were waiting for them, they hoped. They had wanted to travel together as far as possible.

It was a family who worked together, prayed together, and played together. And now they were separating anyway.

Chapter 8

Finding Shelter for the Winter

They were glad that Oklahoma was not as far away as Ohio. They could visit one another. With much difficulty and hard work, they managed to get across the river. William had mentioned that the snowfall in Arkansas would not be so intense, so Phylander was not too worried about a home for his family. After several days of sleeping in the wagons, they found a house with reasonable rent a few miles from town. "We can live here together for now. The babies need a warm place to sleep, and we all need some rest.

"The barn's not the best, but it's big enough to put a wagon inside so we don't have to unload it, and maybe the older boys could sleep in it for a few more nights while we make room for everyone." Phylander got down from the wagon seat. "Let's go see the house."

"I think we could all stay here, even though it might mean a pallet in every corner and anyplace big enough to lie down, at least until the winter is over," Lucy added.

Thurman, Gideon, and their uncles, Moses and Leander, agreed that they would rather sleep in the wagon until the weather got really cold. It was quite a step up from the ground they had slept on for many nights. Once some of the supplies were removed, there was a lot more room. The top mattresses from each wagon were moved into the cabin. With so little furniture, they could use the room for beds.

Lucy and Elmira had prepared mattress covers before they left Ohio; as time permitted, they would be stuffed with clean straw to make other beds. Carrying supplies inside, Thurman mentioned, "Mama needs to rest; she looks tired. Is she sick, Papa?"

"I am glad you've learned to take care of your mother, Son. She doesn't feel well; that is a fact, but it is nothing that a few months won't cure. She's going to have another baby. Sara is only two and requires a lot of attention. Sheridan is four and thinks he can keep up with all of you. You boys, be sure to watch after him when you can. Your mother works hard and worries about all of you, especially after losing Mattie. Be careful not to get hurt, and help her where you can."

"We will, Papa; we're just glad you are with us. She misses you when you're away, and so do we. Will you have to go to work on the river soon? "Thurman asked.

"I've been thinking about that. I started saving for this trip a long time ago. We can hold out for a while. I don't want to leave your mother in a strange place to care for children alone, albeit you and Gideon are a great asset to her. But I plan to stay as long as I can. Maybe I can find work somewhere close by. We'll just have to wait and see."

They all had saved as much as possible and brought as much food as they could load onto the wagons, but they would need to buy some things later on. It would be a relief to live close to any town. Paris had less than six hundred people but had lots of farmlands available nearby.

The house was fairly large, though much of it needed repair. They were allowed to do work on it in payment for some of the rent. "We just might like it here, Mama; I only wish we had Mattie with us. If I had listened to William years ago, she might still be with us." Elmira picked up a baby quilt that had been Mattie's.

"Don't go blaming yourself, Honey. She is happier than any of us. We were where God had put us. Now, we are here because He wants us to heal and carry on. We have to think of our other young ones and your new baby now. We are truly blessed."

"Yes, Mama. I know you are right. I just think of her all the time and can't see how one little girl could have made such an impact on so many in such a short lifetime."

Chapter 9

An Early Spring

Spring was in the air, and the birds were singing. The children were playing in the clear, fresh air and bright sunshine. Winter had passed quickly; it had snowed only twice during the whole winter and never got over eight inches deep. Twice, they had ice sickles hanging from the roof and trees, but it only lasted a few weeks, and then it was above freezing again. The rest of the winter was milder than Phylander had imagined.

"We could almost farm year-round here," he laughed. "It's still February, and things are beginning to turn green in places." He walked outside to see how the boys were coming with the milking and enjoying the warm sunshine in the hill country. The trees were budding, and the sun was gleaming. "Thank you, Lord." He began to feel a strange peace.

Lucy and Elmira straightened up the house and made new window curtains. "It's beginning to look like a home. "

Elmira agreed as she looked at Lucy, "Yes, this might be a good place to raise children. The people seem quite friendly. I am glad we are all together; however, we do need to find a place of our own soon so we can get settled in before William decides to go off to work on the river again."

"He probably wishes he could be home more, also. It is a joy to watch him with the children, and they are soaking up the music! That guitar and fiddle have been well used and appreciated. We are all learning not to take family time for granted."

"There now, this one is finished." Lucy put down her thimble and needle after finishing the lace on the last curtain. She hung it on the window, and then she and Elmira listened to the music as they folded freshly washed baby clothes and planned for the new baby that would be arriving soon.

Elmira put the clothes away while Lucy made the crib ready for the newcomer. Sarah tried to climb into the crib.

"Not so fast, Sarah; this is not for you this time. You're a big girl now. We are going to have a new baby that is too small for a big bed like yours. Do you want to help me?"

"No, it's my bed!" She started pulling on the covers and the crib until Lucy picked her up and held her.

"Come here and let me hold you for a while. It seems to me you need a little extra attention this evening. This other stuff can wait; it is time for Sara!" Grandma held her and talked with her for quite some time. "No one is trying to take your place, Sweetheart. You are too big for that little crib now. The pretty new quilt that Mama made for you would not fit that little crib."

Before long, she was willing to give up her crib for the new baby and went to bed in her bed, covered up with her own special quilt, made by her Mama a few months earlier.

"I have been thinking of a name for the new baby, Mama. If we have a boy, he should be named after William. He has three sons, and none of them have his name. I think Monroe is a nice name; we almost never use it. What do you think?"

"I think it would be good; I'm sure he would like that." On May 19, 1888, they were blessed with another baby boy. Elmira was thankful that her husband had not gone away since they had been in Arkansas.

"William, if our baby had been a girl, I would have wanted to name her Mattie, but since he's a boy, I think we should name him Monroe after you. You have missed out on so much of the lives of the other boys. Do you know of a name to go with it?"

He thought for a few minutes, then said, "Well, how does Madison Monroe sound? That would be as close to Mattie as one could get for a boy. I think it sounds good together." He sat on the bed beside her, looking at their precious bundle of joy. "He seems healthy and happy. We're going to be ok here, Elmira." He held her hand as they admired little Madison and watched him sleep.

"We'll have a home of our own just as soon as you are back on your feet. I may have found a place, but the house needs lots of work. You need some time to get your strength back first. It is good to have your mama so close to help, especially with Sarah. She is a joy, but she is also a handful sometimes. It will be interesting to see how she reacts to Madison."

The children were waiting outside to see their little brother. Grandpa Storts and the children came in to see them. Grandma instructed them, "You can only stay for a few minutes; your mama and little Madison need to rest for a while."

Later on, Lucy gave him a bath by the fire and wrapped him up tightly, then took him back to Elmira before putting him in his crib to rest.

"Papa, do you think Madison needs to get used to music the way Sarah did? "Gideon asked as he opened the door.

"Why don't we wait a little while? Your mama is very tired. They both need to sleep a while, maybe a little later."

Lucy had prepared extra food earlier in the day because she felt sure they would be too busy to think about cooking in the evening. They ate together but allowed Elmira to sleep. She could eat when she woke up and felt like it.

Sarah didn't want to eat. "I want to eat with Mama. "She was worried about her and didn't understand why they needed another baby anyway. She was still not quite willing to give up her place as the baby and didn't want to see him.

It took several days before Sarah would even talk about Madison. Papa said, "We maybe should watch her closely so she doesn't try to topple his crib."

Elmira agreed, "It has been hard for her to endure the trip. She is so young and probably has been affected by our grief more than we realized. If parents aren't happy, it is hard to make children happy. Mattie would have spent a lot of time with her. We must take extra care to make sure she feels loved and secure, especially now with a new baby."

Chapter 10

The Krigbaum Farm

William had traveled down the Arkansas River on more than one occasion and had looked for land that might be of interest to him; however, he could never get far from the river. Traveling by wagon and horseback had opened up a whole new world to him.

He found a place near Paris that he hoped Elmira would like. It had a house that badly needed repairs, but it could be made livable. He took Mr. Storts to see it. "What do you think of it, Sir? The roof leaks and it needs a lot of work, but the boys and I could fix it up."

"It looks good to me if you think you can handle 160 acres. That's too much for me. What'll you do with that much land?"

"Well, I thought that at first, we might try raising several small crops to see what we could handle best; we might try to raise a few cows and chickens, maybe even a pig. Then, I could stay at home with Elmira and the kids, and we could all work on the farm together. The boys will be a lot of help."

"I've been able to find some work here and there. I would make more on the river, but I have been away for too much of the children's lives. Elmira has had to be a mother and father for too many years. She needs me here and a place to call home, Sir."

"It is taking a chance to give up a good job in these times, but it sure would be good to have you home. Life is going to be very different here. I know that Elmira will be relieved."

"I've been saving for this trip for a long time. We can hold out for another year or so if I have to, with careful spending.

The boys are almost grown, and life is too short, as you well know. I want to spend more time with them and have a little more time for music. I feel as if I have almost missed out on their childhood. This trip has been good for all of us; it has given us quality time together. They are doing well on the guitar. Even Sheridan wants to play the fiddle. We need to find a smaller one for him."

"You know, William, they have always been welcomed at our house, but I know they would love to have you home more. This seems like a fine place to raise a family and farm. The land looks good, but a lot of work will be required. Maybe you could use some of it for pasture land. You should have hay enough for both of us."

"I might ride into town in the morning and see if it's still available before I mention it to Elmira. I understand that it is a part of a land grant from the federal government. I might not have to pay much for it. Several places nearby are available if a body's willing to work. I've never been afraid of work, and the boys are good hands as well. They know more about farming than I do. I am not a farmer, but I reckon I could learn as well as the next person."

While leisurely riding back to the house, Phylander said with a thankful heart. "I am glad we came. It has been hard at times, but overall, it was a good trip. The women have been too busy helping each other to have so much time to grieve. The children are almost happy again."

Elmira was overjoyed at the mention of him staying home and working a farm with them. She didn't even mention that they might need the money. Somehow, it just didn't seem important at the time. She and Lucy went to see the house and considered what it would take to make it livable. "Mama, come and see the kitchen! And there is already a stove, and it's not in bad shape. What were the chances of that?"

"Well, that's a double blessing, Elmira: a big house that is already partially furnished. It would be nice if William could be home with you more often. If the Lord will, that will work out, too. He brought us here, and I'm sure He'll find us all a home."

As they put away the supper dishes that night, they talked about the trip, the many things they had learned on the way, and the people they had met. They all agreed that the move had been worth their sacrifice.

A few months later, in 1889, William was able to purchase the property near Paris. It was to be their home. They could start working on it right away. "It has a porch, so I will have to build you a rocker, Elmira. We can't have a porch with no rocker."

Elmira laughed, "It might need to wait until the house is in a little better condition, but a rocker would be nice. You know, we would need two. Mama and I are a team."

"Yes, I already thought of that. Maybe your Papa and I could work on them together." He looked at Phylander.

"I'm sure we could manage a couple of rocking chairs. I have seen some nice willows on this property that would be perfect for chairs. The way this family is growing, we may need another bench for the kitchen table also."

The Krigbaum family was home at last. William had sold their home in Ohio with no intention of returning. He was hoping Elmira would be happy here. The closest town was Paris. It was small but growing. It had a post office and several stores and businesses. Most of the larger farms and even some of the businesses were run by German Catholic immigrants.

They and the town's people, at first, had tried to keep their distance from one another but were beginning to realize that they all needed each other if the town was to survive. Southern hospitality soon became abundant. A few people came to welcome them to the neighborhood. Some offered to help with any building projects. In return, they would expect help from them.

One of the men said, "We're not offering charity, and we don't ask for it. We just like to help each other in this community; it gives us a chance to get to know one another, to know who our neighbors are and what to expect from them."

"This might be a good place. I think we will all be happy here if we give it half a chance," Phylander added. This would be a new life for them as they started to clear the land of lots of trees. The first trees would be used to build a new barn. There would be plenty of firewood without wasting good timber.

"We have a hundred and sixty acres, Mr. Storts. There is plenty of room for your family, at least until you find something that suits you. Just because I am here doesn't mean I want to separate a family that has been together as this one has. The farmland and good pasture should provide enough food for us and for the horses; besides, I need your help. As I told you, I am not a farmer. We could build a second house. We can't separate the musicians."

"I think we'll be okay where we are for now. Lucy and the girls have worked mighty hard to make the house into a home, and the rent is practically nothing since we have put so much into the place. We are not all that far away. We can still help you with your farm. We might need to stay while you're breaking the ground and maybe during the planting and harvest times. It might do the kids good to be separated for a while. They might appreciate one another more. Besides, we probably need to work on one house at a time."

A year later, William and the boys built a guest house near the main house. The well was between them. He didn't ask Mr. Storts to help, but of course, he did. "There's no use letting all these trees go to waste."

Elmira would settle for nothing less than having them move into the new house. "It is either you move here, or you have the kids half the time, and I have them the other half. Sometimes, I can't tell which ones belong to me." Lucy had to agree. It was decided they would be together again.

The Storts and Krigbaum families worked together on the farm. The children attended school as often as possible at a little country school at Paint Rock, about two miles away. The work on the farm was important, but they were to take school seriously and attend when they could.

Elmira and Lucy spent many hours helping each other with gardening, housework, sewing or quilting, etc., as they watched the older boys grow into manhood. Madison was growing fast, too.

Elmira had been sure he would be her last. He didn't seem to take an interest in the music as the other boys did, though he did play the guitar a little.

One evening, she mentioned it to William. "He doesn't seem to have the passion for the music as the others do. I wonder why that is?"

"Music is a pleasure, not a requirement. Talent comes in many forms. There will be something special that they are all good at and enjoy. God gives everyone talents. They don't have to all be the same," William reminded her.

"You're right, of course. He is only four years old and has plenty of time to discover what his is. Maybe the next one will want to play."

"Next one? I thought Madison was our last." He walked closer to her, and neither spoke for a few minutes, trying to read each other's eyes. "Well, is there a next one?"

"It looks that way. The good thing is we are in our own home. The bad news is that he or she will be born in December, and there will be so much that I can't help you with this year."

"That's ok, we can handle almost anything. Your parents and siblings are very good help in the harvest. We'll be fine. We have done pretty well the last couple of years."

As time passed, Elmira began to feel less and less able to work in the fields and took on more of the housework while her mama went to the fields. "Sorry, Mama, this is probably one of our biggest harvests, and I can't do my part. I don't know why I am so tired. It has never been this difficult to have a baby. You are working too hard!"

"I don't mind, Elmira. Besides, we have lots of help; the neighbors are more than willing to pitch in when we need them. Just look at all the food that you've canned!"

"You're doing more than you think. You've taught the children to work. They said that you told them, "A job worth doing is worth doing well." William and your father have a hard time just keeping up with them."

"I am proud of them; they have always stood strong while their Papa was away and never really complained."

"Well, we'll be done before you know it, and soon, we can enjoy a Thanksgiving feast together. I think Sheridan is bringing you a pumpkin to work up when you feel like it. He wants to work hard to finish so he can practice his fiddle. He sure is excited about the small fiddle his grandpa got him. He will be playing as good as Papa in a few years," Elmira added. "He copies his every move."

It became more difficult to get lunch on the table by noon, as was the custom. Lucy would go in early to help her make lunch and whatever else she needed.

Sarah, who was seven, stayed to play with Madison while the others helped with the harvest. "You're a good helper, Sara. I am glad you learned to take such good care of your little brother. Do you remember when he was born? You didn't want to give him your crib. You kept saying it was yours; my, how you have grown!"

"I like to play with him when he's nice. Sometimes, he takes my things and won't give them back. He even broke my new doll, but he said, "Sorry," so I forgave him, like you said, Mama, but I didn't want to! It was my best doll."

"That's good, Sarah; I am proud of you for watching after him. You know, we are about to have another baby. Are you ready to help me teach Madison to share?"

Just then, the girls came in. "Mama, if you need to rest, we can do this. You don't look so good. I think we are about done with the last of the harvest. I am glad!" Lucy laid potatoes on the table.

"Martha added, "Thurm and Gid are going to take some pumpkins and sweet potatoes to market this afternoon. Leander wants to know if you need him to stay here or go with them."

'He can go with them if he wants to. Tell him that I do appreciate his asking, but we'll be fine. Well, we better get lunch on the table. They may be here early; one of you can wash and peel those potatoes, and the other can set the table. I will make the cornbread. The stove is hot, and the beans and ham are done. It won't take long. Baked corn on the cob and bread pudding are in the warming closet. I am so thankful for this stove. With the warming closet and water reservoir, who could ask for more?"

Chapter 11

Thanksgiving Day

Thanksgiving Day was a day to remember for the Krigbaum and Storts families. It was decided that The Storts family would gather at William and Elmira's place.

Elmira had not seen some of her brothers or sisters in years. John Sheridan and Dave had come early, along with her sisters Sarah and Emily and their families, to help with the last of the harvest that William had been struggling to get in before frost. Sarah Jane, Emily, and the wives of John and Dave had been there for a few days helping Elmira.

"You must take it easy, Elmira; we really don't want a Thanksgiving baby. We'll do this while you rest," Emily said as she sat a large bowl of boiled potatoes on the table.

"I love this stove, Sis. With hot water so available from a spout, we can keep the pots and pans washed as we cook, and a warming closet should be on all cook stoves." Sarah Jane was wiping off the top as she admired it.

"Yes, it is a blessing beyond measure. It was in the house. I'm sure glad to have you both here! It seems I have not done my share of the workload this year. 1893 is almost over, and I feel as if I have just waited it out. This baby must be special to cause all this trouble. It's not as easy having a baby when you turn forty."

"That's what families are for. We've missed you so much! I am thankful for the railroad that makes it possible for us to visit." As the rest of the food was being prepared, the children were out in the yard playing horseshoes and other games.

The men were watching a big ham that was cooking slowly on a fire outside while they visited all evening. Elmira heard a knock at the door. "Come on in."

Jamie Temperance opened the door. "Tempie!" Elmira got up and met her with a big hug. "What a surprise. It is so good to see you!"

"We've really missed you, Sis. I know it is probably almost done, but what can I do to help?"

"Sarah and the others are helping Mama, and I think they have it under control; I am just in here out of the way. That seems to be the way I help the most these days."

"That's not like you. How much longer do you have? "Jamie took off her wrap as Martha walked in; "I'll take that for you, Tempie. I knew you would come!"

"Martha! My little sister, how much you've grown! You and Lucy are growing up way too fast!" As they hugged each other, Mama came from the kitchen.

"Hello, Mama. How are you?" she said in a soft, longing voice. "It is so good to see you. I couldn't wait to get here. Thank you for your letters, keeping us informed about your lives here." With a combination of hugs, laughter, and tears, Mama and daughters and daughters-in-law were united, for the first time in several years, preparing a Thanksgiving Feast together.

Madison ran in the door and through the kitchen. "Hold on, little man; where's the fire?" his grandma caught him by the arm. "There is lots of room outside to run. Why are you running in the house? Are you alright?"

He looked up at her. "Grandma, there's too many people out there!" He had not remembered seeing some of them before, though many wanted to talk to him since he was the baby of the family. The more they tried, the less he wanted anything to do with them.

Elmira seemed to understand his dilemma. "Come here and sit with me, Baby. Let me tell you about your family, who've come a long way to see you."

She began trying to relieve his anxiety. Some haven't seen you since you were a baby. They couldn't wait to get here to see you." Soon, he was going to them, asking them questions.

Tables of anything they could make one out of were set up with food of many kinds. Leander had brought home a Turkey. It sat in the middle of the table with a huge pan of dressing. The ham that had been slowly cooking outside for many hours was ready and brought inside. There was corn on the cob, potatoes, gravy, green beans, carrots, sweet potatoes, and bread pudding, along with many other side dishes and desserts.

William said as they all gathered around for a prayer of thanksgiving. "Mr. Storts, would you do the honor of offering our Thanksgiving prayer?"

"Thank you, Son. It is indeed an honor to have most of my children here today. I'm sure Isabella would be here if she could. It has been a long trip for some. I'm so thankful for the trains that make it possible. Moses will be moving away to Oklahoma soon but stayed to help with the harvest. We are truly blessed! We may have a little friction once in a while, but you all come through for each other."

He said a prayer of thanksgiving, and then, one by one, they counted their blessings and gave God thanks. With so much food, they would not have to cook more for supper. That meant that they had time for visiting and music.

"To finish the day off right, we have to hear those boys play. I hear they are quite good." Dave sat back in his chair. "Think you can handle a little music, boys?"

William started getting chairs set up to play. They never had to be asked twice. It took them only minutes to be ready to play. They all got their instruments, and the music of Thanksgiving began. The music circle was more fun than ever.

As the ladies finished up in the kitchen. Elmira said, "This has to be the best Thanksgiving ever! Thank you all for doing so much. Sorry I wasn't more help, but I am so glad you are all here. We should not have to cook for days."

Lucy agreed, "Indeed, this is a Thanksgiving never to be forgotten; our children together again. For that, I am truly thankful. I hope some of you can stay for a while."

Chapter 12

Always Room for One More

William had managed to stay at home and work the farm for the last four years. It was hard at times; Crops didn't always do well, but Elmira assured him that they would make it better with him there than with extra money.

He was glad to be nearby since his wife was having a harder time than usual with the baby. She was sick a lot, and Madison needed to be reassured that his Mama was ok.

"It can't be much longer; I can't take much more," Elmira said as she was sitting up on the bed, not well at all.

The doctor was making his rounds and stopped in to see how she was doing. "This needs to be the last one for you, Elmira. It won't be long now. Just try to rest for a little while." You're going to need all the strength you can get."

In a few days, he was needed again. Gideon went to fetch him. "Papa fears something is not right. Can you come quickly, Doctor?" He grabbed his bag and was on his way.

Elmira was about forty-one, and her youngest child was five. It had been much easier with her other children. "Maybe it's my age," she thought.

As the doctor arrived, Lucy was getting things ready for the new baby and praying that all would go well while trying to assure Elmira that the baby would be there soon.

"Where is Madison?" I hope I'm not scaring him." She fell asleep from exhaustion before anyone could answer. The sleep lasted only seconds, and then the contractions became intense. "I can't do this again! I'm so tired!"

"It will be over soon, Mrs. Krigbaum; take a deep breath and get ready to push. You're a strong woman, and this baby is ready to see you and trying hard to help," replied the doctor.

Lucy put a wet cloth on Elmira's head and tried to calm her a little. An hour later, on December 11, 1893, the baby was born. "You have a boy; do you have a name for him?" The Doctor said as he laid him on her stomach to finish his work and make sure the mother and baby were okay.

William answered before she could say anything. "I think we should name him after his grandpa, who has been a solid rock for all of us. Maybe we could name him Harley Phylander, after his great grandpa Krigbaum also."

Elmira was pleased that William wanted to name him after her papa. "Is he ok, Doctor? I feel as if he had to work too hard because I was so weak."

He handed the baby to Lucy, who wrapped him in a clean blanket, and she laid him in Elmira's arms. "He looks fine to me. He has a good set of lungs, it seems."

"Here is your early Christmas present, Sweetie. He stopped crying the instant I wrapped him; He looks happy to see you. You hold him for a few minutes, and then I'll go get him cleaned up while you rest. You've had a long day. I sent Martha to get your papa; he's been watching all the children and really worried about you."

Harley's grandparents were about sixty years old at the time of his birth. Phylander held him and talked to him a lot. He was honored that he would share his name, Harley Phylander.

A week later, as they were thinking about Christmas gifts for the children, it occurred to Elmira that having William home had been the best gift they could ask for. "Christmas is not about gifts. How about playing a few Christmas carols tonight?"

The boys were eager to play. Thurman was quite good on the guitar, Gideon played the fiddle, and Sheridan played the smaller fiddle that his grandpa had found. The girls took turns with the small guitar. Thurman had bought his own full-size guitar a few years earlier. Madison would not play much at all, though the others tried to teach him.

Chapter 13
Finding Time for Music

As time passed, Harley grew well and was healthy and happy. His Mama got better and spent a lot of time with him. She was glad he was born in the winter, so she didn't have to leave him to work in the fields. It would be months that they could be together all the time.

Madison and Harley grew up in a home with little room, but it was filled with love and trust. "A man's word was his bond," Papa would say. "Be sure to keep your word. Don't give anyone a reason not to trust you."

When the opportunity presented itself, the neighbors would get together for a time of music and games. Everyone was tired from clearing land and working in the fields. The crops would soon be ready for harvest, but before they filled the barns and corn cribs, they made time for a barn dance.

The neighbors and family only needed to hear the word, and people would come from miles away. Wagons were everywhere, with beds made in them for the children if they got sleepy. Many would stay the night; pallets could be seen anywhere.

Festive music filled the air, as did the aroma of freshly cooked food of all kinds; mounds of corn on the cob, potatoes, tomatoes, and other fresh vegetables.

Another table had bread, cakes, and pies made of blackberries, blueberries, and plums, which God had provided, and they had not had to plant. This was a good place.

Tables were set up outside, and everyone brought some kind of food they had prepared for the festive occasion. The fun lasted until up into the night.

Some children played games together, while others joined in the music. By the time Harley was five, he watched as his grandpa and older brother played fiddle. They each showed him a few scales and songs and then let him try to play along. What he lacked in ability, he made up for in determination as he watched his brothers play with his uncles and aunts.

Thurman handed Harley the small guitar that he had first played, thinking he would play along in a short while, which he did, but his mind was on the fiddle. Between the Storts and Krigbaum families, they had more musicians than instruments, so when anyone put an instrument down, another picked it up.

His papa and grandpa saw he was really interested, but his arms were a little too short to note the fiddle correctly. They agreed that he needed to grow a little for that fiddle.

"He's gonna play that thing someday!" Grandpa noted. "Do you still have that little one?"

"I'm afraid it needs a lot of work, a new bridge, and strings, to start with. It has been well-used and has a few cracks here and there. The children have played with it, but not with much interest. They mostly played the guitar after John got a bigger one. I planned to get it repaired and in working order a long time ago but kept putting it off."

"Well, it looks as if Harley has his heart set on playing. Let me see what I can do with it. I have repaired instruments for them before." The morning light brought evidence of much fun. People were sleeping in any place that looked like a possible spot. The women were busy preparing breakfast for everyone while the men got the wagons ready to go back to their homes. The children were to pick up and clean up what they could outside.

Some had gone home, but several still lingered. "That sure was some good music last night, but these late-night hours really catch up with a fellow in the morning. I doubt any of us will be worth much today," Thurman said sleepily. "Hope you have plenty of that coffee, Mama. It sure smells good!"

"If we run out, I'll make some more." How about you go tell everyone we have breakfast ready? I think the table is set outside. Martha and Lucy were working on it."

"Sure thing, Mama; if I don't move around, I'll be asleep again, anyway." He went through the house and yard, waking up anyone still not up, finding some in wagons, under wagons, some in the strangest places. "It's hard to stay up all night, ain't it, guys?" Wake up; the sun's been up for hours! Breakfast is ready but won't wait long."

The food was devoured in a short while. They would need to make good use of the time left before harvest. When they were through with breakfast, the older boys took down the makeshift tables. Soon, the rest had gone to their homes. The farmers would need to get up early from then on, carefully watching their crops. Anything could happen; they stood by to help one another in case any of the farmers had a problem.

The Storts and the Krigbaum families had become a part of the soon-to-be-famous (Southern Hospitality). As the last of the neighbors had gone home, William acknowledged, "This is a friendly place. Neighbors know the meaning of being neighborly. People help one another instead of hiring things done all the time."

The rest of the week was work as usual. But no matter what kind of day they had, music was usually a part of the evenings. One afternoon, when the chores were done, as they sat outside to play and listen to music, Grandpa came out of the house with the smaller fiddle in his hand. "I think it's time you had one that is closer to your size. This is yours now. Take care of it."

Harley's face lit up as he reached for the fiddle. "I will. My own fiddle! Thank you, Grandpa! I promise I'll practice."

Harley put the fiddle up to his chin. It was still a little big, but he could make it work. He was only six and would grow.

Sheridan helped him learn to play a song, and he tried it over and over until he could play it. "That's ok, you're doing fine. Just keep trying; it takes time to handle the bow well," he encouraged.

The music was sweeter than ever that night, and Harley almost learned to play two songs. With Thurman playing his guitar and others playing instruments or singing, Harley learned fast. Papa showed him how to keep time with his feet. His mama and grandma were especially proud of him. A love for music was something Harley would pass on to his children and grandchildren. The family soon could enjoy twin fiddles. His brother began playing harmony as Harley struggled to play as well as he could, but he learned fast.

It was hard for him to put it down for the first several nights, even when his fingers hurt. Mama told him that if he wanted to play, he must learn to obey and go to bed when he was told because there was much work to be done the next day, and it would take all the help, and they needed plenty of rest. She would ask him to play one last song for her before putting up his fiddle and going to bed.

He loved to please his mama. She praised him often, so he worked harder because she was proud of him. Within a few months, he learned to play several songs on his little fiddle, practicing any time that he had an opportunity, and was included in the evening music.

With more people than instruments, the girls and Madison would often just listen or join in the singing or stories of the day. They might even play a game of some kind with the Storts children.

Because the instruments were made available to any of them with a desire to learn, most of them could play at least a little. Some just had a special interest. Harley was one of them.

Walking the two miles from school gave them a chance to maybe bring home a squirrel or rabbit for supper. Mama and Lucy had learned to cook them from the neighbors. At first, it had been unthinkable for Lucy; later, she decided that if she was going to live in the South, she needed to make adjustments.

In due time, she could make squirrel dumplings as well as anybody. Even more surprising, the family ate it like it was good. "Mama wouldn't believe me if I told her," Declared Lucy.

Harley's brothers, sisters, and uncles played together every day. Phylander and William played when they could, with the joy of knowing they would have many years of enjoyment together. Often, friends would join them.

However, music was a way of life for the Storts family, along with his grandchildren, the Krigbaum family. They had a family band that kept them together for many years. When one moved away, he was missed, but someone else stepped up, and the music continued.

Chapter 14
Nothing Lasts Forever

It was almost the 1900s. "Where did the time go? We're about to start another century." Phylander sat at the table, reading a letter from Isabella.

Lucy was finishing up in the kitchen so she could go check on Elmira. She had never really regained her strength since Harley was born and didn't seem to join in the singing as she once did. It seemed that she tired more easily than usual.

William decided it was time to ask the doctor to take another look at her, though she resisted. He wouldn't settle for less. "You have not been yourself for a long time. Something is not right!" Bringing the wagon to the house, he took her by the hand; "Let's go, Elmira. You have to go see the Doctor again. He must be missing something."

She was feeling bad that she had not been able to do much for her mother the past several months and had not been well in a long time. It was all she could do just to care for Harley. Since Madison was five years older than him, he tried to help as much as he could, trying to believe that she would be ok.

The Doctor explored several possible problems, and then one day, he expressed to William that she was very ill. She had developed breast cancer. The word alone was fear enough. There didn't seem to be much he could do. Somewhere in a bigger hospital, they might help, but there was no known cure.

At the young age of seven, Harley learned that his mother was very ill. The doctor said that it possibly could have begun to develop even before he was born.

Madison refused to accept it. He tried to remain hopeful and strong. But later that year, the tears flowed freely from his eyes as the doctor told them it was only a matter of time. She just needed to rest. They were all so dependent on each other. How could they go on without their mama?

"It's not fair! It's not fair!" Harley cried. He could not hide his tears. He and Madison tried to be strong, but their hearts were breaking as they talked to Mama. With five children to leave behind, Elmira was sad to leave them, but Harley was just a baby! This was too much for her. The worry in her eyes was more than visible. She told them how she loved them and wanted them to be good boys and help their papa and grandparents.

Through tears, they told her they would try. That was a mighty tall order for a seven-year-old. Elmira knew that, but it was out of her hands. She said they must accept the Lord's will and be good for their Papa and grandparents.

After the children went to bed that night, Elmira told William that she would write to the children who were away. Without knowing how long she had, she didn't want to waste a moment. She loved her children, no matter how big, little, old, or young, and wanted to be there for them if they needed her.

As she began to write to her children and family who had moved away, the pen left marks on the paper, and tears would smear the words. "Missing you and love you so much! I would love for you to come home as soon as possible. I really need to see all of you." She didn't want to tell them goodbye in a letter.

Knowing that her children would be in good hands, she was ever so glad they had stayed near her parents. It was a comfort to her to have them nearby to help raise them. William would be lost without her, and she knew it. "Harley, will you bring your fiddle and play a song for me?"

The tears welled up in his eyes, but with a heart that was heavy, he brought out his fiddle. It wasn't quite in tune, but somehow, no one seemed to care at the moment. He played for her, and it seemed to make her feel better. So, he promised to play for her every day and to try to learn a new song each week. She mainly wanted time with him; she wanted him to have good memories of her.

He kept his promise as long as she lived, trying to get better and better so she could enjoy the music more. Many evenings, they all cried. Sometimes, they found a way to laugh. One thing is for sure. They loved each other and treasured every moment they had together.

Many of her family and her siblings made arrangements to go visit her as soon as they got their letters. A few of her family that she was sure would not be able to come, she told them in the letter that she only had a short time to live and wanted them to know that she loved them. And asked them to keep tabs on Mama, "She will be so lost, plus have her hands full with so many children."

One by one, she got letters back. They also were tear-stained, and visits started often. Sara Jane came to stay for a while to help her and Mama as they tried to prepare the children.

Elmira Storts Krigbaum passed away in 1900 at 48 years old. She was buried at Paint Rock Cemetery, not far from the school house and church. Harley and Madison would go early and visit her grave every day when he went to school.

Harley lost interest in the fiddle and refused to eat or talk to anyone, overwhelmed by grief. He hadn't found anything that could relieve the sadness until one Sunday afternoon; he got out his fiddle and was just looking at it, thinking about his mama. It seemed he could hear her say, "Play one more song for me."

It was a surprising comfort to him, so he played as if he was playing for her. Wanting to please her, he thought that maybe she could hear him play. Sheridan heard him and said, "Harley, Mama wanted you to keep playing." Maybe she can even hear you.

After that day, he began to find comfort in the music, so he worked extra hard to learn new songs. He was growing to fit his fiddle better all the time.

When he went to bed that night, tears again filled his eyes. "I could learn for you, Mama." He spoke softly. "Why did you have to leave us? I miss you so much! I need you to hold me. It hurts too much!"

Grandma Lucy was nearby and overheard him. She came and sat down beside him, wrapping her arms around him; she assured him, "God is taking care of your mama, and we need to go on and do the best we can. We all miss her. She was my baby just the same way that you are hers. I love you too, Son, almost as much as she did." Lucy held him, and they cried and talked for a long time. It seemed that they needed each other more than anyone knew.

Lucy was glad they lived next door to them to help with the children; however, it was so hard to see Elmira's place so empty all the time. "Harley, your papa probably needs you with him tonight, but you come and stay with us any time you want. We'll get through this together." He clung to her as she held him in her arms and rocked him until he finally fell asleep, so she laid him on his bed and went home to deal with the next part of the anguish that they were all feeling.

Phylander was sitting at the table with some of the children. Most of them were crying. It had only been a short time since the funeral, and he and Lucy needed each other at that moment, but the children must come first.

The cancer had crept up so quickly and viciously; there was much they felt they had not done or said. Martha and Lucy were trying to make something for them to eat; it was hard to do with the tears flowing down their cheeks.

"It's all right, girls; I doubt if anyone is hungry right now." Lucy reached out to them as they came and hugged her, trying not to cry. "It's ok to cry. God sees and understands the tears. He knows the pain behind each one.

If you can imagine how happy she and Mattie are to see each other, maybe it will help. We will all be together again someday. I can't see how we are going to go on without her, but we will. We've been through a lot, and God has seen us through. He will do it again.

Chapter 15
The Choctaw Nation

William was at a total loss as to what to do without his wife. He decided he needed to go back to work on the riverboat, but he couldn't do it living there. Trying to be the responsible parent he was supposed to be, he moved his children with him to Oklahoma, closer to the river and where Thurman and Gideon lived, near the Choctaw Nation. He was thinking it would be best to get them away from where Elmira had been so they could think about something new.

His daughter, Lucy, was not so far away and would help when she could, but he thought they needed to get away for a while. "I can't stay in this house!"

As he told Mr. and Mrs. Storts that he was moving, Grandma Lucy wanted to offer to keep the children but knew that he needed them with him. It was hard to just be the grandma when she had been as close as a mother to them.

"If you need to sell the place, we will find another place to live," Phylander mentioned. We have always planned on getting a place of our own anyway. Splitting the children up just didn't seem fair."

"No, Sir, I don't even want to think about selling right now. If you would, I'd like for you to stay here. Use my house as you need it. I don't even intend to move anything. I just feel we need to get away for a while, and if you want to farm any of the land, that's fine, but don't try to overdo it. Raise what you need. Remember I have half the workers with me."

"It will be good for all of us to see other family. Had they known Elmira was so ill, they wouldn't have moved. I will try to get a job on the riverboat and maybe stay with Thurman or Gideon so I can spend a little time with them. It will do the children good to see them also. Maybe I can send a little money back to you for watching after the place."

Sadly, the Krigbaum family moved to Oklahoma, where William was able to find work. He had to leave the younger ones with Sarah while he worked, being gone for sometimes weeks at a time. "You are carrying a heavy load for a young girl, Sarah. I hope it's not too much for you." They stayed with Thurman until he could find a place for them to live.

They had arrived there in time to be counted in the 1900 census of the Choctaw Nation, but he soon realized that the children needed to be with their grandparents. It was not fair to take them away from them also. They had lost their mama, and they seemed to feel as if they had lost everything.

Harley hardly spoke to anyone. He had lost his mother and also his grandparents. William tried to cheer him but to no avail. "Grandma Lucy needs me, Papa! I saw her crying. She misses Mama as much as we do! Why did you take us away from her, too?" He began to cry uncontrollably. They all missed Grandma and Grandpa. Harley, Madison, and Sara wanted to go stay with them.

The older boys got to work with Papa. But they were too young. "Maybe you should go back and stay with your grandparents. I could come to see you when I have a chance; you could go to school there at Paint Rock. Let me give it some thought." He knew, although he didn't mention, that the Storts family already had a house full, but they would always make room for his children.

"Sheridan, do you want to go help Grandpa with the farm work? Madison will do a lot, but they will be taking on a lot more, too.

"I will go, Papa, but you need someone to stay with you. You won't be alone with Thurman and Gideon so close by. I can help Grandpa with the farm."

Sarah wrote Grandma a letter asking if they could come and stay with them, and Papa posted it the next morning. The evening meal was much more pleasant that night. Sarah made a special supper. She even made a cake.

"You have outdone yourself today. This is very good! I might want to keep you with me."

They all went with him on a riverboat and got as close as they could to Paris. Dave and Leander would meet them and take them home.

They had been working the land for him and watching after his house and property, plowing fewer fields than they had done in years past. Life was unbearable for Lucy at times. The children also had been lost without each other. Their reunion was the first sign of joy anyone had felt in a year.

"Grandma! Grandpa!" Harley jumped from the wagon and ran to meet them. "We get to stay with you while Papa is working. We even get to go to school here!"

Lucy greeted them with open arms, as did Grandpa. Having Elmira's children home made all of them feel better.

"Is that alright with you, Lucy? Harley insists that you really need him. I have to admit, none of them are happy with the Choctaw Nation. Sarah takes good care of them. It is just not home. Harley is very unhappy!"

Grandma Lucy replied, "I've missed them too. And of course, they can stay with us. You're absolutely right. I do need him. We are glad you're back also, at least for a little while, William. We've really missed those babies. Are you all ok?"

Soon, the wagon was unloaded, and they got ready for supper. William stayed for a couple of days, then went back to Oklahoma, where he could work on the river.

He missed his family very much, and he felt as if he was letting Elmira down by sending them back for their grandparents to raise. He worked as often as he could, trying to send as much money back to the family as possible.

The boys were worried about him. "Papa, you need to rest. You're working too hard. We are a lot younger than you, and you're wearing us out!"

He thought about what it meant to leave his children with Grandma Lucy, who already worked very hard. "Maybe I should just move back. Something is bound to work out better than this. Children grow up too fast to grow up with unhappy memories." He began to tie up loose ends on the ship and give them time to replace him and then get back home to his children.

"I would love to take you boys with me. We missed you a lot when you left home. You'll be having children of your own soon, and then you will know what I am saying. It was hard to leave you when you were little; it's just as hard to leave you now."

William moved back to his home near Paris, Arkansas, where Phylander and Lucy had been living in a house built for them, not far from the main house.

In 1902, William met a woman who had lost her husband about three years earlier. He felt she would be a good mother to his children, but he did not want to make the children think he was replacing their mother.

A few months went by, and then he decided to ask her to marry him. They were both alone. Thinking of a way to try to convince her, to his surprise, she said yes without a second thought.

"You will?" All of a sudden, he was at a loss for words. Though relieved, he wasn't sure how the children would react. He wondered how he was going to tell them. She had been there to care for them on several occasions; they all liked her.

William and Widow Moss were married that same year. It was comforting to him to know he had someone who would take good care of his children. She had raised two of her own.

Finding that things would change a lot in their home, but the younger ones stayed every minute they could with their grandparents. It wasn't the same without Mama.

As William's new wife began to take over the house. Elmira's family began to feel as if they needed to move. It was no longer the home of their daughter. Elmira was gone. They just didn't feel right living on the Krigbaum farm.

Phylander told William, "We need to find a place of our own. I think there is an open homestead nearby. I may try to get it if I can. It will require a lot of work, but we can handle it if you think you could spare us here."

"You don't have to move, Sir, but I do understand. She is a good woman and good with the children. But it is hard for them to see her in their mama's place. I do see where it would be hard for you. I am not trying to replace Elmira. No one could do that, but I do care for her. I hope you understand."

"I know, William. We're glad you found such a good woman. We both like her. You don't have to explain anything. I just think it is time we moved on with our own lives. We have to let Elmira go, also. God took her home for a reason that only He knows. It is not for us to understand."

"Mr. Storts, let's go see this land of yours. Maybe if you get it before I leave, I can help you move. I owe you that."

In a few months, William decided he was more suited for the riverboat than for farming. He decided to sell his place and move into a smaller house with his wife. It would be better for everyone. The work was available on the boat, and He would send them money when he could to help care for his children. "We don't need to try to run two farms. My boys can help you, and I'll be glad to help when I can."

"Lucy, I want you to have the kitchen stove that Elmira loved so much. You two cooked a lot of meals on it together. She couldn't have asked for a better mother or friend. She never would have come here without you."

Chapter 16

Grandpa's Homestead

In 1905, Phylander found eighty acres of good farmland with timber in Logan County, which was part of a land grant. Most of the homestead land had been taken. This was only eighty acres. At his age, that would be more than enough.

Although he met with a little opposition because of his age, Phylander was granted a homestead near Paris, Arkansas, about four miles from William's home place. He was not young but in good health and had a family who would help him. There would be plenty of work for everyone, and he counted on them.

With the help of his family and friends, Phylander built a one-room log cabin on the east end of the land close to the creek, giving them quick access to water. They would add to it or build another as they had the opportunity.

It was big enough since most of their children had married and had homes of their own. They would make room for any of the grandchildren when they came to visit.

Madison and Harley were ready and willing to help. They were good at the farm work by then and wanted to help Grandpa.

Sad times would come, as the boys learned, oh so well; however, they also learned that the living had to keep working and do what they could. Watching their grandpa, uncles, and brothers clear the land, Papa helped when he was there.

The boys had learned how to work the land using plows behind oxen, horses, and mules. Each had to be handled differently in order to get the job done right. The first few years were hard for them. Phylander and Lucy kept busy. There was no end to the work.

Then, when they could clear enough land, there would be cotton for a money crop, making sure they rotated the crops so as not to wear out the soil. He reminded the boys that caring for the land would help it to produce well for later years. The abundance of wild blackberries and plumbs were added blessings. The land was good for farming; however, it could not be all good.

The whole place also seemed to grow rocks of all sizes and shapes. Harley and Madison spent many hours behind the plow and picking up rocks, sometimes working from sun up to sun down when the weather would permit.

These had to be removed from the gardens to make the most of their work. Along the side, they decided that each of the gardens was a good place to pile the rocks. It was often Harley and Madison's job to remove them from the rows as they were plowed up.

The piles got bigger and bigger as the years went by. Madison was sure the land must be growing rocks because they never came to an end. Some of them were too big to pick up, and they had to work together, while others were so huge that they could not budge them. Once, it took hours to remove one large one, digging around it and then hooking a chain around it and pulling it out with the horses.

Grandpa told them that the rocks were an added blessing and could be used to build with as they were needed. The piles would make them easily accessible and keep the gardens from washing away in the heavy rains.

This made them feel important and work even harder. Harley and Madison picked up so many rocks that it was a real treat to get to do the plowing, planting, cutting, or stacking hay; albeit, they learned quickly not to complain. It would not be in their best interests, so instead, they tried to make it fun by competing with each other and taking pride in their work.

Eventually, the piles would meet and go the whole length of the garden. There were always rocks to pick up when all the other work was done. They never had to look for something to do. It always found them. Boredom was not an issue because Grandpa had a surefire cure for being bored.

Harley lived most of the time with his grandparents in the cabin they all helped him build, partly because his papa was so often working away from home, and Papa said that Grandpa needed the help.

Adding rooms to the cabin was done when harvest time was over. He was kind of glad Papa had sold the farm, but he missed him so much since he was away.

He and his brothers also loved to play music with the Storts family. An evening of music out on the front porch just finished off the day right. It just wasn't the same at his house with his mama gone. When his papa could be there, it was even better. Sometimes, one of the girls would play, but the boys couldn't seem to put the instruments down.

Chapter 17

The One Room School

"Wake up, boys, get your chores done early. School starts today." Lucy opened their door, and they could smell the hot biscuits and bacon cooking. Grandpa was bringing in the bucket of milk. "Grandpa did the milking already, but there are other animals to care for before you go."

"Ok, Grandma, we'll be there in a minute." They got up and quickly dressed; then Madison went to the wood pile and brought in some fire wood. "Something sure smells good, Grandma."

They washed up and sat down to a hot breakfast, finished their chores, and then were off to school. Madison and Harley attended school at Paint Rock, Arkansas, in Logan County, in a one-room schoolhouse about halfway between William's home and Phylander's. This was to be Madison's last year there.

Though it had only one room, the children were divided into class groups, with seats on both sides and an isle down the middle. It was also used as a community building and church. In the middle of the room sat a much-used, wood-burning cast iron stove. Two windows on each side allowed fresh air in the summer time and provided ample lighting.

In the winter, someone had to come early to build a fire. The older boys in the community took turns going early to build the fire and had it warm before it was time for class.

Each class member's family supplied their share of the wood. Harley and Madison walked about a mile and a half to the school; so, when it was their turn, they had to get their chores done and leave for school very early.

As they walked along in the evenings, the squirrels and other animals were fun to watch, so they didn't mind the walk.

Occasionally, Madison would bring a slingshot to school and try to bring home a squirrel or a rabbit for supper. Mostly, they just liked to watch them.

One winter, the weather had been bad for weeks, and the snow was deeper than usual. Cold air was coming in around the windows, so Madison and Harley stayed after school to help the teacher seal them off better. They forgot about the time and were enjoying the warm fire inside the school house.

The teacher said, "You boys better get home; your folks will be worried. This will be much better when the cold wind blows. Thank you for your help. Would you like a ride home?"

"No, thank you, we can walk," they said in unison. Saying goodbye, they started walking toward home and could still see each other, but the sun was getting low.

It seemed the animals were roaming everywhere, looking for food. Harley and Madison knew most wild animals would not normally bother a person if left alone. A single wolf was not a threat, but if they were in a pack, they might be on the hunt and must be avoided.

About halfway home, a gray wolf appeared out of nowhere. It was only one, so they kept going. In a little while, another came around a tree, then another. Thinking the whole pack was probably nearby; they didn't know what to do, so they stopped for a moment. Realizing they had to do something, the wolves began to move around, watching them.

Just over half a mile, and they would be home. Cold and hungry themselves, they talked about what they could do. With no gun nor even a sling shot, they couldn't fight off the wolves if they attacked. They had to think fast as the wolves were slowly coming closer. The only thing they could think of to do was to climb up into a tree and get out of reach of the animals and hope they would move on. Slowly, they moved over to the nearest tall tree with branches, and then scampered up as fast as they could.

As they started moving quickly, the wolves lunged towards them. The number had changed from three to about six.

They were growling and jumping to reach them, almost reaching their feet at times. "We have to go higher!" Madison said as he pushed Harley up to the next branch. He was older and responsible for Harley. He wasn't about to let the wolves get him.

The snow on the trees was starting to freeze, and their hands were so cold they were afraid of slipping off the branches, so they stayed as still as possible, hoping the wolves would soon give up and move on. Snow was beginning to fall again. They were late for chores and supper. Harley asked, "Do you think they're gone."

"Maybe they are, but we should wait a little while longer to be sure." The sun was going down, and he was hoping someone would come looking for them." If they are still close by, I am too cold to run from them. I think we should wait a little longer also and give them plenty of time to lose interest."

"We can't stay here all night, Matt. It's getting dark." Harley remarked. "Grandma is probably really worried!"

"I know, but let's get our minds on something else for a little while. I'll tell you what I did when I first started school here. I don't think the teacher ever knew. Papa said I had to go to school, though I didn't want to, so when he left, I hid in the wood box until all the kids were inside, and then got out and went back home by myself. Papa was upset, but he thought it was so funny that I didn't get a licking."

They both laughed out loud. Harley wondered, "why would you do that? Wasn't it hot in there? I like school."

"I guess I did it just to see if I could. I don't remember." Replied Madison.

The family was getting concerned by that time. It was not like them to be late for chores or supper. Leander came in from the barn and decided to go look for them. He took the wagon just in case something was wrong. As he drove up the road, he looked for footprints and began calling for them.

It wasn't long before Harley and Madison could see the wagon. They began to climb down from the safety of the tree and ran as fast as they could toward the wagon. Grandma had put a blanket in the wagon, and gladly, the boys climbed in and covered up with it, too cold and scared to talk much. He asked them what happened.

The only reply was, "we'll tell you when we get home. We're just glad you came to get us." They didn't have to do chores that night. Grandpa and Sheridan did them while they warmed by the fire with a cup of hot sassafras tea.

When all was settled down, and they were ready for supper, they told the story of what had happened to them and why they were late. Madison added, "Sorry we didn't do our chores, Grandpa."

"That's ok, Son. We're just glad you are alright. I do think you need to come straight home after school until this weather breaks. The animals are naturally having a harder time finding food for their families in the snow. It makes them a little aggressive. It could be a bear next time."

The snow was deep the next day, and there'd be no school. Grandma was glad and didn't like for them to walk to school. "I'm sure glad you boys took time to think instead of just running. Those wolves might've had you for supper!" exclaimed Grandma.

"There now, Lucy. You needn't worry so." Grandpa tried to assure her that it probably would never happen again. "It's not common for wolves to attack people. But the boys will be sure to come straight home after school during the winter."

If they were going to go hunting, they needed to carry a gun, sling shot, or a bow and arrows. Having lived in the Choctaw Nation when Harley was very young, he knew a little about making a bow and arrow, but Madison had learned a lot from the Indian culture and understood how to choose the right wood, notch the ends, bend the bow just right to give it the most power possible. He helped Harley, and they each made a bow that was the right size for them.

Then, arrows were carefully made from the straightest sticks they could find. Arrow heads were plentiful in Grandpa's place, so they tied them on end and made arrows for each of them. For the rest of the winter, they would carry some sort of weapon to school.

Grandma Lucy thought they should have some time to play and have fun when the chores were done; Harley was glad, but if he ever found a book he hadn't read, he would cut his play time short because he loved to read and studied hard, even at home whenever he could, though it was mostly by lantern light.

He loved to read about other cultures since his Great Grandma (Hall) Storts was from Ireland, and his grandpa had come from Germany. His Great, Great, Great Grandpa Conrad Krigbaum had come from Holland back in the early 1600s. One of his great-grandpas had come over on the May Flower, so the stories go. Some of the Krigbaum family were Cherokee. As he had it figured, he was about a quarter Cherokee himself. "Quite a mix," he thought.

Fascinated that he was from so many places, he wanted to know about his ancestors; how they lived, and how they came to be together. Harley had been very sad and confused when they lived in the Choctaw Nation because he missed his mama and didn't feel like playing with the other children; however, he was glad to have memories and education from them. He had learned things that he wasn't aware of.

They went to school for three months in the winter and three in the summer. The school was closed during planting and harvest times because the crops had to come first or many would go hungry; however, being the hard worker he was, Harley was not giving up his education or his music either. He found time to practice the fiddle every night. It reminded him of his mama.

He loved it when Sheridan would be there and played twin fiddles with him, and he really missed playing with Papa when he was away working.

Every time he came home, they had a grand time with music. "Mama would be very proud of you, Harley. So am I. You have come a long way since you got that small fiddle." Thurman would sometimes try to visit if Papa could let them know when he was coming. Sheridan and others would get together for a musical or square dance.

Grandpa Storts loved to play fiddle, but with so many musicians, he spent a lot of time dancing and listening to the music and sometimes would sing or dance as Harley played, which always made Harley feel proud.

As the years passed, they continued to attend school there and spent much, maybe most of their time, with Phylander and Lucy, working the farm with them.

Chapter 18
Finding a Job

Madison had graduated eighth grade and was working on farms and wherever he could get a job, in addition to working for Papa and Grandpa. He worked wherever he was needed.

Harley still had another year or two in school and would like to go on to the Academy in Paris, but knew that could not happen. After graduating eighth grade, he still read every book he could get his hands on and practiced his arithmetic skills by calculating crop production, making furniture, putting souls on shoes, or helping make wagon wheels or horseshoes, along with many other tasks.

He soon realized that almost every job had to do with arithmetic in one way or another, and he needed to try to keep his mind sharp. An education was something that never stopped anyway, so he would learn what he could where he could.

In 1909, Harley was sixteen. He had been looking for a job, and there didn't seem to be any work available during the winter, but he was determined to find work somewhere since he was not needed on the farm for a little while. Finally, he was offered a position as a house servant for someone. They didn't expect him to accept.

He didn't accept it that day. It was not what he had in mind. As he thought about it that night, he thought to himself, "Oh, well, I can handle anything for a little while." He went back the next day and told them he would take the job.

He was such an outdoors person that he would be ready and willing to help his grandpa with the farm work when planting season came. He would love to help his Papa, too. He missed him, but he had been gone for months this time, and no one even seemed to know where he went.

They had not heard from him since he had last left on a steamboat. "I sure hope Papa is alright. He should have been back a long time ago." He tried not to worry but did.

Meanwhile, he wanted to earn a little money and would try to spend it wisely or save it for when he really needed it. He didn't think he would ever get married, but his grandma had said he should not be so quick to say never. "Falling in love is not something we plan. God is the only one who really knows our future. Marriage is a good thing with the right person."

He thought about what she said, then decided that if he didn't get married, he might have to do housework for the rest of his life. He couldn't always live with Grandma.

By planting season, he had served his time as a house servant and wanted no more of it; though, he had only worked a few months, feeling that he was much more apt to handle a team and a plow.

From then on, he would work at blacksmithing, carpentry, or anything else he could find. Housework was not for him; although he didn't mind helping his grandma now and again. Actually, he loved to spend time with her doing anything, especially helping her in the kitchen, but he wouldn't advertise that anywhere.

Chapter 19
Laura Graham

About four miles away from Harley, in the Barn Hill community, lived a young girl named Laura Graham. She attended a larger, two-room school at Driggs. It also doubled as a community building. Church services were held there, as well as dances or musicals. This was another community that believed that if you worked together, things could happen.

Laura's birthday was April 1, 1893. She was one of ten children. Her parents were John Slater and Amanda Louise Graham.

Her father, John Graham and his first wife had divorced shortly after they married. He later married her sister, Amanda Louise Anderson.

Their children were Andrew Jackson (AJ), Boyd, Lula, Bessie, Ollie, Mattie, Rosie, Holland, Daniel, and Laura.

Their home was in the Barn Hill community. Laura had been raised much the same way as Harley had been, with much love and hard work. She had gone to school at Barn Hill for some of her life, but she had also gone to Driggs for several years.

They had to walk two miles to school unless her father was teaching then they could ride in the wagon or walk along with him. Both her parents had been schoolteachers. They had both taught at Driggs at some point, but Laura was one of the younger children. Her mother had given up her teaching career in order to take care of her own children.

Her father, born in 1848, was in his fifties by the time she started school. He was also a farmer, as most of the neighbors were. Having homesteaded several acres, he had to work the land as a part of retaining it.

Everyone had to provide food for their own families. They could trade some things with each other. But for the most part, they all must raise food to eat.

The school terms were three months in the summer and three in the winter. During planting season and at harvest time, they were all needed to work at home. When Laura and her brothers and sisters didn't get to go to school, they were taught at home whenever there was an opportunity.

What they were taught first and foremost was to be kind to each other and be friends as well as siblings. Ma told them that if they worked together in harmony, the job would get done better and faster. They put it to the test, and she was right; if they would team up with their chores, it wouldn't seem as much like work.

Pa told them they could take it easy or take it hard and make it hard on themselves, but either way, they had it to do. With all the chores of milking the cows, gathering eggs, cutting and hauling wood, feeding the chickens and other animals, gardening, and many other things, they understood what he was saying and learned to depend on each other and enjoyed each other's company at the end of the day.

Not to say there wasn't an argument now and again, but disagreements never paid off and would usually make it harder on everyone and could cause a late supper. Ma wanted harmony and peace at the supper table. They would just wait until everyone was in good humor to eat, even if it meant no supper at all.

Pa stood by her and respected her ruling. The girls helped with all the housekeeping, cooking, and canning, so the boys had to do more of the outside chores, but they worked as teams on many assignments.

The weekends were full; work on Saturday, but total rest on Sunday. It was the Good Lord's Day. Rest was not an option. The whole family would rest on Sunday. They often went to church, and then the rest of the day was spent with relaxing games, a nap, or music. "Even the Good Lord rested on the seventh day." Pa allowed He wanted everyone to take one day off for rest, as well.

On Sunday evenings, Laura or one of the others sometimes played the pump organ while the others sang or just listened as they rested.

If the children refused to obey, even the punishment would wait until the next day. But it would come as sure as rain. A whipping after Pa had rested a full day was not a good thing! It would be better to be in trouble any other day of the week. It would be the first order of the day on Monday.

A game of checkers or maybe marbles was ok; however, games that require lot of physical activity were not allowed. The work week depended on rested bodies.

Since graduating eighth grade in Driggs School, Laura had considered becoming a teacher herself, but life seemed to lead her in other directions. She loved learning and had confidence that she could teach her own children at home, if the need ever arose. She had a special love for history and reading.

Laura and Harley met when they were young and had seen each other at community musicals and other events, but she didn't pay a lot of attention to him. There were several boys her age in both communities. He and Holland had become good friends. They helped each other and hunted together. He had been to their house many times, had eaten with them when they worked at the Graham farm and still had not thought much about Laura.

It was not until a year after they graduated that he began to talk to Laura. Having similar interests and lifestyles, their conversations brought them to realize they might be of great help to each other.

Laura liked to read and enjoyed school, but it was hard for her to put too much heart into anything. Her home life was devastated by the untimely death of her mother.

Being one of the youngest children, Laura had lost both her parents. Her mother died of breast cancer when Laura was fifteen. She was thankful to have Ollie still at home to help her. Daniel was only ten years old at the time their mother died. Laura and Ollie felt it was their responsibility to help raise him.

The loss of their father less than two years later was hard. Then, soon afterwards, Ollie married, leaving her at home with two brothers, Holland and Daniel.

Most of her brothers and sisters were married and had families of their own. Daniel could have stayed with any of them, but he thought Laura needed him also.

Her oldest brother, A.J., was living near Driggs, and his children attended school where Laura had gone. She had not wanted to leave her home; however, it was not the same anymore. Playing the organ as she had for years was just not the same, either. Laura's heart was filled with sadness. It seemed that Harley took some of that sadness away.

Laura's brothers and sisters, though they had lost their parents, stayed in close contact with each other, visiting often, depending on each other for many things, and appreciating time spent together.

More and more, they came to appreciate their parents' teaching them to work as teams. "Help one another, and you will have help with your own work." If one was building a house, they didn't think of hiring help; the family and community came together to help. Laura knew they would always stay in contact with each other. She had helped them with their children, expecting that if she ever had children, they would be right there to assist her, also.

"It sure is a good thing Ma and Pa insisted we learn to help each other," She thought. Her memories of her mother in the kitchen were happy, yet sad. She had taught all the girls to cook and keep a clean house. Laura was quite at home in the kitchen; however, she was left the only woman in the house with two boys when she was seventeen. They expected her to cook and clean for them just like their ma had done.

Since she had all the housework, cooking, washing, and ironing, the boys said it was only fair that they did the outside chores. Most of the time, she would build her cook fire herself to get the right heat for the food she was cooking.

Laura was glad to do the chores; it's just that it seemed like a heavy cloud was hanging over the house. Even her brothers and sisters didn't seem to come over as often. "It is so lonely here; I can't put my heart into anything!" She spoke out loud to herself as she was washing the dishes. "God, I don't understand why you took them? I guess you know best, but the house is too empty! What did we do that was so bad?"

Laura went to her room and lay across her bed, and tears began to flow. She had thought she was past the crying. It was as if the pain was starting all over again. Forgetting about the time and the kitchen, she cried herself to sleep while holding a picture of her parents.

Holland and Daniel thought she must be sick, so they cleaned up the kitchen for her and let her rest. Daniel went in to check on her, finding her lying on top of the covers, still in her day clothes, with a handkerchief in her hand. Then he saw the picture she was holding.

"Are you ok, Laura? Can I get you anything?" He sat on the side of her still-made bed, seeing that something was really upsetting his sister. "I miss them too, Laura."

She opened her eyes, realizing she had fallen asleep. "Yes, I'm fine. Guess I better get up and get the dishes done," she said as she sat up on the bed. "I was just—well, the house is so empty without Ma and Pa.

I was thinking about Ma and how she cooked, cleaned, or sewed all day, and nobody noticed or really appreciated it; then, it all had to be done over the next day. I try to do what she did, but I can't! I really miss her! "

"Why do you feel you have to fill her shoes? It's not your place to take care of us; we are not your children. You need to get out more. Have some fun now and then." He continued, "Don't get me wrong, we are glad to come home to a home-cooked meal and a clean house every day, but you are only seventeen. You need a life of your own. Holland and I can carry our own weight."

"I really don't have anything to do, and I don't mind the cooking." She got up and went into the kitchen to clean up.

"Well, who has been working in my kitchen?" Laura laughed. Guess you weren't kidding! Maybe you don't need me."

"Oh, I guess I should have told you; we did the dishes. But, that's not true, Sis. You know we need you, but we want you to be happy, also."

Since the cleaning was done, Laura decided that she would go back to bed. She told the boys thank you and good night and then went back to her lonely room.

The next afternoon, Harley came over to visit with the boys. They often helped each other with certain jobs or went fishing together. She noticed he was looking at her often but thought nothing about it. As he was about to leave, he stopped at the door, "Laura, there is a barn dance this weekend; would you like to go?"

Surprising herself at her own response, "Well, I don't see any reason why not. It's not like I have a lot to do except housework. Guess I don't have to ask permission. Sounds like it might be fun." She was surprised that he had asked her and even more surprised that she had accepted.

"Great, I will pick you up around 5:00. Will that be ok with you? Oh, by the way, that was a good supper. Thanks."

"You're welcome; one more mouth doesn't make much difference when you feed boys with hollow legs. Glad you enjoyed it." They all laughed; Dan and Holland were a little embarrassed.

He left shortly, and Laura began to think about what she should wear. She had not gone anywhere but to church and to her siblings' houses in over a year. She thought, "I suppose I really should wear one of these pretty dresses that Ma made for me; she worked so hard on them. It just makes me so sad! I know I can't just sit here forever."

Laura had graduated from school two years earlier. She had been quietly grieving and had turned down several invitations to go places, not interested in ever leaving her home. She never wanted to marry, so why go through the trouble of dating? Somehow, at that moment, she felt differently. "Ma and Pa are gone and are not coming back."

Besides, there is no harm in going to a dance. Harley seems like a nice enough boy. He will probably be playing his fiddle most of the time, but I can find something to do. I am really tired of playing nursemaid to a couple of ornery boys that are big enough to fend for themselves."

Friday night came, and Laura wanted to back out, but she had to keep her word. A person is only as good as their word. She would have to go; she already said she would. Picking out the prettiest dress she could find, she got dressed and waited for Harley to get there.

"Wow, Sis! We better keep an eye on you at that dance, or Harley better leave that fiddle alone tonight. We'll have to swat those boys off like flies."

"Stop it, you two! I dress like this when I go to church sometimes. Maybe I should just not go. Harley will be playing music most of the time anyway."

Daniel said, "We're just teasing you, Laura. We'll be there too. If anyone bothers you, just let us know. We'll take care of them for you. You'll have a good time.

I don't know why I told him I would go. I don't really feel like being around a lot of people, and I don't know what came over me."

Holland put his arm around his sister, "It's ok, Laura, I hear a wagon; it's probably him. You can't back out now; just go and have a good time. We'll be there by the time you are. You deserve a night out once in a while."

Harley came to the door, dressed in his Sunday best. She had not thought of him as handsome before, and now she wondered why she hadn't noticed. He was quite dashing in his shoes that shined like new money and his stiffly ironed shirt and with his hair so neatly combed.

Handing her a corsage of red roses, he said, "Hello, Laura. Wow! You look stunning! Shall we go?" He extended his arm to her as she grabbed her scarf and closed the door behind them.

"Thank you! It's beautiful. I wasn't expecting flowers."

He helped her up onto the wagon; though she thought it was needless since she got in and out of their wagon all the time without help. But it seemed to be the thing to do. He was trying to prove himself a gentleman. She would respect that and allow him to help her as he wished. "I hope I don't forget," she thought. "Did you bring your fiddle?"

"I never go far from home without it. That doesn't mean I'm going to be playing it all the time. I invited you to a dance. I am hoping there will be enough musicians without me. I wouldn't want to leave such a pretty maiden unattended at a barn dance."

Blushing, Laura didn't know what to say to that, so she just smiled and didn't say anything for a few minutes. It seemed as if she was seeing him for the first time. Harley had been to her house many times, but she had not paid a lot of attention to him since he was usually doing something with her brothers.

A strange new feeling stirred within her chest. "My, he does look handsome!" she thought to herself. "You look very nice also," she said.

As they rode along in the wagon, Harley seemed to be in no hurry. The horses walked along at a leisurely pace while they talked about one thing or another. "The dance may be over by the time we get there at this rate, but I sure do like talking to you, Laura."

"I'm having a nice time also. Thank you for inviting me. Is it going to be at your grandpa's?"

"No, it's at a neighbor's barn. If it had been at Grandpa's, it would have been harder to get away for this long. I'm so glad you came with me. It may be a chore keeping you to myself. Maybe I won't have to play much tonight."

"It's ok if you play; I love to listen to you. It is good to get out for a change. I haven't really been anywhere much since, well, since my Ma passed. Dan and Holland have been telling me that I need to take time for something besides housework and cooking for them. Did they put you up to this?"

"Of course not! I have wanted to talk to you for a long time. You didn't seem too interested, and I know you have been having a hard time, so I didn't want to make a nuisance of myself. I don't know if I have thanked you properly for the times you have set an extra plate for me at your table, often without knowing ahead of time."

"I don't mind at all. You are welcome any time; Ma has always spoken highly of you, and I like you too. Besides, it gives the boys something to do besides pick on me."

"Well, here we are. That was a short trip." Harley got down as he was saying, "Wait there, and I'll come around and help you down."

Laura had not enjoyed anything so much in a very long time. Her mother had been ill since Laura was a child. They found out she had cancer when Laura was thirteen. It was only a matter of time; so, it was hard to be anything but sad.

Her mother had tried to help them make the best of what they had and seemed happy for the time she had with them. "We mustn't waste the good times worrying about the bad. God has given us another day. Let us be thankful," she would often say.

But tonight, Laura realized that she had been sad and lonely most of the time. Many days, she just went through the motions of housework, cooking, sewing, and anything else that she deemed her responsibility.

Her sisters were all married, and she didn't want to bother them, though they loved it when she went to visit them, which she sometimes did whenever the boys were going to town in the buckboard.

The dance lasted several hours, and Harley played a song or two now and then when he was asked to, but most of the time, he danced or talked with Laura. They left early just to have time alone together. Harley went to get the wagon while she waited inside with some friends.

Harley returned and helped Laura onto the seat. "I don't know where my head has been! This has been the best time I think I have ever had. Guess I've been too busy to notice you. Well, I did notice your cooking, you know, and I always thought you were the prettiest girl around. But tonight, I feel as if I would love to spend the rest of my life with you, Laura. May I see you again?"

Laura blushed and smiled. "I guess I haven't noticed much of anything. Ma and Pa left us alone, and I just try to get through each day the best I can." She was still grieving the loss of her parents, though it had been almost three years.

"I have also enjoyed this evening, Harley. Thank you so much for inviting me. And yes, I would like to see you again. Maybe I could cook supper for you next week. I will make you something special if I know you are coming."

"I would like that very much. This time, I won't be doing things with the boys. What will they think of that? Daniel has been telling me that I need to take some time for myself. I can see that he was right. Both boys are just as capable of cooking as I am. Ma saw that when she realized she was not going to be here to care for us. I guess that I just need to feel needed."

They got to the house, and Harley walked her to the door. "I won't be able to sleep tonight without dreaming of you, Laura. Thanks again for a most enjoyable evening. Would you like a ride to church on Sunday? I would be glad to come and go with you."

"Are you sure? Isn't it somewhat out of your way? Guess I could feed you to make up for the extra effort. You would have to bring the wagon instead of riding your horse. Or we could just walk from here. I often do. Then you could ride your horse."

"That's thoughtful of you; it might be nice to walk to church. Besides, Grandpa might need the wagon. I better be getting back now. You have a good night, Laura."

"Good night, Harley." Laura went inside to find the boys waiting up for her and wanting details of what she had done that night. They had left the dance early, too, and rode straight home.

"Did you have a good time, Sis?" Daniel noticed a pleasant look on her face. It was a welcomed sight. She had looked so sad for a long time. They all missed their folks, but Laura seemed to take it harder than all of them. "That smile looks good on you."

"Yes, I had a very nice time. It was good to get out. Ma and Pa are not coming back. We need to somehow pick up and move on."

They all agreed that they would have to make the best of what they had, just like their parents had taught them. That night, Laura slept better than she had in a long time. She went to sleep thinking about what to fix Harley for Sunday dinner. She had cooked for him before, but nothing special. "I think I will bake a blueberry pie," she whispered.

Laura and Harley spent many hours and days together after that day. It seemed that it took a long time to ride four miles in a wagon. Harley rode a horse to see her most of the time.

A few months later, they were going for a walk in the woods behind Laura's house; Harley said, "You know, Laura, I can't stand being away from you. We live four miles apart. When we are together, I think I never want to leave you; when we're apart, I wish to see you. My grandpa asked me what was wrong." I forget what I'm doing and am sometimes late with my chores. It almost has to be love.

Grandma said we don't choose to fall in love; it just happens. It seems to me that it would make sense for us to just get married, so we don't have to be apart for so long. If I asked you to marry me, what would you say?"

"Oh, Harley, I don't know, I really have not thought much about marriage. I would need to think about it for a while. I wish I could talk to Ma. It scares me a little. I think that is what has bothered me about being without parents. There is no one to tell me right from wrong or good from bad. I do enjoy your company. You have helped me more than you could possibly know. I would hate to leave the boys."

"I am sure they can manage. If need be, Daniel could come and stay with us. I know Holland already has a girlfriend. He might be thinking of marriage himself."

"I never thought of that. But that would leave Dan alone. He's only thirteen. Let me think about it for a while. That is a lifetime commitment and should not be taken lightly, parents or no parent. Don't you agree?"

"That's why I love you, Laura; I'm sure you would be a good and devout wife because you are devoted to anything you undertake, and with no one to say you have to."

Laura had an idea, "How about if we don't see each other or talk about each other for a couple of weeks or so? If we can bear to be apart, then maybe we need to stop seeing one another so much and make room for other things. What do you think about that?"

"I think I will go insane without you, but we can try it. And if we really can't stand being apart, then will you marry me, Laura? You really have captured my heart, you know."

"You are not even eighteen yet. We can talk about that later, depending on the next few weeks."

The next week seemed longer than either of them had expected. They both missed each other more than even they could imagine. "Harley, are you and Laura feuding? You haven't said a word about her all week." Madison asked.

"No." He had agreed not to talk about her, so he got up and went on about his chores and then on to anything that could keep him busy. He didn't want to talk about anything.

"I don't need two weeks or even one, but I promised her, so I have to give her time. What will I do if she doesn't want me? She can't possibly say no! Can she?" he thought.

The longest two weeks of Laura's life finally passed. Her heart was pounding, hoping he would come, but she would have to wait for him. He might not feel the same way she did. He was on her mind day and night, hoping he had not found someone else. Her brothers tried to comfort her, thinking she was missing Ma and Pa.

Daniel asked, "Why hasn't Harley been here lately? Is something wrong? Do I need to talk to him?"

"No, that won't be necessary. It seems I have to make my own decisions." She walked out of the room. "

Then, one day, Harley rode up on his horse. Laura was outside doing laundry. She dried her hands and waited for him to dismount. Neither of them spoke for a few minutes, wondering what the other was thinking.

Finally, Harley said. "Laura, this has been the hardest two weeks I have ever spent. I don't want to live the rest of my life without you. I hope you feel the same way."

"It has been hard for me also. I was counting the days. I was afraid you would not come back; maybe we are pretty well suited for each other. "I'm happiest when I am with you."

They began to spend as much time as possible together, and a few months later, he asked her to marry him again; and she gladly said, "Yes, I would be honored to be your wife."

Chapter 20

Wagon Trip to Oklahoma

Laura really enjoyed her time with Harley's Grandma Lucy. Still missing her own mother, she was glad they lived near her.

Harley and Laura were eighteen years old when they married in 1911. They lived in several places but never ventured too far from Driggs or Paint Rock. One of the few journeys they made was to Oklahoma in their covered wagon, traveling with some of Harley's family who were on their way to California. They thought of staying there for a while.

Harley had family they wanted to visit, and it would give them a chance to make a little money picking cotton in the many large cotton fields. Picking cotton was something they were both accustomed to. The cotton fields in Oklahoma were plentiful, so they heard.

He managed to purchase a wagon and team with the money he had saved from working at odd jobs during his lifetime. Not quite having enough money, he was able to work out the rest. The wagon needed repairs, but that was no problem for Harley. His grandpa had made sure he knew how to repair any part of a wagon.

Dealing with weather and other obstacles, they would pick cotton as often as they could, sleeping part of the time in the wagon and other times with family members whom they had not seen often. Neither of them wanted to make many long trips, so they would try to visit all his relatives living nearby.

As the wagon bumped along, Harley asked, "Did I ever tell you that I lived in Oklahoma for a while, Laura?"

"Not that I recall. I thought you were raised near and with your grandparents."

"Well, for a few months after Ma passed away, we lived in the Choctaw Nation. I was seven at the time she died. Wanting to try to make a new life for us, Papa moved us to Oklahoma. We went to be near my brothers. Anyway, I don't remember much about it. I was so sad about Mama dying, I suppose."

"Papa found he could not make us happy there; so we moved back home to be near Mama's folks. He still had the home place a few miles from them. I mostly stayed with Grandma Lucy after that. Papa was gone a lot, working on the steamboats, sometimes for weeks at a time."

"Well, how time flies when you are having fun! We're here. I hope they got our letter that we were coming."

Harley's brother, Thurman, met them at the wagon. He was so glad to see them that he took off a few days from work just to spend time with them and play music together. "How're you doing on that fiddle, Harley? It has been a long time since we played together."

"Well, go get your guitar, and let's find out." Without another word, Harley started toward the wagon and took out his fiddle. They met under a shade tree where chairs were arranged already. "Looks like you were ready for us. Do your kids play?"

"Sometimes, some of them are getting pretty good. How is it that you thought to bring your fiddle along anyway?"

Seeing the excitement on Thurman's face, he said, "I never leave home without it. There is something about a good fiddle tune that makes the day end on a good note, but I sure miss your rhythm on the guitar."

"So do I. The only time I have a fiddle to play with is when Gideon comes around. That doesn't happen often. It sure seemed a lot easier to find time to play when we were kids. Some of my kids play guitar, but no one has picked up the fiddle yet.

This feels like old times; I am so glad you came! Stay as long as you can, I'm going to take time off so we can make up for lost time. Maybe Jack will be here soon. I know you can't go to see everybody. This could be a good meeting place. There's always room for one more. I have a big watermelon that has just been waiting for a time like this. I almost cut it earlier; but I knew it was too big for just us."

Harley replied, "Sounds good to me; Jack and I were together so much when we were young that people thought we were brothers. I sure wouldn't want to leave without a little time with him."

Laura and Mary went into the house to make plans to feed everybody. Laura was having a good time; although, it reminded her of the times with her own family. She realized that maybe the pain of losing her parents would someday not be so hard. She loved her brothers and sisters a lot, and today, she felt especially blessed to have married into such a loving family. She said a quiet prayer of thanksgiving.

"It might be good to have supper early so they can get back to the music. Makes me want to dance, as if I had the time. Do you play anything, Laura?"

"Not really, I used to play a pump organ some. My father taught me to play when I was very young. Mother loved to listen to us. They both passed away before Harley and I married. It was not as small as a fiddle or guitar, and I thought it might be too cumbersome to move with us, so I left it there."

"That's too bad. Do you think you will ever get it? You and Harley could play together." Mary Suggested.

"Harley doesn't know that I play, and I don't think I am going to tell him. We are just renting a small house and have no room for such a big instrument. I don't want to make him feel bad about it. I guess it belongs to my brothers now; though, as far as I know, no one ever plays it."

"Maybe you should reconsider. I'm sure that Harley would try to find a way to get it for you."

"Yes, I'm sure he would. That's why I don't want to tell him. It wouldn't be fair to ask him. 'Oh, by the way, it really is good of you all to go to so much trouble for us. Harley has looked forward to this trip for some time. It looks like we came to play music, but we are hoping to pick a little cotton while we're here."

They both laughed and looked out at their husbands so cheerful in the front yard. "Harley has really missed playing with Thurman. My family lives close by, and he plays with John and the others, but I think he misses Thurman."

"I think this food will be ok for a little while. Why don't we join them for a few minutes? Thurman is glad that Harley brought his fiddle, even more so that he plays so well. Jack should be here any time."

They took their aprons off and strolled out to enjoy the music. Just as they were closing the door, Jack and his wife came up the walkway.

"I'll be! What a surprise! So good to see you two! Papa, are you going to cut that big watermelon you've been saving? We wouldn't want them to miss out on it."

"We've already been talking about it. We might try it tomorrow afternoon after it's cooled in the spring for a while, if you'll take it down there after supper."

"No problem. Harley, do you want to come with me to the spring? That is if you can take time out from the music. You've really gotten good on that fiddle. I knew you would with that determination of yours. I haven't seen much you couldn't do."

"Grandpa always says that if a job is worth doing, it's worth doing well. Learning to play the fiddle was a job for sure, one of the hardest I ever tried, partly because I was so young and not big enough to fit the fiddles, I reckon. It actually feels good to have a full-size one now and know that I won't outgrow it."

"Oh, and sure, I will go with you to the spring. I just sort of landed in the yard, and the music took over. We could go now if you want to, before supper. We need a break, I imagine."

Jack and Harley had a wonderful time just talking about the many years of growing up together as they walked along to the spring. They all enjoyed an evening of music, singing, dancing, and visiting, with plenty of good food.

Thurman said, in almost a sad voice, "I hate for this night to end. It sure has been fun; but we better get a little rest so we'll be able to make the best of your visit. I wish you could just stay. Wish Willi could have been here, also."

"We will go see him a little later," Laura added. "We can't make these trips often; we have to make every minute count and see everyone we can."

"Laura insisted we put a nice straw bed in the wagon so we could take our time. She has it made up fit for a king, with fresh, clean sheets and Quilts. It doesn't feel like camping when she's along. She has it feeling like a cabin instead of a wagon."

"Well, you can just leave it made up; you're not sleeping in the wagon tonight. There's a comfortable bed ready and waiting for you in the house. It's not open for discussion. I hung the quilts out to air this morning." Mary spoke firmly.

In a few days, they would pack up the wagon and head on to see other families, but first, they would go to the cotton field they had planned to work in for a little while, in order to make some cash money to help pay for their expenses.

Jack was not thrilled about picking cotton; he would rather just visit, but he was very familiar with the fields and knew where the best patches were. "Let me get my sack, and I will go with you. We can make five dollars in a day in the right patch without having to bend over so low." He was still talking as he came out with his sack.

'That's what I wanted to hear. It is about all we can do at home to make five together in a day. We need to save some of our time for visiting and music. It sure is good to get to work with you again, Jack! I hope Thurman didn't lose too much time at his job."

"He wouldn't have done it if it had been a problem. He can make it up if he needs to." Jack went on. He is a good worker, and his boss knows it. He used to go with Grandpa to work on the steamboats. He said he was really tired by the time he got home, but he did it to spend time with him."

"I was not really aware of how hard Papa had to work. All I ever knew was that he was gone a lot. Then, when he came back here to live, he remarried, and I was haunted by the loss of my Mama that I really didn't spend a lot of time with him after that."

"Wow! You're not joking! Looks like this field is covered with snow! Think they'll let us pick?" Laura asked.

"Sure, there are a lot of pickers, but this is a big field. Let's go see the man in charge. He can tell us where he wants us. I've picked here before. He's good to work for."

Jack introduced them, and within minutes, Laura handed Harley the long cotton sack that she had made for him. They were soon picking in tall cotton; unlike the cotton patches they were used to in the bottoms in Arkansas.

Working as hard as they could, they worked rows next to each other and visited as they picked, taking advantage of every minute they had together. Family time was something to treasure.

Before they knew it, their sacks were getting heavy, and it was time to weigh out. "We're not even halfway to the end of the row! Can you believe this cotton?" Laura declared.

"Laura, don't you go out picking us now! We men have a reputation to protect." Jack laughed. "I still have to work in these fields after you leave!"

"She might; she can stay up with me. She is no slacker, that's for sure. I'm a lucky man." Harley added, and they all laughed as they headed for the scales.

"If it makes you feel any better, I can put some in Harley's sack," she laughed. As the last of their cotton was weighed at the end of the day, Harley had made almost six dollars. Jack had made six twenty-five, and Laura had made six seventy-five. Jack looked at her in disbelief, while Harley just laughed. "I told you, she's no slacker at anything!"

"It's not my fault - the two of you spent more time talking and visiting than picking. We were picking in the tallest cotton I ever saw, and I wasn't going to pass up this chance just because you wanted to talk."

It was hot and tiring, but they picked a couple of days to make a little cash money and would like to have stayed and picked longer; however, visiting with other family members was more important. Maybe they could work in another field before returning home.

The cotton sacks were tucked away for later use, and they said goodbye to Cousin Jack. As they sat on the wagon seat, Harley paused. "Jack, do you have any plans to go on to California with the others? It seems as if several of the family are going together."

"I am still thinking about it, Harley. Seems like a long way to travel. If I go that far, I would probably go on to Oregon around where Grandpa lived. Speaking of traveling, I hope the weather holds for you. The storms here get a little rough sometimes. If we do have bad ones, be sure to find shelter. Almost everyone around here has a storm shelter. Don't try to ride it out in the wagon."

"Will do, take care, now. Thanks again for everything. Come see us when you can, Jack. Glad you could pick with us these few days. It's like old times."

"I will; you two enjoy the rest of your trip." Waving to them, he watched as they started to find Jack's brother Willi and his family.

Harley and Laura were on their way again in the bumpy wagon. Harley had to stop once or twice to tighten up some spokes. He had brought an extra wheel, just in case.

After a few weeks of working and visiting with as many of Harley's relatives as possible before some of them went on farther west, they both agreed that they would never venture that far to see any of them.

It was time to go home. They'd had a wonderful time, and the weather had been bearable, for which they were thankful.

Packing up their supplies that night, they would head out in the early morning. Seventy miles was a long way to travel by wagon, but it gave them a place to sleep at night when they needed it. If Harley had gone by himself, he would have ridden horseback, but he would never have asked Laura to do such a thing. She would not like the idea of sleeping on the ground, and they would need supplies for the trip.

The last night was at Willie's house. Harley had been anxious to see him. They all enjoyed their special time together. Again, they slept in the house on a nice comfortable bed. The wagon bed would not need to be made in the morning. "It is getting late," Harley stated. "We have a long ride tomorrow. Today has been a good day."

"Yes, it has, Harley; you are getting really good on that fiddle. I knew you would be someday. Your Mama knew it, too. She was mighty proud of you," replied Willie.

"I still play the last song for her, it seems. I appreciate the time John, Papa, and Grandpa took to teach me. We play together often. I really miss Thurman and his guitar."

"I'm sure you do. I am glad you are staying close to help Grandma and Grandpa." He added, "Say hello to them for me and tell them I love them."

"I will. Thanks for putting us up. We've had a great time." The team had been fed, watered, and hitched to the wagon; they all waved goodbye and were on their way, having enjoyed time just to spend with each other and the visit with family, but were glad to be going home.

Harley and Laura Krigbaum were soon on their way to their home in Arkansas.

Chapter 21
No Place Like Home

As they rode along, they talked about their families and other things while enjoying just being together.

"Family time is important; I'm glad we are able to visit some of your relatives. We must be sure to look after your grandparents when we get back. They have been through a lot, it appears to me," said Laura, thoughtfully. "Grandma looks sad sometimes, yet she is always so gracious."

"That's true, in 1900, Mama, who was only 48, passed away, leaving all of us devastated. They were still grieving from Aunt Mattie's death. I guess you never get over losing a child.

Five years later, we lost Aunt Temperance, who was only 51. They were dealing with a lot, trying to take care of grandchildren from both families. It was difficult to take on two extra families in five years when they had children of their own. I was only seven when Mama died and twelve when Aunt Tempie died."

"We stayed with Papa part of the time, but he was gone a lot, and it just wasn't the same without Mama. He did remarry, but we were so used to staying with Grandma Lucy and thought she needed us. Now that I think about it, maybe she could have used the break, yet she never would have told us that." They both laughed.

Papa went back to work on the steamboats and left me with them most of the time. Grandma Lucy said I had no business on that boat. Sometimes, he would take one of the older boys, but most of the time, he left us here to help with the farm.

There was really no way to get ahead. Papa tried to give them some money when he came home, but they used it all on us or gave it to us."

"I'm glad you're such a family man. I guess this would be a good time to tell you that our little family is growing. How do you feel about being a father?"

"Well, uh------ I guess. I haven't thought about it much. Are you sure? How long have you known?

"Pretty sure, I guess life will change somewhat for us. I will need to start making baby clothes, and we will need a crib when you get time. I think we should have about seven months, so there is no hurry."

He sat quietly for several minutes and then pulled under a shade tree to rest the horses. "You out picked us in the cotton field! I'm not sure what I think of that. Why don't we get off and stretch our legs? There's a creek close by. I'll water the horses, and maybe you could see if you can find us a bite to eat."

He unhitched the team to let them rest and took them to the creek. Laura had a meal put together by the time he arrived. After eating, they took a little walk, then rested themselves on the soft mattress stuffed with clean hay that had made traveling a lot more bearable. "I sure am glad you talked me into this bed."

"So am I. It's doubtful that I would've come without it." After about an hour, the sun had gone behind a cloud and made them realize that maybe it was time to be on their way. Soon, the wagon was back on the trail and on whatever road they could follow. The horses were refreshed, and it seemed they knew they were going home.

It was then decided that wherever they lived, they would just have to keep in touch with family, mostly by mail. The trips were too long and hard to make often.

Upon arriving home, Harley made the statement that is so often spoken, "There is no place like home." He was so glad to be home that he made a little wooden plaque with the words carved in it and hung it over the front door. (NO PLACE LIKE HOME)

Laura added, "True, but I think home is where the heart is." He didn't really understand that she was just coming to grips with her sadness over losing her parents and leaving her home and then, finally, beginning to be happy again.

Harley and Laura lived in a number of houses, mostly in Logan County. The little wooden sign went with them to every house and hung over the front door.

Harley added a few words as he nailed it up the third time. "You are right; home is where the heart is, and my home is with you, Laura."

She smiled and, with a deep feeling of satisfaction, felt that she, indeed, was at home with Harley. It really didn't matter where they lived as long as they were together.

As I see it, they heard so many hard luck stories about travel, weighed the cost, and decided that it was best to stay where they were and make the best of it.

Family ties were very close. Laura didn't want to get so far that she could not see her family often. They helped each other with many things, quilting, canning, gardening, and just talking while they rested.

Though many of his family lived in other states, they kept in touch the best way they could. A few trips would be made to visit, and they could count on Jack and Willie coming for a visit about once a year, but letters were their main means of keeping in touch. They were not going to California, they agreed.

Chapter 22

The New Family Life

On March 3, 1913, their first baby boy was born. They named him Cloyal Oren. Just as proud as could be, Harley brought in the new crib from the barn. He had put rockers on it and painted it brown. "I painted it because I figured this wouldn't be our last. The crib needs to survive through several years of use. We're only twenty years old; we could need it several times."

"You rest now, Laura, just like the doctor said, and let your sisters and me take care of things for a while. You will have time enough with him."

Laura's sisters, Ollie, Bessie, and Mattie, took turns helping Laura while she took time to regain her strength and spend time with her newborn son. "It is our turn to help you, Laura. You have always come when we needed help, they agreed."

Laura could expect to see Daniel about once a week, and he helped out a lot with Cloyal. He had never had a little brother, so they really enjoyed each other. That little boy filled a void that neither of them knew they had.

She wished her ma was there to share her joy, but the love for that baby overpowered the grieving for her parents. She was happy and complete for the first time in years. Life seemed to get better for them.

For the last several years, William, Harley's papa, had been home a lot more. "Papa, I'm sure glad you are close by. Being a father is a big responsibility. I may need a little advice or even help. But mostly, I'm just glad to see you more often. I always missed you when you were gone. I don't think I ever really thanked you for teaching me to play the fiddle."

"You were easy to teach, Son; you're a natural. Your Mama knew you were; she told me you needed that small fiddle when you were young. I guess mother's instincts are pretty accurate. You did well. Now you have a son to pass the skills on to. How about we have a little music and get that boy of yours used to it? What do you say?"

"Sounds good to me; you'll need to play guitar, though, if you don't mind. I don't do so well on it. I want him to hear it played right for the first time. We need to train his ears early. The way you play, he may pick up guitar instead of fiddle." They laughed.

"I have kept you all to myself, and Cloyal needs to get to know his grandpa. I'll hitch up the team for you when you are ready to go. You can visit with Laura and your grandson."

Harley took his time as he hitched the team to the buckboard; Papa stayed in and visited with Laura and the baby for a little while. After a pleasant evening of music and supper, Papa said goodbye and headed home with a tired but thankful heart.

Laura said, "I am so glad your father is home again. He's proud of his grandson. He has worked too hard, and he looks tired. You may need to be sure to help him more."

"Yes, I think you are right, as usual. He is a good father; I spent more time with my grandparents, I guess, because I was so young when Mama died. I maybe didn't realize the loss he was feeling. My own hurt was too great.

Madison spent more time with him. He was older and understood his needs better, I think. Now that I have a son, I think maybe he needed me with him more."

"Well, you both did the best that you could do at the time. He was more concerned that you be taken care of properly; he also knew that you would be of comfort to your grandma. After all, she had just lost a daughter. He is a good father, one to be proud of. He puts the needs of others before his own."

"I always enjoyed working, hunting, or anything else I did with Papa, but what we always seemed to enjoy the most was music. He can play about anything, I suppose. He taught Thurman to play guitar when he was very young. I think maybe he thought it might help us to stay together as we got older."

"You get together when you can, and it is a joy to watch you. I understand how you must miss the ones who have moved away. Madison has sure been a blessing. Do you think he will ever get married?"

"I don't know, it's not looking too promising. I wish he would take more interest in music. He can play guitar but won't play much."

"Now you have your own son to teach. He can't play yet, but he was listening. I was watching him. He really liked it!"

"If you say so, you're the mother; you probably have those instincts also. Guess I better start looking for a small guitar. There is plenty of time; it is getting late. We need to get some sleep if you plan to get the rest of the fields ready to plant."

They were soon fast asleep, with the baby snuggled in the new crib that Laura had rocked him in while they talked. For the next couple of years, their lives were full and happy; even Laura had to take time off for Cloyal instead of working so much in the gardens and fields.

He was growing up so fast that she began to miss having a baby. He had outgrown his little crib a long while back and was almost three years old. He loved his time with his grandpa Krigbaum, and Laura appreciated the break as she was getting ready for the second addition to their little family. It would not be long.

She would be glad when the baby arrived. It was getting harder to care for her son like she felt he needed. She had done fine and was feeling ok, but she could tell it was close.

In 1916, Harley and Laura had a precious baby girl. They couldn't have been happier. God was blessing their family. The baby girl was healthy.

Laura loved having a son, but there was just something special about having a baby girl. They named her Clossie.

Grandma Lucy came often, and Laura's sisters helped her for a few days until she was back on her feet. They wanted to make sure she didn't overdo it.

Laura was glad to have them with her, not that she thought she needed help, but she loved her time with them and was thankful for such a loving family. They often took time to thank God for their precious gifts and children.

Chapter 23

Papa Talks of War

In 1914, there was talk of another war. It seemed the whole world was being drawn into it. Harley went to check on his father, who was really disturbed by the news. He remembered the civil war and what it had done to the country, fearing that if it didn't stop soon, the US would be pulled into it. As news of the different countries getting involved, he began to tell Harley of some of the horrible situations he had seen and heard of in the civil war. He had not talked about it much before; he was just thankful he had survived, but he was sad because of the many who didn't.

"This country can't stand another war. No one wins a war. I was on what was called the winning side. I lost a cousin and other family members. They didn't win anything! They paid more than should have been required of them."

"Many of our family are in the military already; I have a brother, cousins, nephews, and son, and, as you are aware, I probably will have several more. These young patriotic boys and girls want to do their duty, along with families all over!"

"Oh. It's not a bad thing, mind you. If we lose our military, we lose our freedom; that's for sure. I just hate the thought of all the useless killing. There ought to be another way to settle things!

This country has already started a draft, just in case. War is a terrible thing. Don't–if you don't have to." He took Harley by the arm. He looked very worried and tired.

"Ok, Papa." Harley saw he was really worried and wanted to ease his pain. "We will do what we have to do. You know that. Maybe it will end soon, and we won't have to worry about it."

With the nod of his head, Papa left it at that and tried to go on with the music. They couldn't seem to make music happen much that night. Playing a few songs at Papa's house, Harley decided he better get home to Laura, who had stayed home to keep Cloyal in for a while. He was getting a little harder to handle, and she needed to rest, as they had worked in the garden while watching him and the baby all day. "Life sure changes when you have children," he thought.

Harley came home a little earlier than he had planned. Laura had put Cloyal and Clossie to bed and met him at the door. "Is your Papa ok?" She reached out to take his hat and watched the expression on his face, seeing that he was disturbed about something.

"Papa is worried about the other war, I think. He has never really wanted to talk about it. It must have been terrible for him. I was not aware that so many of our family had been killed and wounded.

It seems as if several countries are involved in fighting at this time. Papa doesn't look so good! I don't think he could survive if any of us had to go to war. I've not seen him like this."

"I don't think he's looked well since he lost your stepmother. His mind went back to when your mother died. Maybe he shouldn't be left alone so much."

"I just pray that the war will end soon, and we don't have to become a part of it. Maybe, he needs to see the doctor. He is only sixty-four; has been a hard worker all of his life, yet he doesn't seem to hold up for very long at anything." Harley added.

They got ready for bed, and Laura checked on Clossie. She was a year old and would climb out of the crib if she got half a chance, so Harley would need to make Cloyal a bed so they could have the bigger crib with taller sides for Clossie. They both were growing up too fast. Every day was a new day.

The next day, Harley went back to see how his father was feeling. "Papa, how would you like to invite some of the neighbors for music this weekend? I haven't heard you play your fiddle much lately. "Harley opened the case for him.

"I really don't feel like playing much, Son. As a matter of fact, Harley, I would like you to have my fiddle. Sheridan has a good one that he purchased himself. The other boys have guitars. Someday, your children will want to play."

"Laura wants me to bring you home with me tonight. She says you spend too much time alone. She has supper almost ready." Without any argument, he got his hat and was ready.

They didn't play at all that night; instead, Madison, Harley, and Papa sat and talked until very late. "Madison Munroe, my namesake, for some reason, you don't seem to play much on any instrument. Is there a reason? I want to be fair to you. You're such a good son and are always doing things for others. What do you need? What can I do for you?"

"I don't need anything, Papa. I love the music. I don't have to play to enjoy it. I am proud to be your son. You gave me your name. That is the best gift of all." They all smiled kindly. "You and Grandpa have taught us to love, live peaceably with each other, and work hard to make a difference in this world. What more could I want?"

For the next several weeks, Harley, Madison, and Laura spent a lot of time with Papa. Sheridan and his family came as often as they could.

He seemed to be getting a little used to hearing about the war overseas. At least he was going on as life would let him. He never went back to work but spent most of his time with his family. They tried to avoid talk of the war with him.

A few weeks later, he passed away quietly in his sleep. They never really learned what was wrong with him. The doctor thought it must have been his heart.

He was buried at Paint Rock Cemetery beside his first wife and the mother of his children. It was a sad day for all of them. The family stayed together and visited for a few days before going back to their homes.

William Munroe Krigbaum had left a legacy of love and music that would follow through many generations. The little guitar and fiddle that had changed the lives of the whole family, would be passed on to any of the younger children who were interested in learning to play and would be repaired many times.

Chapter 24
WW I

On April 6, 1917, the United States was drawn into the war. It had become the First World War, leaving much of the farm and factory work, again, to the women and elderly men and sometimes children. It seemed that everyone was either in the war or had family members who were. Many friends and members of the Storts and Krigbaum families had enlisted in the armed services or registered for the draft.

Harley and Madison didn't know which needed them the most, a hurting family or their country, so they registered for the draft. They would let God decide what they should do. Harley sure hated to go off and leave his wife and elderly grandparents if he didn't have to.

Grandpa had fought in the Civil War and said it was horrible and wouldn't talk about it much. Then, some of their children and grandchildren were in the military already.

They could do nothing but pray. All the talk of a world war was just too much for Phylander and Lucy. The news was never good. Thousands of Americans had been killed and thousands more wounded, including some of their own family. A few they would never see again, and others missing in action. Injuries got some soldiers sent home early.

"It is sad when you have to be thankful for an injury," Laura commented. "I just wish this whole thing would end. We teach our kids not to fight and to be good citizens, and for what? So, they can draft them and send them off to kill other people! She usually was not so outspoken but feared for her family, friends, and country.

The Storts and Graham families lost family members, but many of the Krigbaum men were soldiers. The number of casualties and injuries in their family was greater.

Many generations of the Krigbaum family had been in the military since the Revolutionary War, and several had enlisted since this war started, including a few of Harley's brothers and uncles; therefore, it would come as no surprise if some might not come home.

It was reported that at least two of their family members were missing in action and may have become prisoners of war. Several were injured. Most of them did come home after the war, some with permanent injuries. Many more still made careers in the military; though for some, it was difficult because their family had come from Germany.

There were stories of victory in spite of the odds. One of which was that of Captain William L. Krigbaum, Company A. 124th Machine Gun Battalion. On Oct. 9, 1918, he mounted and captured a German machine gun in a major battle and successfully stopped a counterattack that had the platoon totally surrounded, saving the lives of many in his platoon.

Not all the stories had been so pleasant. On May 20, 1918, Marcellus Krigbaum, a resident of California from Ohio, was accused of being a German Spy; although, he denied it. I didn't find anything that said he was convicted, only accused. Someone had overheard a conversation between him and another man that triggered the investigation.

His German mother-in-law, who was living with them, had not registered as an alien enemy woman during the war. He said they had simply overlooked it. She spoke such a mix of German and English that they couldn't get her to understand the need to register.

It must have been very difficult for the citizens who had family in other countries to fight against that country. Some of his family was from Germany, and some still lived there. The stress that the American people faced was great.

The Krigbaum, Storts, and Graham families were trying to hold on to what they had and help each other while praying for those in battle. The music stopped again. No one felt like playing while others were in a horrible trench, foxholes, or worse. Many were praying for them and all the soldiers to come home, listening for any news.

By the end of 1918, less than a year after the US entered the war, it was over; however, the cost had been great.

There was much rejoicing when they returned home, in spite of the sadness that many would not return. No one knew what lay in store for them. What they did know was that they should be thankful for what they had and the time to be together.

As the soldiers returned, these words were repeated over and over, "There is no place like home!" Harley polished up his sign that hung over the door, grateful to have a home.

The Storts and Krigbaum families loved to find a time to meet and have meals and music together with neighbors once again. Sometimes, Laura's brothers or sisters would join them, especially A.J. Graham. He played guitar and would try to get with them every weekend if possible. The more, the merrier. Any instrument or voice added just made the music better. It seemed that with the music, one could forget about the worries of life for a short while. It seemed to give the minds a rest.

One evening, they met at the Storts' homestead. Harley thought of his Papa as he played his fiddle and called the square dance. It was hard to have a good time with so many sad times still hanging on, but for that night, all was well and peaceful. They would address the hard times later.

Money became even more scarce. Then, as sometimes life is, they met with really hard times. Harley and Madison tried to help, but neither of them could come up with the money to help them. What little money they had was needed just to buy basic food and other things the family and animals needed.

Grandpa and Grandma were doing the best that they could. It just was not enough. One thing led to another. The war had taken its toll. He was not able to do anything about it. Though it broke his heart, and Phylander felt as if he was letting his family down, taxes had to be paid, and he wasn't able to come up with the money to pay them. He lost the homestead.

"I'm really sorry! My hope was to pass this farm down to all of you someday. You've worked too hard to make it a good farm. I just can't find a way to keep it. If either or both of you can, you can have it for the cost of the taxes. I'm going to lose it soon."

"Grandpa, I'm sorry. I have no money. We could try to sell something; few people around here have money either. Most are just barely surviving. Why didn't you tell us earlier? No need to answer that; we should have known. We thought we were helping you, but we have depended on you and Papa to provide for us way too much!"

Madison stayed the night with them. Harley was late going home that evening. He had stayed with Grandpa to help him with whatever he could and just to try to think of something that could help. There didn't seem to be anything to do.

Laura didn't know what to say to Lucy. "You know you can stay with us. It would be a real treat to have you here."

"Thank you, Laura. I'm not sure what we will do yet. Phylander has to have a little time to deal with losing our home. He feels as if it is his fault when we are supposed to be in this thing together! Life is not always what we think it should be."

A few weeks later, as Harley and Laura sat quietly at the table after supper, Harley bowed his head in despair. "We should have been able to help them. He lost it for the price of the taxes! I am going to do all I can to get it back for him someday!"

"They did the best they could. That's all anybody can do. It is nobody's fault; just the way life is sometimes." You still have each other; that's the main thing. I miss my Ma and Pa to this day and always will. I lost both parents and grandparents before I was eighteen. I am just thankful to have your grandma and grandpa. The land doesn't matter that much."

Neither of them felt like talking anymore. They went to bed early but couldn't sleep. Laura was almost relieved when Clossie made a sound. It gave her a call to check on her.

Grandpa and Grandma Storts never moved far away. Living here and there, making the best of what they had, and being thankful for whatever that was, especially for their children and grandchildren.

Chapter 25

The Late Letter

Lucy was concerned about Sarah Jane. She and her family had not been to see them for months. "It is not like Sarah to go this long without writing; something is wrong." She sat down and wrote her a letter, but before she could get it finished, word came that her daughter, Sarah Jane, had passed away.

Sarah had known her mama had so much to worry about, and she didn't have a lot of warning. "There is nothing either of us can do, and I need to spend time with my children. I want to see Mama and Papa, but neither of us is able to travel." She thought as she had begun to write to her parents.

My Dear Mama and Papa,

I really miss you and hope you are well. The kids are all doing fine, and they come by often to see if I need anything. They talk about their grandparents a lot. I hope they can spend some time with you all soon. I'm sure their father will want to come too.

I wish there was an easier way to tell you this, Mama; but the doctor says that I only have a short time to live. I just found out myself. Hope you can understand; I am not strong enough to come and see you. I guess that is why I have been so weak for the last several months. I kept thinking I would come and tell you in person.

Maybe it is better this way. You can remember the good times. I know this hurts you, and I am sorry. You have had to deal with more than your share of losses. God has brought us through losing Mattie, Elmira, and Temperance; He will carry you through this. I love you both so very much. Please try to trust God and don't grieve forever.

Give the rest of the family my love. By the time you get this, I will probably be in heaven; God has planned a meeting place for my sisters and me. Don't you think so, Mama?

All my Love,

Sarah

Well, if life had not been hard enough, Lucy was about to reach her breaking point. Why was she not allowed to see her daughter at a time when she was needed most? She didn't want to outlive all of her children. "God, why are you doing this?" She realized that Phylander was not able to travel well enough to even go to her funeral. His heart was not functioning well.

It was too late now, anyway. Sarah's children needed her, and there wasn't a thing she could do about it. She would have to write to them. Her heart was breaking, and she was wondering whether Phylander's heart could bear such a blow, so she put the letter aside to find the right way to tell him. She couldn't hide it. Her tears and actions would tell the tale shortly. He had always been the strong one; now, it was her turn.

Lucy fixed supper and tried to see that her husband ate in a calm setting, even though she was not hungry and could only eat a few bites. Waiting until they had settled down for the evening and he was in his chair, she told him about the letter as gently as she knew how. Then she gave it to him to read for himself. Fully expecting to have to send Madison to the doctor, she had told him a little earlier so he could be prepared.

For whatever reason, Phylander was not overly alarmed. It was as if he had not heard her. It was not soaking in. She was worried about him and asked Matt to keep a close eye on him.

Going to bed that night, they talked about their children and the lives they had lived. "It has been a hard life but a good life here, Lucy." I really hate that we lost Sarah, too. We'll get through it together, just like we always do, won't we, Dear?"

Lucy could hold her tears no longer. She lay in his arms and cried as if her heart was breaking. "I'm sorry; I tried to be strong for you. You are always the strong one. It was my turn. How much can one family handle? Why are we outliving our children?"

"Lucy, we've just come through a very hard year for many who have lost sons who were fighting for our freedom. Some were not much more than children. Maybe if we pray for those families, we could see how blessed we really are. Sarah is okay, with no pain now, sweetheart, and I am sure that she doesn't want us to grieve so much."

Chapter 26

Sharecropping on the Homestead

Harley had lost his ma as a young boy, and his grandparents were very important to him. Knowing they had lost the homestead that they had worked so hard for, just made Harley more determined than ever. They stayed with or near family.

Harley and Laura had rented homes and were eventually able to live on the old homestead as sharecroppers. They had to work extra hard to provide enough food for themselves and the animals because half had to go to the owner of the land. But they were still in the home his family had built and were thankful.

Madison was not married and was always nearby. He worked for different people in the neighboring communities, often staying with them until the job was done.

Sometimes, he would work for room and board just because someone needed help. When he was not working somewhere else, he stayed with Grandpa and Grandma or Harley and Laura, helping them with the farm work as if it was his responsibility, especially when they lived on the old homestead. He always wanted to earn his keep, but really, he loved the memories of growing up there.

"You know, we are going to miss Madison if he ever gets married," Laura stated to Harley as they sat down to supper. "He takes a lot of work off everyone."

He was known as Uncle Matt to many. Cloyal had been born on March 3, 1913, and their daughter, Clossie was born about three years later.

Finding it necessary to move to wherever they could find work to provide for their growing family, Harley learned to do many things and worked wherever he could.

He quickly discovered he was a man of many talents, out of necessity: from blacksmith to shoe cobbler, to wheel right, or farmer. Making or repairing leather harnesses became almost a weekly chore for one person or another. Whatever the need, he could do it or learn to do it because always in the back of his mind was that someday he wanted to get his grandfather's homestead. He would not give up on the hope that he would someday get the land back for his grandpa.

The person who bought the land did not have a large family to help him and could not work the land by himself. He had put a notice up in town that he was looking for sharecroppers.

Harley didn't even have to think about it. He went straight to the owner. But without working for money, how would he buy the homestead? First things first, they need to get Grandma and Grandpa back home again.

"Pa, is this our cabin?" Cloyal asked as he watched him chink the walls and tighten the shutters.

"No, Son. I'm afraid it's not. I wish it was. It used to be Grandpa's." We are going to try to get it back someday. You see, Grandpa and Grandma came here a long time ago and homesteaded this land, farming it for several years."

Harley had been raised on that land and promised himself that someday he would buy it back. None of them had money, but he was determined. "Where there is a will, there is a way."

Phylander and Lucy would stay with family, or rent places nearby, but would never go back to Ohio.

They had taught their children and grandchildren never to give up on a dream so they could not go back. Trying to keep their chin up, they spent lots of time enjoying their grandchildren and working anywhere they could.

"Harley and Laura moved into the cabin that Grandpa had built," Laura said, "They put their whole life into this place! It would be good to be back home, even if it wasn't theirs. They should live here. We need to move them in with us."

I agree, and I will ask them, but you know they would never agree to that; Grandpa has too much pride for that. We just need to get the land back and build them a house.

Madison had managed to find them a small house for rent about a half mile away. It was about the best they could do under the circumstances. They could visit often; Lucy would help Laura with the children, and Grandpa could help with farming or cutting and stacking hay. He would help whenever possible; albeit Harley and Madison tried to see that he didn't overdo it.

Harley and Laura had been married for six years and had two children in 1917. Cloyal was four years old, and Clossie was one. He would never forget how his grandparents took care of him and his siblings after their ma had passed away. Lucy more or less became his ma. He loved to spend as much time with her as he could. In the evenings, he told his children stories of growing up with them.

Though sharecropping, he was glad for the opportunity to live in his homeland, even if it did belong to someone else. They had moved into the log cabin on the East end of the property, down by the east creek crossing. The garden next to the house was for their use. The house had been there for a long time. It was the first cabin that his grandfather had built on his homestead. Harley didn't mind that because it brought back fond memories of when he was a boy.

It needed lots of repairs. The wood shingles needed to be replaced. Keeping the roof from leaking and the log walls chinked was an ongoing chore after a hard day in the fields. Harley would have to find time to work on the house before winter set in. Fall was fast approaching, with much to do in the fields.

Laura had lots of canning to do, so the food did not waste and would feed them through the winter. Wood was needed, fences needed mending, and harvesting was taking longer than usual.

They did not have enough hands to do all that needed to be done. Hay for the horses and cows had been stacked tightly around long poles that had been set in the ground, so that it did not ruin in the rain, and it would soon be butchering time at the neighbor's houses and their own.

It was important that they all worked together because it was a lot easier on everyone and faster in the long run. The meat must be salted and cured or smoked to make it last as long as possible. The smokehouse had to be kept in good shape with plenty of green hickory wood for smoking.

The roof would just have to wait, though the shingles were beginning to break more and leaked during heavy rains.

Harley thought of his grandpa and the hard work he had done in that place. Maybe he could get it back in livable shape soon, in time for him to appreciate it.

He wondered if he had helped him enough. Remembering the love they had for each other as he thought of his own children. He was trying to provide a good home for them. It would take a while; by spring, the children would be able to help Laura a lot more with the gardening. She would be able to do more, also.

Cloyal and Clossie were getting big enough to help a lot, and Madison was a lifesaver. He spent days splitting and stacking wood. Maybe the weather would hold until they could get the roof fixed. There was too much to do and so little time.

Christmas came, and the snow began to fall. Laura didn't remind Harley of the roof, because he was doing all he could. She thought maybe it would hold until the spring rains ended and just kept buckets handy to catch the drips when it rained heavily. The snow would not be a problem unless it thawed too fast.

They had both been busy making gifts for the kids and for each other. Laura was not in any condition to travel at that time, so several members of both families came to their house for Christmas dinner, and the women helped her do the cooking.

Her sisters did not let her stay on her swollen feet but insisted she sit down and peel potatoes or whatever she could do sitting down because soon, she would have another baby.

They always enjoyed being together, and the house was full, and the table was set and filled with lots of food.

Harley and Madison made sure the women had plenty of wood to cook with; although, they each had brought some foods already prepared. Laura was glad she had sisters nearby. They really loved being together.

Bessie and Ollie lived in town. Mattie lived between Paint Rock and Driggs. AJ lived at Driggs, and Boyd lived in Paris. Holland and Daniel lived in the home place where Laura grew up. It saddened her to go there because she missed her ma and pa more and more, as she had babies of her own; yet it had been her home and held many happy memories. She still, sometimes, took her children to see where she had been raised and to visit with her brother.

Chapter 27

Snow in the Cabin

During the Christmas season of 1918, Laura had been a little limited as to what she could do that winter because it was almost time for her baby to be born. She remembered her own mother and the meals she had prepared for all of them as children, not forgetting to care for the unborn baby, realizing that it was a precious gift of love from God.

The New Year was exciting but challenging for them. Harley and his grandpa were out in the barn working on some harnesses that needed mending before planting time. Mostly, they just enjoyed the time together. Only in the winter did they have the time to visit with each other with such pleasure.

"You think the hay will hold for the rest of the winter? It is difficult raising enough for so many." Phylander put some hay in the manger for the cow so Harley could milk her.

"I hope so. We tried to make it tight around the poles like you taught us. Maybe what we do have will be kept. The horses are enjoying the rest. They earned their keep during harvest season. I don't know how you ever managed with the oxen. Do you really miss the farm, Grandpa? You can help as much as you are able; I just want you to not overdo it."

"I don't regret coming here at all. It has been a good life for us, even with all the sadness, but I still miss Mattie and your ma as if they left yesterday. I know you think about her, too; I can see it in your eyes at times, especially when you play your fiddle. At times, I think you are playing just for her."

"Do you reckon she can hear us talking? I sometimes can still hear her ask me to play the last song for her. That's why I always play, just one more, before bed."

"Well, maybe she can, and if she can't, the Good Lord can. Surely, He will let her know you played for her. She loved you a lot, son. So do we. You're a lucky man and a smart one, too. You proved that by choosing the wife you did. She takes mighty good care of the children and you. Wish your grandma and I could do more to earn our keep."

"Earn your keep? You already paid for yours and mine! I want to tell you something, Grandpa. Laura and I have been putting a little money aside; anytime we get a penny extra, we save it. I am going to get this place back for you if it's the last thing I do!"

"Well, you do what you need to do for you and Laura. I can't do much with it anymore. It has been a joy to live near you, in the place where we all worked together for years."

"Harley, I don't know how to tell you this, but my time is getting a little close to the end here. I don't feel so well anymore. You do understand that, don't you?"

"Grandpa, you have lots of time left. Your grandchildren need you an awful lot, and I need you more. One grandchild hasn't even seen you yet. Just look at them playing. You and Grandma put more glimmer in their eyes than snow on a sunny day! They really love you!"

The weather was mild, yet they had lots of glistening snow. The children loved to play out in it with the sled that Pa and Grandpa had made them for Christmas.

The warm scarf and gloves that Grandma Lucy had knitted kept them warm, and she painted a pretty picture as she watched them play from the window. "This is such a beautiful place, especially when it snows."

"It certainly is," replied Laura. "I am glad we at least get to live here; even though it seems there is no way to get ahead. Harley has such fond memories of growing up here with you. His heart is set on buying it back someday, you know."

"I do wish you could. It broke our hearts to lose it the way we did." Lucy sighed and looked away from the window, and closed the shutters. "God has been mighty good to us to allow us to live here near you and in a cabin that we built. Speaking of our house, we need to get back home soon. Do you need some help before we go? It has been good just to visit, but you look miserable! How much longer do you have?"

"The doctor said it should be a few weeks yet. I feel fine." "Ok, let me know when we need to get the kids or whatever else you need. Even young folks need help at times."

"I will, don't worry. Thank you, Grandma Lucy. My parents are gone. Harleys are gone, yet you are a mother to both of us, and our kids have grandparents. We are truly blessed."

The men came into the house, and Pa gave his grandma a hug. "We should be giving you another grandbaby in a few weeks. Hope the snow is gone by then; it's fun to play in for a little while. Thanks for the pie. We've got the wagon ready to go when you are."

"Love you, Son. It's been a good day. I'll see that Matt comes back soon in case you need help?" Lucy replied.

"He's going to help me tomorrow with firewood. We'll be sure to cut some for you as well."

They got in the wagon and drove home. Madison was waiting for them and took the team and wagon for them. "I'll get this, Grandpa; you go on in where it's warm. I made a nice fire before we left; it should still be warm."

"Thank you, Matt. I do feel a little tired. I just don't seem to be able to do what I used to. You seem to always be where you are needed the most. I am proud of you, Son. You are a good man." He helped Lucy down from the wagon, and they went inside a warm house and got ready for bed while waiting for Madison to return from the barn.

"Madison, I am always glad when you are here. I know you are trying to take care of us, and I thank you. But Laura doesn't look so good. I think it might be good if you stayed closer to them for the next few days. They may need help with the children. Laura will want them out of the house while the baby is being born. Someone will need to go get the doctor."

The next few days, Laura seemed to have unexplained energy, and knowing her time was approaching, she cooked extra bread, beans, and baked some sweet potatoes, and made other extra foods, wanting to make sure that her family had plenty to eat; because, she would have to be in bed for a little while. With so much cold weather outside, the extra heat from the cook stove was helpful.

Her thoughts were on trying to get the kids ready to go to Grandpa and Grandma Storts' house. They could not get out in the weather, as they were both in poor health and frail.

If Harley got back in time, he would take them. Her time for delivery was drawing near. If the weather permitted, one of her sisters would be there soon, she was sure, but the snow was getting deeper. "We've not had snow like this in several years." Laura worried the weather was getting worse.

Harley was trying to get in more wood, unaware of any need to hurry. He had been too far away from the house, and Laura began to have what she knew were contractions. She tried to keep the effects of the pain from the kids, but Cloyal noticed anyway and began to try to help her.

Laura didn't know what was keeping Harley and didn't want to send him out in the cold and take a chance of getting sick, but she needed help and the kids out.

"Cloyal, can you get your coat and boots on and go find your Pa? Tell him I need him as soon as he can get here."

"Ok, Ma. What's wrong? Are you ok?"

"Yes, now hurry. There is no time to waste. Take Shep with you. She didn't want to send a six-year-old out in the cold, but it was either that or having them both in the house when the new baby came. "Pa should be in the barn by now."

Before Cloyal could get his boots on, Pa opened the door and asked, "Where are you going, boy? "That wind is really blowing hard, and the snow is getting deep."

"Ma needs you quick, Pa!" He was glad Pa came in. Harley saw that Laura was in a bad way when he came through the door. She was lying on the bed in severe pain and wanted Harley to take the kids to his grandpa's house, but there was not enough time.

He needed to get the doctor, if possible. This was not her first baby, but something could go wrong. "Matt will get the doc. I'm not leaving you."

"What do we do about the kids? I should have let them go with Grandma this morning. I thought you would get back in time."

"Don't worry, we'll make it. It will be ok. Try to relax and wait for the doctor if you can." He noticed the aroma of hot foods. "You been cooking all day?"

Laura just nodded. The snow was falling and getting deeper. North winds were blowing hard, and it was turning colder by the minute. Meanwhile, that baby, unaware of the cold, was getting persistent!

Madison had been clearing the path from the barn to the house and came in, shaking the snow from his boots, and started to take them off by the door. "It's getting colder by the minute."

Harley said, "You might want to leave those boots on. One of us has to go to the doctor."

It only took a second for Madison to decide which one, and he was on his way. He saddled up one of the horses, who seemed to be a bit confused.

"I know. I just took your harness off, and you've worked hard at hauling wood, but we've got a baby coming! No time to argue or explain. This one more time, and you can have all the hay you want. I'll even give you extra grain later."

He headed toward town about three miles away, so they had to go as fast as they could when the road and the weather would permit. "Lord, we could sure use a little break in this weather or some way to get the doctor faster. I'd appreciate any help you could give. Harley can do a lot of things, but delivering a baby?"

Before he got more than a mile down the road, he met the doctor in his buggy. "Hey, Doc. Am I glad to see you! Where are you headed in this kind of weather?"

"Well, having delivered several babies in my life. I know they usually pick the most inopportune time. With the snow and wind like it is, I figured Laura might need me to pay a visit."

"You're thinking right. I was just coming to fetch you. Laura's sisters had gone home before the snow, but a neighbor, just up the road, had been there earlier that day and saw how she was feeling, so she came back to check on Laura.

She knocked on the door, opened it and went on in. "Laura, I had a feeling you were overdoing it today. How are you feeling?" They looked at each other. No more words were needed. If you don't mind, I will stay here with you or try to take the children home with me for the night. Got to tell you, though, that wind is mighty strong! I almost could not walk in it. Which would you like me to do?"

Laura wanted her to take the kids, but the snow was blowing in drifts at times. Neither of them needed to go far. She felt it was dangerous to be out in it.

The doctor was on his way, but the wind and snow were blinding and cold. The baby was getting in a hurry. Harley was sure, hoping he would get there on time.

"I would appreciate it if you stayed here until the doctor gets here." If need be, I will take care of the kids, and you can help Laura. You're more qualified than me."

As Laura took a break in between contractions, she noticed that her bed was getting wet, cold, and white. "Harley, it's snowing on the bed!" The wind was howling and they heard a cracking on the roof; the hole had just gotten bigger. It was too late to worry about that by then; other factors were more important.

The horses fought their way through the storm and finally were at the door. "Doc's here, Harley. He was already on this road when I met him. Are we on time?"

"More like just in the nick of time, I think. Good to see you, Doctor; thought we might have to do this without you."

Uncle Matt spoke, "How would you kids like to help me take care of the animals in the barn?" It seems a little crowded in here. I promised some extra grain to the horses after the hard ride. "Get your overcoats on; it is cold outside. Stay close to me. I cleared a path to walk in earlier; maybe it's not too deep."

Laura was glad he was there. She had worried about what to do with them when the time came. Clossie and Cloyal were worried about her and didn't really want to go. Pa told them to go with Uncle Matt, who was pushing them out the door.

The doctor walked over to Laura and saw he had no time to waste. He looked at the lady standing by and asked her to bring hot water, then realized she had everything ready and waiting. "You seem to be in good hands without me, Mrs. Krigbaum."

Surprised, he noticed the piling snow on her bed and then looked up at the ceiling. His eyes met Harley's, but he did not say a word about it. Neither did anyone else. He went on with his work as if the snow wasn't falling.

Once in a while, one of them would wipe the snow off the bed before it melted on the bed from the warm heat of the wood stove.

Most of the work was over by the time the Doctor got there, but he delivered the healthy baby girl, checked to see if her heart, lungs, and everything was working properly, wrapped her up, and placed her in Laura's arms.

Laura was more than glad to finally get to hold her precious baby. "She had us worried for a little while, Doc. I'm sure glad you could make it."

Madison and the kids soon came back into the house as they heard the baby cry. Cloyal was very happy to see his new sister, but Clossie wasn't sure about the whole thing. She didn't want to share so much of her time with Ma.

Ma assured her that she was the big sister now, and that made her feel important. "Her name is Clara Alene. When she gets a little older, you can help me with her. "She is our baby, not just mine." Clossie seemed to be ok after that.

Grandma and Grandpa Storts are going to be surprised when they come tomorrow, aren't they, Ma?" Cloyal chided.

They will be here in the morning to get you two to spend the night. I hope they're not upset we didn't send for them.

As soon as Laura was able to get up for a few minutes, the bed was moved, something was put over the wet part, and dry sheets were put on it. Harley put a bucket on the floor to catch the snow where the bed had been. As it melted, they could use the water for cleaning. It seemed that something good could come of about anything.

Madison suggested they get more snow from outside and melt it on the stove. That would be one bucket of water they wouldn't have to draw from the well and a little bit of snow that was gone.

They filled dish pans with snow and set them on the stove to melt for washing dishes and floors. It was water that God had provided, and they were thankful. They all survived the snow that year.

Harley kept it as warm as possible in the little log house. He was never one for sparing the wood in the wintertime. As he waited for the snow to stop falling, he went to work making new shingles for the roof.

Laura had suggested he make some of them in the lean-to. He was surprised but would welcome the warmth of the cabin while he worked. She didn't have to say it twice. He would have to wait until the snow was cleared from the roof in order to repair it. The heat from the house would melt it quickly. Meanwhile, he needed time to cut the short pieces of logs into shingles.

Chapter 28
Repairing the Roof

In a few days, the weather was clear, and the snow was almost gone. Harley said, "One blessing of living in Arkansas is that the snow and ice don't stay nearly as long as in Ohio."

Grandpa and Grandma Storts were not in good enough health to do a lot to help, but they were glad to see them repairing the cabin they had built and wanted to help where they could. He would put new shingles on several places that had been blown off by the storms of the year; then secure any loose ones that were still in good shape.

It was worse than he had thought. A large section of the roof had been blown loose, and some were broken. So he spent the biggest part of the day checking and repairing shingles while Cloyal and Madison went up and down the handmade ladder, bringing him shingles and nails, and Grandpa helped with whatever he could from below. Harley was very glad to see that his son was growing up to be a good worker.

"Grandpa, you already built this cabin once. You're working too hard. We can finish up. Why don't you go on in by the fire? We are in good hands here. Look at that boy's work, just like you taught him yourself! We can handle the rest."

Phylander knew he was right. He was really getting tired and cold, but he was not one to leave the work to others. After a little coaxing, he went on into the house with Lucy and Laura. Clossie was glad he came inside. She loved her grandpa's time.

"Are you alright, Grandpa? Harley and Madison can do the roof work." Laura noticed he was a bit pale.

"Yes, I'm fine. Harley and Matt thought I needed to come in so that Cloyal could do my job. He can, too! He's a good boy. I know you're proud of him. So am I."

Pa only allowed Cloyal to help a little while at a time because of the cold. Ma did not want him to get sick. Each time he went back into the house, he carried in an armload of firewood. "No use wasting steps," he would say.

By late afternoon of the third day, the task was completed, and they were glad to go into the warm house. Next year, Harley would check the roof before the weather gets cold. "Roofing is not a job for wintertime," he thought.

When they finally got some time to rest, Pa Said, "You did a fine job, Son. You and Grandpa make a good team. You took a lot of work off of Uncle Matt and me, also. Thank you. You will be a good man someday."

"We all make a good team, Pa. We worked together, just like you said. Next time, can I get on the roof?" They all smiled.

Why don't we pop some popcorn and maybe have a glass of warm milk? We can talk about that when the time comes. Would you like that, Laura? We have kids that are growing into real helpers. It would have taken me a lot longer had I not had such good help."

"Yes, they are." The baby lay sleeping in the crib, and Laura sat up on the bed. "Do you want me to get up and pop the corn?"

"No, I think we can manage. You just rest and get well. The doctor told you to stay in bed a few more days." All the while, he knew that doing nothing was very hard for her. She was always so busy with one thing or another. "Clossie, will you get us a pan while I stoke up the fire?" "Sure, Pa, I can get it by myself." She knew where they were because Ma sometimes allowed her to help dry and put them away. They had a good evening in a warm house as Pa told them stories of when he was a little boy.

They noticed that Grandpa told a few stories but seemed rather quiet.

"Are you ok?" Lucy asked him. "Do you want to go home and lie down?"

"You can sleep here if you want, or I will drive you home. I'm not going to let you walk. I know you are tired. I can't thank you enough for your help."

"Glad I could help. I think I will take you up on that ride, Son. It has been a long day. I'm not what I used to be." "Clossie, come here and tell me about your new sister while your pa is hitching the team."

Harley hitched up the buckboard and took them home. "Thanks for your help, Grandpa. Working with you again was a real treat. Kind of made it seem like fun instead of work. It brought back many good memories."

Good night, Harley. Glad the roof got fixed. It's a good house, worth saving, even if it doesn't belong to us.

"It will belong to us someday, Grandpa. You wait and see. The owner can't work it by himself. He will sell; by then, I will have saved enough money to buy it. Good night." He went straight back home and wanted to rest as well. "Thank you, Lord, for the roof and Grandpa and Grandma."

It was soon bedtime, but first, they put away the pots and buckets that caught the leaks. "Now the rain can stay on the outside," Clossie exclaimed.

"That is where it belongs," Ma said with a smile. Sleep came quickly for all.

Phylander and Lucy (Place) Storts

Chapter 29

Grandpa Becomes Ill

The new baby was doing fine, Clossie was playing with a rag doll Ma had made for her, and Laura was trying to catch up on some much-needed sewing. It would be gardening time soon, and she needed to be ready for it.

Cloyal would be six years old in a few weeks. Ma wanted to make him a little cotton sack that was small enough for him to drag in the cotton patch. He always wanted to help but had to put his cotton in someone else's big sacks. Wanting to surprise him, she only worked on it when he was out with Pa or asleep. She needed to measure the strap but didn't want to spoil the surprise, so she measured a pair of his overalls. "That's about as close as I'm going to get."

Harley went to check on his Grandparents to see if they needed anything from town. He was going to make a trip to Paris. Grandpa might want to ride in with him. Sometimes Grandma would want to come too. Lucy heard the wagon and already had the door open by the time he got to the step. "Hi, you're out early."

I need to get a few things from town; do you or Grandpa want to go with me or send for anything? I hope to be back soon. I just need to get some seeds and a few supplies from the hardware store, but I can go wherever you want me to go.

Lucy was not sure what to say, knowing that Phylander had not been feeling well for several days. So, she went into the living room and asked him if he wanted to go with Harley. She thought she knew the answer, but she would ask.

Phylander didn't get up, "No, I am pretty tired. Maybe I better stay here today. Thanks for asking."

"Grandpa has not been up and around much the last couple of days, Son." If you see the doctor, maybe you could ask him to pay us a visit when he gets a chance."

"I will, Grandma. Love you. I will be back soon." Harley thought she looked worried. She was always a positive woman of faith. Why was she so worried this time? He said goodbye to them and didn't waste any more time.

Grandpa would never complain about anything. Something was not right with him. Starting the horses at a gallop, as soon as he got away from the house, he made record time getting to town.

The first thing he did was find the doctor and tell him about his grandpa. "Maybe it's nothing, but Ma seems worried, Doc."

"I have to see one other patient this morning; then I will head out that way. I need to go see them anyway. How long are you going to be in town? We might be able to drive back together."

"I won't be long. I just have to pick up a few things from the hardware store. I will be done by the time you are. I'll meet you back here in, say, an hour, and we can drive along together. Will that be ok? I would like to be there when you see him anyway. He hasn't been himself lately."

They were soon on the way to the farm, neither of them driving slowly enough to talk to each other. Phylander was a kind, hardworking man, and everyone around there thought a lot of him. The doctor was in deep thought about the many things they had been through together and the hard times he had seen Phylander and Lucy endure and still come out smiling. Their faith and courage were strong. His heart was heavy as he drove along.

Some of the families were living in other states, some in nearby towns. Harley was thinking of a way to get word to them that Grandpa might feel better if they would all come to see him. He really enjoyed the grandchildren. They all loved him as well.

"Maybe we should have a birthday party for Cloyal since he and Grandpa had worked so hard on the roofing together," he thought. He could invite everyone and have a fun get-together before planting season instead of harvest time this year. Maybe we could even do both. "Grandpa has a right to see the family he loves so much. I know he misses them terribly." He spoke aloud.

"You say something, Harley," the doctor shouted. He slowed down enough to hear him. I was in my own world and thought I heard you."

"I guess I did. Sorry, just talking to myself. I was thinking. Grandpa hasn't seen many of his kids or grandkids in a long time. I know he misses them. That is why I could not leave here, no matter what I thought would be good for us. He put his whole heart into that farm. I want to get it back for him, Doc."

"I know, Harley. You are blessed with a loving family. Not everyone is as fortunate. It probably would do him good to see any of them, especially the grandkids. Kids have a way of lifting anyone's spirits. Your kids sure do love him, it is easy to tell."

"Yes, they do, and he loves them. But right now, we need to get there. I will try to keep my thoughts to myself so we can get there faster." They chuckled softly and were back to a fast trot, sometimes even a slow gallop.

By late morning, they were there. The doctor grabbed his bag and headed toward the door. Lucy met them at the door. "Glad to see you, Doctor. Phylander is not feeling well today at all. He's in here; come on in."

"Thank you, Ms. Lucy. Harley tells me he has not been well for several days. Any fever? Tell me anything you can that might point me in the general direction."

I haven't noticed any fever; he just seems to be so frail. He hardly gets up except to come to the table or maybe the porch swing. Something is not right. He is always so cheerful in spite of every situation. He has lost his appetite also, or I'm losing my touch as a cook." She struggled to try to laugh.

Harley spoke up, "That is not the case, I can assure you, Grandma. People come from miles around just to taste your cooking."

"Well, let's go take a look at him and see what we can do." They found him sleeping on his bed; he had not noticed them. Mr. Storts, are you awake? With no answer, he gently shook his shoulder. "Phylander?"

"Hey, Doctor. Sorry, I must have dosed off. I will get up. Just give me a second."

"That's ok, just lay there, I came to see what has been ailing you lately. Ms. Lucy and Harley seem a little worried about you. What's going on?"

"I think I am just tired and can't seem to get enough sleep. My energy is gone! There are so many things I need to do. It'll soon be planting time. I keep thinking if I rest, I will feel stronger, but it's not working out that way. Doctor, I think I am all used up. I want to be of help to my family, but I feel like I am more of a burden to them. I am blessed to have Harley here. I don't know what we would have done without him and Laura."

"Grandpa! I am the one who's blessed. You have always been strong for me, no matter what. You never left me when so many others did, and you always knew my needs before I did! How can you feel that way? We all need you. You know that I count on your wisdom. I would not be half the man I am, had it not been for you. We're a team, just like Cloyal said.

Remember the day we worked on the roof? Cloyal still talks about the great time you two had together. He will treasure it forever."

The doctor checked everything he had the ability to check and could not find anything major wrong except his weakness and short breath. "I'm going to give you a little something to boost your energy level, but you need to try to eat a little better. You have your wife thinking she forgot how to cook." He tried a chuckle out loud.

"Well, she should know better than that. I married her for her cooking, and she knows it. She has just gotten better over the years. I'll try to do better, Doc." Thank you for coming all this way."

"It wasn't for nothing; I came to visit an old friend. We've had a lot of good times together, haven't we? I'm not even charging you for this visit. Just came as a friend. By the way, I hear your great-grandson is having a birthday party. Make sure they invite me, will you?"

With a smile from both of them, he got up and packed up his bag. I'll be back soon. The medicine should help a little."

"Goodbye, Doctor. Thank you for coming. Good to see you, my friend." Phylander didn't try to get up. He just laid there thinking about what a lucky man he really was, as Lucy and Harley walked out with the doctor.

"What do you think is wrong, Doctor.? This is just not like him," Harley continued.

"I wish I could tell you both what you want to hear. I am sorry. The truth is he is worn out. He has worked harder than most his whole life. I think his heart is giving out. That is why he is so weak. These bodies are not made to last forever on this earth. You know that He is in God's hands. I will do what I can, but my skills are limited to what the Good Lord allows."

"Thank you, Doctor, for being honest with us." Lucy walked back to the house.

In anguish, Harley asked, "What do we do then, Doctor? Just sit by and watch as he slowly fades away? I can't do that again!"

"I think a birthday party is a good idea. He would love to see his kids and grandkids again. Tell them he is ill. There is no way of knowing how much longer he has left. They will want to come. I would like to see them myself. I will try to bring a little gift for both the kids. Many others will, too. And try to be cheerful around him. He deserves to be around happy people."

With those words, he got into his buggy and drove back to town. As he slowly drove away, he was in deep thought of what they were about to face again. This time, the strong one in the family would not be there to lift them up. He wondered, "What will Grandma do? She has to be about eighty-four years old. She will be lost without him."

Laura was at home waiting for Harley and wondering what had kept him so long. After putting the baby in the crib, she met him at the barn as he unhitched the team and decided to wait for an explanation of the day, seeing he looked so heavy-laden with something. "Are you ok?" She finally had to ask. He was so quiet.

"Yeah, I think we need to have a big birthday party for Cloyal and invite all my family. Do you think you could write some letters as soon as possible?"

"I'm sure I could, just as soon as you tell me what is going on." She stood there waiting for Harley to get the words to tell her that Grandpa was dying."

"It is short notice, but I will get right on it." She went into the house and began to write to Harley's family members and explained to them that Pa and Grandpa needed them. But the party was for Cloyal. He was six years old and loved his great-grandpa.

Not all would be able to come, of course, but she wasn't leaving out anyone if she could help it. To keep down confusion, she invited some of her folks. No matter; they also thought a lot of Grandpa Storts.

It is a little cool, but they could build a big fire outside and circle the wagons to try to keep out part of the wind. The party will only last for a short time. Mostly, they would go to visit Grandpa and Grandma Storts, a few at a time.

March 3, 1919, was a big day, with a big party! Most of Phylander's children and grandchildren came to see them. One by one, each family went by to visit Ma and Pa Storts; some a day or two before and others earlier that day. The party would not be until the afternoon, to give everyone time to visit with them.

Cloyal was excited as they decorated for his party. Parties were not a common practice. They usually got a cake and maybe a little gift from Ma and Pa.

Soon, everyone brought out their instruments. They played for Grandpa as if it was the happiest day of their lives. Having them all together again brought joy back into his eyes and laughter that was heartfelt. "Lucy, I have really missed having all of them together. Isn't this great? I wish they didn't have to go home. We have such a talented family. Even some of the kids can play music! Dance with me, Lucy, one last time. Please!"

"Phylander! Well, ok, but they are going to have to slow down the music! I'm too old for what they're playing! Besides, the doctor said you should take it easy."

Jack walked over to see how they were doing. It's sure good to see you again. "Can I get either of you anything? I think they are talking about cutting the cake soon. "

"Yes, you can get them to play a slow waltz for the lady here and myself to dance to. The spring in our step is a little sluggish, but the music is still in our hearts. Can you do that, Jack?"

"I would be glad to. A waltz is more my speed, as well. We might all enjoy it. These guys have missed each other so much they are playing with the excitement of playing together. What would you like to hear? On second thought, I know one."

As he walked off, Phylander and Lucy got up from their seats and slowly walked into the inner part of the dance floor. All talking stopped, and all eyes went on them, just waiting for the next move. Jack told Harley they wanted to dance. His heart almost did a flip. "They can't do that with his heart!"

Jack said, "Then you tell them! I wouldn't tell my grandpa he can't do anything!"

"Ok, we need a slower-than-usual waltz. How about the one he wrote for Grandma Lucy many years ago? Just keep it slow and smooth. He will be surprised, and it will have special meaning to both of them."

"That's just what I was thinking," Jack interjected. "He thinks we've all forgotten it by now."

Harley started playing the fiddle; soon, everybody joined in. It had three verses, and they played the whole song and an extra chorus.

Lucy had tears falling down her cheeks. She was a little embarrassed until she looked at the crowd around them. Almost everyone was crying. Phylander laughed and said, "What is this? Everyone is crying over a little old love song? Lucy, every word of that song is still right from my heart."

"Boys, can we do that same song one more time? I'd like to try and sing it. They're already crying; we might as well give them words to cry about."

He sang the one and only song that he had ever written to Lucy as if they were the only ones in the world at that moment: the sweetest, most beautiful picture of love that anyone could ever hope to see. He was eighty-six, and she was eighty-four. They had an army of children and grandchildren and great-grandchildren, several of whom they had helped raise, yet they still loved each other as much, if not more, than the day they married.

Sheridan walked over to them and put his arm around both of them. "I am so glad to have you as my grandparents. Ma was always so proud of you. Now I know why. Your love for us and for each other has carried us through many battles and trials. I love you both very much! Thank you for everything!" He kissed Grandma and hugged Grandpa, then walked away, giving room for others.

Seeing what was about to take place, Laura asked Martha to take them some chairs. "This could take a while."

In a little while, Phylander said, "Where is the birthday boy?" Reaching out to call Cloyal over to him, he said, "Happy Birthday, big boy! I noticed you're watching that guitar mighty close. Think you would like to play?"

"Yeah, I wish I had one. Pa's is too big for me. He says if I just watch, I will learn a lot. That is how he started learning the fiddle."

"Well, maybe he's right. I am about ready for a piece of that cake, how about you? Let's see if we can't get this party headed toward those presents over there."

With that statement, the attention turned to Cloyal, the cake, and the presents. He and Grandpa and Grandma got the first pieces. They ate theirs, and then, while others were being served, he got to open presents.

Laura said, "Cloyal, open this one first. It is from Grandpa and Grandma Storts." They all gathered around and stopped what they were doing for a few minutes. It seemed they all were waiting to see what they had gotten him.

"Oh, my goodness! Ma, Look!" He could not get anything else to come out. Trying to say thank you, no words would come. He leaned the little guitar down carefully on his chair, as he had seen the others do, and went over to give them a big hug. "Thank you! You're the best grandparents ever! I already know some chords. Pa taught me."

"They stopped everything, and Pa came with his fiddle. You want to try to play a song with me right now?" Everyone cheered, and he couldn't wait any longer. Pa knew the chords he was ready to play, and talked him through the changes.

To everyone's surprise, he could actually keep a pretty good rhythm. The cords would take a little work to get them clear, but they would come in time. Phylander and Lucy were not surprised, just happy that they had managed to get the little guitar.

He went on opening presents, but none could compare with the guitar. This night was shared with his hero, Grandpa Storts. The cake was not enough for so many people, but they were prepared with two others. It was a wonderful day that none of the family would forget.

The doctor was watching the whole event and keeping a close eye on Phylander. He had brought a present for Cloyal and one for Clossie, just as he'd promised. He was right; several others brought gifts for her also. "What a wonderful way to end a day!" He said to Harley as they began to go to different places to spend the night. "If you need me to put some of your family up for the night, I will."

"Thanks, Doc. He's been happier today than I have seen him in many years. And wouldn't you know that he would be the one to think of finding a guitar? I should have, but all I could think of was him. I don't want to lose him," he sighed. Taking a deep breath, he continued. "Anyway, I'm sure glad we did this. You are more than our doctor; you are our friend. How can I ever thank you for being here and for what you do for all of us?"

"It's my job. You work hard at yours." He, Madison, and Harley decided to follow Phylander and Lucy home. He could see he was getting tired. "Lucy is apt to need a little help with him tonight. I think I will look in on him on my way home.

Laura came over to say good night to them as they were leaving. "It was wonderful of you to get him that guitar. Thank you again. You're so good to us that sometimes I feel as if you are my own grandparents. Hope you get some rest; you both look tired. I think Gideon and his family are going to stay with you tonight, but is there anything you need me to do?"

"Thank you, Laura, and we are your grandparents too, and proud to be," Phylander replied.

Lucy continued. "We'll be fine, thank you; it looks as if you will have your hands and house full too. It is wonderful to see all the kids again. I hope no one has to leave soon. This is the way a family should be. My, how they love the music! I didn't realize how much I missed them. I am so glad you and Harley live here."

"So am I. Here they come with your wagon. Be sure to rest now. Goodnight."

They said goodnight to everyone and hugged the birthday boy, "Happy Birthday, Son. Was that a cotton sack I saw? You will be able to pick twice as much if your sack is your size. Your ma must expect you to earn your keep. You have a good Ma there. Do as she says, Son."

"Yes, Sir, I will try." Thanks again for my guitar." Cloyal watched as they left for home.

Several spent the night with Harley and Laura; others went to other places. Some went to help Phylander and Lucy Storts, wanting to help their Ma but not make her feel a need to care for them.

Phylander went into the house with a little help from Gideon and Harley. He was feeling very weak and tired again. "It has been a good day, boys, I can't thank you enough. I know you did this for us. It's so good to have my children and grandchildren close by. I have a family that would make any man proud.

"Harley, be sure to teach that boy to play that guitar. He has a real talent that will help him deal with pain the same way your fiddle helped you when you needed it the most.

Children have real pain, too. Never forget that. You must be strong for him. He's going to miss me a lot; we're a team! When you lose a member, it hurts. I wish I could spare you the pain that you are going to have to bear in the near future, I feel, but we all have this step to take."

"We all love you, Grandpa," Harley said, and then he and Gideon said good night. "You both try to sleep if you can. It's early, but you've had a long, busy day."

"Some of us will be right here if you need us. It has been so wild for the last couple of days that I'm sure you could use a little quiet time," continued Gideon. "We'll try to keep it down."

They all stayed close by. The doctor decided he ought to hang around until he settled down a little. His breathing seemed a bit labored. It was early in the evening. They enjoyed just visiting with each other because he had grown up with them and seemed like one of the family.

Phylander and Lucy talked about the evening and the song he sang to her. "I can't believe you still remember the words to a song you wrote so many years ago. I really love you, Phylander Storts! I have to be the luckiest woman God ever put on this earth! I have a husband who loves me after all these years and a wonderful family. I feel as rich as a Queen!"

"Sorry, I lost your palace, Queen Lucy." He uttered with a halfway smile.

"Oh, well, that was only material. What we have is so much more. We have something that even death can't take away. We've lost children, but we kept the wonderful memories. I have you to thank for helping me see that. You're my rock and my life's stronghold in any storm."

"Lucy, you know that I'm not going to be here to help you with the next one, don't you?" He reached up and put his arm around her ever so gently. "You also know that my love for you will never die." We have wonderful children and grandchildren. Let them help you. They love you too. I don't want to leave you, but I'm pretty sure it can't be too much longer."

Tears began to flow down her cheeks as she laid down beside him, and they cuddled up in each other's arms. "You're going to be ok. Let's get some rest. I will be right here with you. It is my turn to help you until you get better. Thank you for the dance tonight and for that beautiful song you sang for me. I will never forget it as long as I live. There is no place on earth that I would rather be than in your arms. I think I will just stay here for a while and rest also."

It was early, and several of the families were there in the house. Lucy couldn't leave him to visit with them, and she knew that he needed rest. The others would understand and could fend for themselves. He was the one who needed her at that moment.

She laid there and watched as he tried to sleep, but his breathing was difficult, and he kept waking up. Each time he did, he would pull his arms a little tighter around her as if trying to keep one of them from falling. As she reached up and kissed him gently, he managed a smile and a faint whisper, I love you, Lucy."

About eight o'clock that night, Lucy noticed he was really struggling to breathe. So, she got up to give him more room and propped him up higher with her pillow, hoping it would help at least a little. Sitting on the side of the bed, she asked, "Are you in pain, Phylander?"

"No, –just- can't- breathe. Stay–with me, -Lucy." He reached out for her hand.

"I'm going to see if the doctor is still here. He and the kids were visiting when we laid down earlier. I'll be right back. I won't leave you."

She opened the door and found that almost everyone was there, sitting quietly so as not to wake them. "Doctor, can you come and see if you can do anything for him? He seems to be really struggling to breathe."

"Yes, Mrs. Storts, I will be right there. Did you get any rest? You two surprised all of us with your dance this afternoon. It was a sight to behold."

"Yes, we both slept some. His breathing woke me." Then they were back at his side. Lucy reached down to take his hand.

"Phylander, how are we doing? We can sit you up a little straighter. Just try to relax and exercise that faith of yours that has - you and your family through so many difficult times. Here, take this, and maybe it will help you rest a little better."

He sat by his bed and watched him for a little while. "There is not really a lot I can do, as I'm sure you know. You are in God's hands now. Most of your children and grandchildren are here. You sure made one of those little ones happy today with that guitar. He's already making chords. He'll be playing in no time. He was trying to play the song you sang tonight. He'll have it down soon."

"Phylander struggled to speak. He has- Krigbaum- blood, I know- he'll be- playing- in -no time. He may get some of his talent from the Krigbaum side, but he gets his determined, persevering traits from you, Mr. Storts. He won't give up until he masters that guitar, just like his pa did with the fiddle." Phylander nodded and tried to manage a smile.

The doctor left Lucy there with him and went out to talk to the rest of the family. "It is only a matter of time, now; not long, I think. If any of you want to say anything to him, now would be the time. But let me warn you, he isn't really able to talk much. He needs all his strength just to breathe. He knows you're all here, and he's had a wonderful day with all of you."

Harley, Thurman, Martha, Lucy, Sara, Madison, Sheridan, Jack, Gideon, and others, including some of the children, in turn, went in to see him for a few minutes. Some just wanted to tell him goodbye or that they loved him.

They went out to give Lucy and him what time he had left together. She sat on the bed beside him and put her arm around him for the last time. Then, just before midnight, he took his last breath.

Harley spoke, "This has been a sad but happy day. Grandpa danced with his true love, sang the song he wrote for her many years ago, and then died, all on his great-grandson's birthday. We will not soon forget this day."

He then went over to Grandma Lucy, put his arms around her, and held her. She had already cried until there were no more tears for that day. Much more would come later, but for the time being, she sat there in silence. It would be a long time before they could find a way to deal with his passing. He had always been the one who made things better.

Phylander Storts was buried at Paint Rock cemetery. "Life is hard, and you have to take the bad with the good; the living must go on living until it is their time to go," Grandpa had often said.

Laura brought Lucy a cup of tea. "Grandma, would you like something to drink? You didn't eat anything but that little piece of cake. Is there anything I can do?"

"Thank you, Laura, I'll be fine. I just can't even imagine going on without him. We've been married almost our whole lives. He has been my stronghold."

"You can't stay here alone. You must come and stay with us, at least until things get settled. Harley will help me make you a nice place to sleep at our house. It is our turn to help you. You have been our stronghold. Allow us to help you."

The families went back to their respective homes, and Lucy moved in with Harley and Laura. "Laura, you should have the stove I got from Elmira, I don't plan on doing so much cooking anymore. It needs to go to someone with a big family. You are just getting started. I think Harley would appreciate it about as much as anyone. Maybe you could sell the little one of yours and add to your savings."

"I'm sure it would help Harley to feel closer to his mama and you. That stove carries a lot of memories for him. Thank you. You can stay here with us and cook on it as often as you like." Madison and Lucy would move in with Harley and Laura. He and Harley moved their things out of the rented house. Some items would need to be stored in the barn loft for a while.

Harley and Laura kept a close watch over her for the next several months. She did whatever they asked her to and never complained about anything; however, she had lost her smile for sure and even her will to live. It seemed she had become so sad that even the grandchildren could not cheer her. She was kind to them, but it was as if she was feeling nothing.

"Doesn't Grandma love us anymore, Ma? I miss her almost as much as Grandpa." Clossie had been visiting with her, trying to make her feel better.

"Sweetheart, of course, she does. She is hurting right now more than we could imagine. She and Grandpa were together almost seventy years, almost their whole lives. Give her some time. Let's try to keep it quiet in here for her, some of the time. She has lost several of her children, but he was always there to help her get through it. Now he is gone. We must help her."

Chapter 30

Too Little Room in the Cabin

After living with Harley and Laura for several months, Lucy began to be more herself. She had always wanted to put the needs of others before her own. "I feel that I am taking up space that is needed for your children, Laura. With another baby coming, you need the space. I can go stay with Martha. She asked me to earlier. I really just like being with the children. It is too quiet in a house without them."

"You are not in the way. We love having you here, but you can do as you please. Harley is trying to find us a place to live that has more room. If you want to go stay with her until we get moved, we certainly want you to come back."

"Maybe I should. I can't do much right now, it seems. I am trying to find the strength to do some things with the girls. I want to give them good memories of us together. They're so young."

The log cabin was getting pretty crowded as the Krigbaum family continued to grow. Lucy decided to stay with Martha for a little while. Harley's sister Lucy would stay with her part of the time while Martha worked. The two girls had grown up as sisters. Lucy was her second mama.

Martha came to pick up her mother. "You can stay with me as long as you like, Mama. I really miss you, anyway, but I am not always home, in that I work during the week, but either Lucy or I will try to be close by if you need us."

Harley spoke as he thought Grandma wanted but would not say, "Only take what you really need to Martha's house. We will move the rest of your things to the new house. We won't move until after the baby comes. The bigger house near here should be empty by then. The family is moving out in a few weeks. It has lots of room, even a kitchen, separate from the rest of the house.

It might be best if you don't watch us move from the homestead again. No matter how small our house is, we will always have room for you and Madison."

On June 21, 1920, Harley and Laura had another son. Alene was eighteen months old. Ma was thankful for Clossie, who, though was only four at the time, played with her and kept her happy.

Uncle Matt was one they all could depend on to help with any chore on the farm, and he depended on them, as well, to give him a place at their table and a place to live and sleep.

He stayed with them and had been such a big help with the kids when the last baby was born that they named this one Madison Monroe, agreeing that he had earned a namesake. Since he had no children of his own and apparently no interest in marriage, it seemed fitting. Ma was happy he was a boy and she was glad to finally hold her new baby. They would call him Matt.

Harley hated to leave the homestead again, but they needed to find another place to live. Just down the road on adjoining property was a house for rent, still vacant and close enough to work for the owner of the homestead, and maybe he could earn enough to pay their rent.

So, they loaded up the wagon and moved their belongings to the new house. It was hard once again to leave their home, which they had put so much work into.

"Well, at least it got a new roof," Cloyal announced. They were able to laugh a little and agree. They were durable and soon realized that sometimes things happened that were out of their control. Laura often said that it was the Good Lord watching over them and that He knew their needs before they did. Before long, they were settled in and found it wasn't so bad.

Harley and Madison put all of Grandma's belongings into one bedroom. They would organize it and have it nice for her as soon as they all could find the time.

The older children had beds of their own. The baby's crib sat next to Laura so she could make sure he kept warm and safe. Ma's stove was moved to a kitchen big enough to hold it. It soon felt like home, and Laura was thankful for the new kitchen, a small room all to itself. No bed in the kitchen. "I could learn to enjoy this," she said to Harley.

"Grandma should do better here. We need to get her room ready and make her feel at home. I have her bed made and clothes put away, but I need you men to help me move a few pieces of furniture."

"I think we should wait 'till the weather settles. We might get wet before we get back." That evening, as they sat outside watching the clouds, Harley was playing his fiddle; he stopped playing and mentioned that it could get kind of rough by nightfall. The weather had been very unsettled for most of the day. It was hot and not much of a breeze. "We may miss that cellar tonight."

They kept their shoes on and tried to prepare for a storm as best as they could, expecting a lot of wind and rain.

It soon began to rain very hard, and the wind was blowing from all directions. Laura thought of the cellar they had at the other place, but they didn't have one there so they must do the best they could. The rest was up to the Good Lord.

"Come here, children. Let's sit here together until the storm passes. The glass windows might break, so stay away from them." They had never had glass windows, so they kept going to them and looking out at the storm.

It was different from the shutters they were used to, but they liked the light in the daytime. It was amazing to the kids that light could be inside the house in the daytime, even with the windows closed.

It became very dark and still. Then suddenly, the wind blew, and the rain came down almost in buckets; they waited for the storm to pass. Just as they thought it was about to end, there came a deafening crash of thunder. Something outside had been hit by lightning. The children were getting scared, and the little ones began to cry. Laura told them not to worry, "God is watching over us." She held them as close as she could.

Harley looked outside as far as he could see; nothing was burning, so maybe it was ok. He would have to wait until morning to see what had been hit. As he sat down, both girls climbed on his lap. He began talking to them. They were soon okay, and began to fall asleep in his arms.

Laura put the baby in the nearby crib, took Alene from him, and went back to sit by Cloyal, who snuggled up close against her.

They sat and talked for a little while as the storm began to lose some of its rage; then, they put the children to bed.

The next morning, Harley and Laura realized just how blessed they really were as they walked outside to assess the damages of the storm.

There was a huge tree beside the house. It had split right down the middle; most of it had fallen to the ground, just missing the house by inches! Harley and Laura stood looking at each other with a prayer of thanksgiving on their hearts, knowing that, once again, God had protected them. Neither of them could speak a word for several minutes.

A part of that big oak tree stood for many years as a reminder for Laura (Ma) to show her grandchildren and tell them about the storm that caused a lot of excitement, but God had protected them. She believed that there was a lesson to be learned in every trial. The Bible says, "In everything, give thanks." They had much to be thankful for.

Chapter 31
Precious Memories

It seemed that Lucy was doing better in a few weeks. Laura would need her help because of having the new baby. She moved back to their house and seemed to really enjoy time with the children, helping the girls with sewing or knitting. Sometimes, they would cook a special meal together.

Harley or Madison would come into the kitchen and pretend to steal a bite of what they were cooking. The girls giggled as Grandma would say, "Oh, no you don't! This is our surprise for supper."

Harley was glad to find her enjoying the girls. He would wink at her and grin and then go over and kiss her on the cheek. "Something sure smells good! You girls pay attention, and you will be a good cook someday, like your grandma."

Laura had been trying to take it easy since having little Matt, but she had lots of canning and preserving to do before winter. Canning season was not the time to be in bed so much. Her sisters also came as often as they could to help her when they could find time from their own canning.

Lucy worked closely with the children, teaching them to peel apples and pears safely without cutting too deeply. "We should be careful not to waste the fruit that God gave us."

In the evening, when Pa and Cloyal played music, Lucy, Laura, and the girls would shell or snap beans, peas, or whatever was needed at the time.

Harley would only play for a little while, then would say to Cloyal, "Son, I want to teach all of you music as much as possible; however, during the summer and through harvest time, everyone has to carry their own load. We have loads of corn to be shucked tonight. The girls help us; we help them; that's the way it should be. Go put the instruments up and wash your hands well. Ma doesn't want dirty hands touching her corn. She says it will make it spoil."

For the rest of the summer, Lucy seemed happy as she helped the girls sew their own dresses and make surprises for their ma and pa. She prided herself in how fast they learned. "Look at this, Laura; Clossie has almost finished the baby quilt for Matt. He can sleep under it by the end of the week."

"That's nice; you're doing really well, Sweetie!" She looked up from her own work. "It's fun working together and also important that you learn to do things. You may have a family of your own someday. You and Grandma make a good team." Laura was glad to see Lucy doing much better. They had been worried about her, but it seemed she was doing ok.

"Grandma, I'm so glad you are here with us. We're going to have to share you next week. Sheridan and Sarah are coming. Think you're up to it?"

"Sure, I was so hoping to see them. Been thinking about them lately. We can count on the music to pick up a bit. Harley loves to play twin fiddles with him. Sheridan taught him a lot, and that girl of his sure loves to sing. Now, if only Thurman and Gideon could come and bring their instruments. That would be a real treat. Cloyal needs them."

"Well, maybe I could post them a letter and see if there is any way they could come also. We need more family time."

As it happened, both families were able to visit for a few days. Lucy seemed very pleased. Each one spent special time with her, trying not to overwhelm her all at once.

The kids all had a great time. The boys made places to sleep in the barn loft so the hay would keep them warm. Some of the older girls slept in the wagon that was pulled inside the barn.

Mealtime was a little noisy but fun. They were so excited to be together that sometimes they forgot the rule (one talk while the rest listen). Several conversations seemed to go on at the table until Sarah brought it to their attention.

"I think we have all forgotten our manners. There is more noise at this table than on a playground. Sorry, Laura, thank you for sharing your house and your food with us." Embarrassed chuckles could be heard around the table.

Things settled down, and they finished their meal in an orderly way while listening to the one who was talking at the time. That week was filled with laughter, music, and fun.

Cloyal learned a lot about the guitar in that short time. He wouldn't get the chance often, so he soaked up every minute of Uncle Thurman's playing, who, at times, would take him aside and give him undivided attention, amazed at his deep interest and determination.

Lucy was very good at hiding her own pain for the sake of others. She didn't want them to remember only sad times with her. Apparently, many of her smiles were superficial because, inside, she must have been grieving herself to death.

It was a cool evening in October. Lucy went to bed early. "I think I will turn in. It is really too late to do anything much tonight. Harley, if you and Cloyal want to play music, don't mind me. I'd love to hear you. I don't have to go to sleep; I just feel that I need to lie down."

"We don't have to play if you want to sleep," he replied.

"Really, I would love to hear you. Play Phylander's song for me again. It seems I can hear him singing it at times. Cloyal has been working on it. I am so very proud of you all. Your grandpa was also."

"Ok, Son, go get your guitar. Let's play Grandma to sleep." Up he jumped and was back in a flash with the guitar and the little one he handed to the girls. They had been taking turns trying to play along. Pa tuned up the instruments, and then they played Grandma's song first.

She cried quietly in her bed until Laura came in to check on her. "Are you ok? Can I get you anything?

"I am just fine, Laura. It has been a good evening, and it is so good to hear them play again. Elmira loved to hear Harley on the fiddle when he was Cloyal's age. I wish she could hear them now. Good night, Laura." She closed her eyes and finally went to sleep.

They soon put the instruments up and went to bed. "I hope that song wasn't too much for her tonight." Harley worried. "She seemed much better today, don't you think, Laura? Maybe she will be ok soon."

The next morning, Pa was up early, as usual, to go and do the milking before breakfast. He put wood in the stove for Laura before going out. "It's getting sort of cool out. This fire feels good."

Breakfast was ready, but Grandma wasn't up yet. Harley went to wake her. "It's time for breakfast, Grandma." She opened her eyes and looked at him but didn't say anything.

"Are you ok?" She shook her head yes. "I'm not hungry. You go ahead and eat. I think I will sleep for a little while longer if you don't mind."

He kissed her on the forehead as she patted his hand. "Ok, Grandma. Laura will save you some for later." He went out and closed the door. They ate breakfast quietly so they would not wake her.

Laura cleaned the kitchen and took Lucy some juice and a cup of coffee. As she looked at her, she realized that she had gone to sleep for good, ever so quietly and alone.

Laura called for Harley and Madison, "I can't believe it! We were all right here, in the same house, and she died alone!"

"That's the way she wanted it. She wasn't alone. She was on her way to meet her husband, parents, and children. She went to meet as many as she had left behind. She said she didn't want to leave us sad but wanted the children to remember the happy times with her. Remember those times, children. Your Grandma loved you as much as anyone ever could. Never forget that!"

The family was growing, but it seemed that for everyone who was born, another died. There were fewer to inform of her death, yet they could not leave anyone out. Madison went to send the telegrams to those he could. Others would just have to be informed by post. Some of them had expected the news anyway.

Lucy (Place) Storts, daughter of Joseph (Joe) Place and Sarah (Noland) Place, died October 29, 1920, and was buried beside her husband in Paint Rock Cemetery.

As the minister began to talk about Lucy, he began to mention her husband, Phylander, and her children, who had preceded her in death. Little Mattie, who died in 1885 at age eleven; Elmira, Harley's Ma, in 1900; Temperance 1905; Lucy had taken on those grandchildren. Sarah Jane died in 1918; Phylander on March 3, 1919; then her son David on May 5, 1919; Her daughter Isabella Christine (Storts) Beebe had passed earlier that year, in 1920.

"Most of her children have preceded her in death. She was ready to go to be with them. Let us try to rejoice in that she is able, not only to be with the Lord but is also having a great time with those who it broke her heart to lose. Can you imagine the hugs and even laughter she is enjoying right now?"

"If in this life only, we have hope in Christ Jesus, we are of all men most miserable. Her hope and faith were in the Lord. I have seen her express that hope more times than once. My heart goes out to all of you, as I know you are grieving like never before. The Bible says to sorrow not as those who have no hope. The angels are rejoicing. God will give all of you strength in due time.

Let us remember the happy times and the times that your Ma and Grandma helped you through the hard times. You need to help each other now. It is your turn to love and to give the young ones a reason to go on. They are the future. They need to be strong, and we need to give them hope."

Life was not quite the same for any of the family for a while, well, maybe forever, but life goes on. One of the children asked Ma, "What are we going to do without Grandma Lucy?"

"We are going to pick up our sad hearts and march on, if not for ourselves, then for others. Let the Good Lord help you."

Chapter 32
Great Treasures

It seemed that they were unsettled in the house where Grandma had passed. Pa had found one on the side of Wildcat Mountain with even more rooms than the one they lived in.

He wanted to save money to buy the homestead back, so he decided to go to work at the box factory. Factory work would pay cash money. He had to leave very early in the morning and got home late at night.

After several weeks, Laura had enough. She was the mildest-mannered person one would ever meet, but he was going to know how she felt about this one. "Harley, how long are you going to do this? The children almost never get to spend any time with you. Cloyal especially misses you."

"I don't know what else to do, Laura. If I don't make more money, how are we ever going to get a real home for them? I get some blacksmithing and woodwork. But I need a shop and the right tools to do much of that. I'm doing the best I know how."

"I realize that Harley, but being together is more important than where we live. It seems to me that when you have to travel so far every day, well, it just makes more sense to make less money and have a happy family. At least when we were sharecropping, we could all work together as a family; not to mention, we were already living on the land you wanted to buy. The house is small, but we could make do."

"Guess you're right, as usual. I will give them my notice. It would not be fair to the other workers for me to just not show up. They need time to replace me. Besides, it will be spring soon. I think Ben is already looking for someone to help him this year. I'll go see him on Saturday. Meanwhile, I am tired and hungry. Is that stew that I smell? Hope you saved me some."

"Yes, and of course we did. The children wouldn't eat theirs until they saw we had plenty left for you. They love their pa." She got him a big bowl of stew and sat it on the table with cornbread and a cup of buttermilk.

"The kids did the milking tonight. I don't think all of it got to the house. The younger ones wanted to help. I believe Alene was wearing most of it. No use crying over spilled milk." They tried to keep their laughter quiet so as not to wake the children.

Dan and Harley had been accustomed to helping each other with different projects, but he also would often come by just to visit with Laura. "I'm glad you and Harley are married, Laura, but I still miss you; life was not the same after you left. I was so young when Ma and Pa died that you took Ma's place for me, I think. It wasn't fair to you, but I love you for it. I don't think I ever thanked you for that. At least we can visit often."

Laura replied, "What else was I to do? I was just glad you were there. You and Holland kept me going when I felt like giving up. You made me feel needed. I should be thanking you. I should also thank you for talking me into going to that dance with Harley. He is a good husband and father."

"He's also a good friend, and he has always been one we could count on. That is why we were ok with you going with him. We knew he would be good to you. But if he ever isn't, though, you let me know," Dan said with a smile. They had a really good visit that day, as usual.

Dan went home that evening before dark. He told her that he had some work to do with a new horse that he had been working with for a few days.

Laura was to face another tragedy in her young life. She got the news that night that her brother, Daniel, had been thrown from a horse and had died. She couldn't bear to talk about it. He was only twenty-four years old.

"How much more can we stand?" Her grieving was compounded. God had taken her parents and then her source of comfort.

Harley didn't know what to say or do. "Sometimes life just throws curves that only God understands." He comforted her the best he could. "You couldn't have asked for a better brother."

The tears once again fell down Laura's face. With children to care for and another on the way, she had to pick up and keep going as best as she could. He was buried at Paint Rock.

(She really never told me exactly what happened to him. She didn't like to talk about such sad things, so I got very little information about her brother Daniel's accident.) He held a special place in her heart, and she clung to the good memories, trying not to think about the bad. "The Good Book says we should think about the good things."

Harley and Laura had another girl, Leatha (Lathy), born on April 4, 1922, just missing Laura's 30th birthday. God was truly blessing their family, and Laura was so thankful that God had blessed them with children. They helped ease the pain of losing her precious brother and kept her busy.

"The Lord giveth and the Lord taketh away, blessed be the name of the Lord. He certainly has a way of filling the empty spots in a body's heart." Laura acknowledged.

The Bible says that children are a heritage of the Lord. The awesome responsibility that God had placed in their hands was not taken lightly. They had been entrusted with great treasures.

Ma always reminded the children that it was the Good Lord who took care of them; He made the gardens grow, and they all had to do their part and never be lazy because the Good Book taught that it was a sin to be lazy or unkind to others.

Then, in 1924, they had another son. Laura was glad it was a boy, as she wanted to name him after Harley. It seemed only fitting since Matt was named after his uncle. They named him Loren Harley.

Lathy was not exactly ready to share her spot as the baby, but they would give her the extra attention she needed. She would be a big girl, sleep with her sisters, and give the crib to her little brother.

Clossie and Alene made her think they were excited that she was big enough to sleep in the big bed with them, for which Ma was truly thankful.

She loved her children and would give Lathy all the attention and love that she could. She was still a baby also.

Cloyal was (12), Clossie (9), Alene (6), Matt (4), and Lathy (2) when Loren was born. After the evening chores and supper were over, it was time for family time. It was important to Ma and Pa that they had some quiet family time and talked to each other after a long day of either school or work. Ma read the Bible or another book to them, and then later, closer to bedtime, Pa would get out his fiddle.

Pa had a full-size guitar that Thurman had given him, and Cloyal was learning to play better all the time. "You're getting pretty good on that guitar, Son." Cloyal smiled with pride, and they kept playing. "Pretty soon, I can play the big guitar, and someone else can play my little one. I know it was a birthday present from Grandpa, but I think he would want me to share. I sure miss him, Pa."

"I know you do, and so do I, but at least you have memories of him. I wish the other children did. He was the man many wish they could be. I hope you won't forget the things he taught you and maybe pass them on to the younger children as you get the chance. They love to listen to stories; we must give them some reason to think of him and know who they are. He is the reason we are here."

Cloyal and Pa had begun to try to teach the other children a few chords on the guitar. They all were allowed to try to learn as they were able to learn the chords. No instruments were ever kept away from children. They were just reminded to be careful with them. Music was an important part of many days, and anyone with a God-given talent to play or sing should use it.

Martha Storts and Harley's sisters, Lucy and Sarah, came by to give Laura a hand with the children. They had taken their turn helping with Phylander and Lucy and figured that it was their place to help out with the children. Laura had her hands full and welcomed the help.

Somewhere during that time frame, Ma had managed to get a treadle sewing machine. As was Ma's custom, if she had something, it belonged to all of them. Besides, they all needed to learn to sew on the machine since they had been blessed with one. They knew as much about it as she did.

(This doesn't actually fit here because it happened years later.) As the story goes, when Clossie was about 16 and Lathy about 10, they both wanted to use the sewing machine one day. It was hot inside, so the girls took it out under a tree.

Clossie needed to make herself a dress. Ma had got her a pretty piece of material since she had outgrown most everything that she had to wear to church or out anywhere, but Lathy wanted to sew first. She told Clossie that Ma had been teaching her to sew on the machine.

Ma wanted all of them to learn to sew with it; it makes sewing a lot faster and with better stitches, but she expected them to be careful with it so it would last them and that no fingers would get caught by the needle.

Clossie sat down to sew, and Lathy became upset and started pulling her hair and demanding that she be first. Instinctively, Clossie reached back and pulled hers. It turned into an argument.

Seldom were any problems between the girls, so, as they were arguing with each other, Pa didn't say a word; he just picked up the machine and took it back into the house. Neither of them got to sew that day. Fighting was not acceptable, but it was dealt with calmly and rationally and never lasted long.

They would both learn to sew, but as Ma would always say, "We must be kind to one another, and we must always share and give over to the little ones."

Chapter 33
Planting Time

Without the factory job, Pa would not be getting the cash money to pay rent. He didn't want to use up all his savings, so they decided to move back to the homestead and make the best of it until they could afford to buy it. The owner still needed the help, and it was almost springtime. The ground was not yet prepared for planting.

Harley had been helping him, but it was so far from where they lived that it was taking him away from home again. "This is defeating the purpose of quitting the box factory, Laura." She knew he was right this time.

"Is the sharecropper job still open? I could take care of a lot of the garden by the house, even with the babies, while you and the older children handle the fields."

"Yes, he already asked me to come back this spring. The people he had last year did not want to stay in the little cabin. It's still small, you know. We can't change that."

"We can manage. The barn loft is still available, isn't it? We stored stuff there before. Madison doesn't seem to mind sleeping up there when he's here. May as well make an extra bed there for Cloyal, too; he'll beg to sleep with him."

When the children overheard them, they wanted to move back home. "Please, Pa; we want to go home." Harley knew he would have lost any argument if he had one.

They had said exactly what he had hoped to hear, so they packed up the wagon and were back in the little cabin with more children than they had when they left because of not enough room.

With barely enough time to get moved in, He moved his plows and tools first. Making sure to move the heavy cook stove when he had lots of help. It was extremely heavy and took up a lot of space, but no one minded. It meant more to them than any piece of furniture ever could. Laura loved the warming closet and hot water reservoir.

He would have to get started breaking the ground as soon as possible and help Laura with the unpacking in the evenings. "Laura, don't do too much, I will help you when I get home tonight. Cloyal and Clossie can help you. I won't need them until I start planting."

"We can handle most of the straightening and cleaning. Don't worry. We'll work together like a family should."

In the early spring, Harley plowed furrows in the garden close to the house, giving Laura easy access to it. With the children so young, he wanted to help her as much as possible.

Alene wanted to help Ma set out tomato plants. Ma said she could help but gave her only a few plants to be her very own to weed, water, and take care of, and then she would be able to pick the tomatoes from them later, but she had to allow Cloyal or Clossie to help her with the first two.

Cloyal was eleven and had been helping plant the garden for several years. Alene worked for almost an hour on her plants to get them to stand just right. She would plant one and then find something else that caught her attention. He was getting annoyed trying to help her, but Ma said it was ok; she was too little to do much; that he could just go on with his own planting.

As they planted the beans, potatoes, okra, and whatever else, Ma walked behind them with her hoe and covered the seeds as they dropped them. Soon, it was all planted.

The next day, Pa would plow a field for corn. As the table was being set for breakfast, Pa mentioned, "I sure could use some help. Cloyal, how'd you like to go drop the corn in the rows for me? You did a good job yesterday."

"I guess so. Are Ma and Clossie going to help, too?"

"No, I don't think so. It will be a long day and too much for the babies. They will need to stay closer to the house.

Ma fixed them a jug of water to take with them. Cloyal knew how to plant corn in the rows after Pa plowed them. It would be a special day with just him and Pa.

Pa got the furrows all plowed, and Cloyal was dropping the corn three cornels at a time, just like he had been taught.

Pa got to the end of the last row. You are doing a good job, Son. Do you think you could finish this by yourself? I will come back in a little while and cover them after I put the horses up and help your Ma. You can come on to the house when you get all the corn planted.

He looked at the large bag of corn. "All of them?" It seemed like a lot of corn to him.

"Yes, don't stop planting until the bag is empty. Ok?"

"Ok, Pa. But that's a lot of corn!" Pa assured him that he was big enough to handle the task. It should fill all the rows.

As Pa drove the horses on towards the barn, Cloyal thought about how long it would take him to plant every kernel and figured he'd have to work fast.

Soon, he became hot and tired. With instructions to plant all of the corn, he started putting four instead of three in about every other place. Still, there was a lot left. Pa had told him not to come home until it was all gone.

Well, there just happened to be a dead stump with a big hole in the middle of it that went clear to the ground. Without another thought, when he got to the end of the row, he went straight to the stump, dumped the rest of the corn down into the hole, and then started to the house.

"Well, are you done already, boy? You will be outworking me before you know it." Pa went back to finish the job a little later. But when he got there, he seemed surprised that there was a row with no corn. Maybe he miscalculated. He saw that some holes had four or five, so he didn't say anything about the empty row.

Not a word was said about the extra row in the cornfield until later in the spring when the seedlings began to sprout and grow. Pa noticed the stump that he thought was dead, but it had something green growing out of it, and went to see what it was. He had to laugh in spite of himself and then went on home to eat supper. "Have you checked the corn fields, Son? I need you to help me weed the corn tomorrow."

Cloyal had forgotten all about that stump. So, he said, "Sure." He and Pa got the hoes and headed for the corn patch.

Seeing the stump as he looked up from the end of the first row, he stopped dead, still in his tracks. "Oh, no!" Cloyal thought, "Every one of those kernels must have come up! I'm going to get the licking of my life!" He had no idea what to say to Pa, so he just stood there and waited, looking at it.

Pa wanted to find a good way to punish him that would help him in the future. But the whole thing was so funny he could not keep a straight face. "Has this taught you anything, Boy?"

"Yes, Sir, next time, make sure no dirt is in the stump?"

They both laughed so hard that they sat down on the ground. "We're going to have to address this little issue, seriously; you know you can't get by with this, don't you? But right now, it is just so amazing that so much corn can grow in one little stump! It's probably going to burst the stump! How much did you put in there anyway?"

"All that was left in the sack; I really have no excuse. I just did it without really thinking about it." Cloyal wanted to ask him not to tell Ma, but he knew it would do no good and probably make things worse. She would know the instant they left the supper table, maybe before, if Pa was still laughing. He would just take the licking he deserved and hoped they would soon forget it.

Clossie was a hard worker and could keep up with the boys at about anything they could do: milking, gardening, or picking cotton. She was the oldest girl. Alene was always helping Ma in the kitchen or working in the gardens. Lathy worked wherever she was needed. As in all families, each had their own personality and needed to be accepted for who they were. Their children were indeed their greatest treasures.

Chapter 34
Moving the School House

Harley and Laura's children went to school at Paint Rock, where Harley had spent many hours. He told them stories of his school days and about playing his fiddle at church there.

They were amazed that he had gone to the same school that they were attending. It was one big room with several classes. The hillside that it sat on was steep, but no one ever mentioned it.

A better place became available for the schoolhouse, with level ground that was much more suitable than where it stood. Land for the cemetery had been donated, and the community began to question whether to build a new building and what to do with the one they had; maybe they should tear it down and rebuild.

There had been talk of consolidating Paint Rock School with Driggs. They hoped it would not happen, but if it did, they would still need a church and a community place to meet.

Several in the community met at the school to discuss any ideas that anyone might have come up with. Every house was filled with the events of the day at the supper table. Some thought they should just build a new building.

After much consideration and several meetings of the community, it was decided that they would move it, but how? It would be a major issue and needed careful planning.

Madison and Harley, along with friends Tilden Biggs, Gomer Harper, and several others in the community, would help with the planning and moving of the schoolhouse.

It was decided to get Mr. White, a local man who had moved a few houses before, to move this one. All who were able would help him. It was to be a community effort. Most of them had experience with skidding logs. So, they had some idea of how it might be possible to roll it over cut logs. They would cut logs as close to the same size as possible, trim them as smoothly as they could, haul or skid them to the site and close to the building, and then pull them one at a time underneath the front with ropes or chains. Once they got a few logs under it and two or three in front of it, they would need some strong teams pulling together in order to pull the building onto the next logs.

It would take many hours and maybe several days, if not weeks, but everyone agreed that it would be a worthwhile venture. If they didn't try, they would never know if it could be done.

Mr. White said, "Let's go home and get plenty of rest tonight. It may be the last real rest we get for weeks."

All the families were up early the next morning and eager to get started. Some came from close to Driggs to help. The logs were cut and brought to the school.

After a lot of effort and time, they managed to get the first log under the front. It was a tight fit, but soon had another. A horse or mule on each side of the logs was used to pull the logs back as far as they could get them, and then a few more were added to the front again.

It was a very slow process. One wrong move could damage the building or get someone injured or even killed. Next, they pulled the foundation stones out from under it and then moved the front cornerstones out of the way, allowing the building to rest on the logs.

"We're ready to start rolling!" called Mr. White. "Hook those two teams of mules and horses together. Put the horses in front. They will know what to do. Better yet, we may as well start with three teams. Which teams are the strongest and work best together? Let's see if we can do this without getting someone hurt or damaging the church."

Using the first three teams, pulling as hard as they could, it didn't budge, so they added another. "Has anyone moved a building like this before?" Tilden asked.

"I don't know, but where there is a need and a will, there is a way. You got a better way?" someone replied.

"No, but it's not moving. Maybe we need more horses." They hitched up another team of mules, needing the strongest possible. The horses would cooperate better and were put in the lead, but they needed the strength of the mules.

Five teams were pulling together. It still didn't move, but it budged a little. "Now we are getting somewhere," Madison added. Finally, another team was added; they had six teams of horses and mules pulling together. The building moved a little and then a little more.

The cheering began. "It moved!" Harley exclaimed. "We might just move this building after all!" They all seemed a little surprised, even after all the effort it took to move it. The building began to roll over the logs, a few inches at a time.

The boys tried to stay alert and help the men in any way they could, trying to carry their own weight. If they couldn't do a man's work, they would have to go stay with the children, knowing that one childish act could get someone badly injured.

When one log was free in the back, someone with a mule or horse would skid it around to the front, and they would then roll the building upon that log. Working together was the secret to getting such a task done. With the workers in one accord, the schoolhouse would eventually be in a much better place.

Some had thought it was a chore too great to be accomplished; others had no doubt. However, they were all right about one thing, it took several days to complete the task; actually, it took about two weeks, but they eventually got it to the new place about one quarter mile or so from where it had been built.

After it was moved to where it stands today, the foundation was put back under it, and the logs were pulled out. The support beams would need to be checked for any damage caused by the move, but it looked a lot better than many expected.

"Wow! We did it! We actually moved the school!" Several other boys talked about the job with great satisfaction for the rest of the evening. "This is a story you can tell your grandchildren," Harley exclaimed. "You don't move a schoolhouse every day."

"Even the horses seemed to be glad it's over. They deserve a day or two off, too," acknowledged Madison. Though extremely tired, all were glad they had been able to accomplish such a difficult feat and took pride in their success. The people in the community appreciated the schoolhouse even more, and everyone wanted to preserve it for future generations.

With more room around the school now and away from the woods, the logical thing to do was to build a porch on the front and a second outhouse. Finally, there would be one for the girls and one for the boys. One was moved from the other site, and another was built nearby.

The children were anxious to go back to school that year, happy about the two privies, and didn't want to move to Driggs School. They hoped that after moving the building, the boards would change their minds.

Before school started, a few of the boys decided to carve signs for the doors, one for GIRLS and one for BOYS. "We should get the new one after all this work," one boy exclaimed.

"Maybe so, but you know we'll have to switch it and give it to the girls when school starts; we might as well do it from the start. The teacher thinks we should be gentlemen and give over to the ladies," another added.

"Guess you're right." They nailed the signs to the doors. The year they moved the schoolhouse, Harley was introduced to a lesson he would never have thought possible and confirmed his thought that a man is never too old to learn.

He measured his abilities by that venture after that. If a schoolhouse could be moved with horses, then surely, anything that needed to be done could be done if a person tried hard enough and if the Lord willed it, of course.

The community got together and moved the building. The heart of a community makes a difference in anything.

Many have worked together through the years to keep the building usable and have attended school in this building, including my grandpa and his brothers and children.

This is Paint Rock School and Church, as it was when it was pulled over the logs by teams of horses and moved to the place where it sits today. It has been repaired many times and always had a purpose in the community, such as a school or church.

Chapter 35
Rose Catherine

Realizing her time was drawing near, Ma began getting things prepared for a new baby. Pa brought the crib from the barn loft. Ma and Clossie cleaned it up and put padding and clean bedding on it. Lathy and Alene helped them wash the baby clothes as they talked about the coming of the new baby. Clossie told Alene about the snow that fell on the bed as she was being born. Alene asked, "Ma, did the snow get on me?"

"No, of course not! We wouldn't let it snow on you. You were just a baby. We have to take care of our babies. It did snow on the bed, though. That doctor never even said a word about it. They just kept it off the best they could until the bed could be moved. We were all just focused on getting you here safe and sound. Not one flake got on you."

Ma was a hard worker, but no job ever compared to being a mother. She thought it was the highest calling she had ever had, with much greater responsibilities than any other. Using the time with her girls, she wanted to instill in them the pride and joy of taking good care of the special little gift sent by God. They never doubted her love for them.

A few weeks later, in 1926, Laura gave birth to a beautiful baby girl and named her Rose Catherine, after her sister, Rose, whom she had lost a few years earlier.

She had not had a hard time carrying her. The doctor came, helped with the birth, and said she was a fine, healthy baby and told Laura that she should take it easy for a few days and get her strength back. He said, "It looks like you have plenty of help; take advantage of it and enjoy your baby."

Harley agreed that she worked too hard and insisted she follow the doctor's orders. She loved being able to hold and rock little Rose in the rocker that Pa had built for her before their first son was born. She was a good baby, much easier to care for than some had been.

That year, Ma took care of Rose and the smaller children as she worked in the garden close to the house, letting the girls do more in the cotton fields and corn patches or whatever else was needed. It was a treat to them not to have to stay in to watch the baby, they thought. They competed with the boys in picking cotton, beans, peas, or other vegetables or fruit, working hard to keep up with the boys. They had a couple apple trees and a few peach trees.

No matter who picked the most, more work got accomplished when the girls were in the fields. Pa said ,"Don't forget to save enough time and energy to do chores at the house and barn. The cow needs to be milked, and animals need to be fed before supper. You girls will still help Ma with supper."

Ma, Loren, and Rose spent a lot of time just talking to each other. Of course, Rose wasn't doing a lot of talking, but Ma knew what she was thinking. She was thinking how wonderful it was to have Ma there with her instead of out in the fields or milking cows.

She smiled a lot, and Ma's heart warmed beyond measure as she explained to her two-year-old how God had given them a new baby, and they had to take care of her. Nothing could take the place of being a mother.

One day, Loren was asleep, and Ma looked at the clock. "Oh my, I forgot about lunch! Sorry, Rose, but I also have other children to feed." Putting her in her crib and moving it into the kitchen, Ma got to work on the noon meal. She knew they would be ready to eat right at 12:00. She was late! Putting in some dry wood that would heat fast, Laura was thankful that the stove was still warm and that she had been cooking a pot of beans all morning. She would make a pan of cornbread as quickly as possible. The fire picked up fast. Setting the iron skillet of bread on the top of the stove would get it hot faster. It took a hot fire to make good cornbread. When it was bubbling around the edges, she put it into the oven and hoped it would cook in time. Quickly, she peeled potatoes and put them into the pan that was already hot.

It was noon when they all came streaming through the door, expecting to sit down at the table and eat. To everyone's surprise, the table was not set. Ma had a stack of plates sitting on the table and was a little embarrassed that the food was not ready. Pouring the beans into a bowl, Ma said, "The potatoes were almost fried. Cornbread will be done in about five minutes. I am so sorry, I lost track of time!"

"It's ok, Ma, we can help," Lathy replied. They got cleaned up and set the table. Lunch was on the table in no time, and they all had a good laugh about it. They asked if they could have a few minutes extra off for lunch. Ma said that it seemed only fair.

Pa agreed. They got an hour and a half to rest that day instead of an hour. It had been a custom to rest for an hour after lunch every day. Pa said they could get more work done if they were rested, so it wasn't wasting time.

What they actually did was spend the extra time playing with Rose and Loren. Rose was beginning to really notice them, and they all loved to make her laugh. The girls would hold or play with her all the time if they could.

Loren was sometimes jealous, so they would try to give him a little extra attention. Cloyal said, "Come here, Loren, you can play guitar with me." Handing him his little guitar, he tried to teach him how to strum it. He could not do full chords, so Cloyal showed him partial Chords, as Pa instructed him. "You will be able to play someday." He strummed and sang whatever words came to his mind. Even at such a young age, he seemed interested in the guitar.

After resting, they went back to the fields. Pa had unharnessed the mules so they could rest, also. So, he went first to re-harness them.

Several months later, Rose was getting older, and was a lot more fun. She was a year old and was learning to walk. With so many brothers and sisters to do anything she wanted, she was getting a little spoiled, but was never a real problem.

The children each took turns watching her and loved having their turn. Loren often noticed when she was being occupied with the others and wanted Ma's time.

She would smile and pick him up and hold him as if he was the only baby she had at the time. "No one could ever take your place, sweet baby; your Ma loves you very much!"

While rocking Loren to sleep at night was their special time. She would put him to bed and then rock Rose for a while. Ma was thinking that she might not have any more children. She better enjoy this one, and she did. Ma and Pa loved all of their children, and they all knew it.

They had been very blessed. God had been more than good to them in giving them such a family. Laura remembered the times she had growing up with her brothers and sisters and thought about how close they still were. Always in the back of her mind was the desire to train her own children to stay close together and help one another as her ma and pa had taught them.

She looked at Rose as she was rocking her and wondered if she was instilling in her children the love for each other as she had been taught by her parents. Saying a quiet prayer of thanksgiving, she asked the Lord to bless her children and fill their hearts with love for each other, filling in any gaps that she might have left unattended.

After laying Rose in her crib, Ma spent time with the other children. They would talk about the events of the day or whatever was on their minds, often reading the bible to them or listening as one of them read. "We must always read the Good Book and live by it, even when life gets hard to bear. Don't forget that Jesus is your very best friend!

Rose had her second birthday. Clossie wanted to make her a cake. Ma was glad she did. They didn't do much in the birthday department, but they usually tried to at least make a cake and acknowledge that everyone had a birthday. Ma had made Rose a new dress from one of her old ones. Since she was outgrowing the ones that she had, she would make the other girls an apron with the leftover material.

Ma fixed her hair, washed her face, and put on her new dress. Rose was very excited! This was her day! The boys played with her while the girls helped Ma get supper ready.

She loved to play with them because they would get down on the floor with her as if they were the same age. The girls treated her more like Ma did and dressed her up as if she was a doll, always fixing her hair and washing her face. Sometimes, Rose was convinced that her face was clean enough.

Supper was ready, and they had a pleasant but noisier supper than usual. Rose was happy and got the first piece of cake. They each had made her a little something. Ma also made her a new quilt that was just the right size for her new small bed since she had outgrown the little crib. Pa had refinished the small bed because it was quite used by then.

That was a day to remember. The children had a good day at school and a good supper with cake for dessert. But what they enjoyed the most was seeing their baby sister so happy. She danced around and around in her new dress as they played music that evening. They clapped their hands, and she thought she was something special; they all agreed.

Winter was coming, but plenty of wood was in the shed for several weeks at least. The harvest was over, canning was almost all done, and they were ready for a rest. They finally had time to visit with neighbors and go into town as a family. As often as they could, the families nearby got together for a musical or a barn dance.

The kids all loved to play with Rose; she was such a pleasant baby. Ma never really had to watch out for her because all the kids did. She wanted to be right in the big middle of them and usually was the center attraction.

One or another of the girls was carrying or holding her about half the time. They noticed that one of the children, several years older than Rose, started coughing. Her mother thought she might be allergic to something as she had not shown any signs of being sick.

She was holding Rose at the time. Her Ma told her to put Rose down and stay away from her just in case she was getting sick. "You wouldn't want to share a cold." Her daughter agreed and immediately moved away from all the others. They decided it was best to go home just in case.

A few days later, the report was that the girl had a Whooping Cough. It wasn't bad, but needed attention. She soon recovered, but all was worried about who she had exposed. She and her mother felt worse than anyone and had no idea where she had caught such a thing. She had never coughed so much in her life!

Ma was watching for signs of coughing from her children. They waited, and sure enough, it was Rose who came down with it. She was strong and healthy, so they wouldn't panic. Others had gotten over it in about two weeks or so.

Ma would put everything else aside and take care of her. A tent was made, and water was boiled to sit under the tent in order to help her breathe. They called the doctor, who came right away. "Laura, you're doing all that I could do. She should be ok in a couple of weeks. I'll be back tomorrow."

The children were worried. She seemed so sick. Ma assured them, "It won't be long 'till she's better. Some of you had the same thing. Only the ones who had had whooping cough were allowed to get near her.

The younger ones wanted to see her, but Ma and Pa said, "No!" One at a time was enough to worry about. They could not take the chance of passing it on. "The doctor said she should be getting better any day now," Harley exclaimed.

The doctor came by every other day by then. Something was not right. He started coming every day. She was coughing way too much, and it seemed so deep within her lungs. He did some more tests and reported that Rose had developed Pneumonia.

No one slept much, especially Rose. She could not get her breath nor stop coughing long enough to sleep. Ma would not leave her side. Pa and Clossie had to insist she eat something to keep up her strength. She couldn't eat because Rose couldn't stop coughing long enough to eat.

Ma's heart was breaking insufferably! How could she help her baby? There had to be a way! The other kids had been fine in a couple of weeks with the same sickness. What was she doing wrong? She had so many questions, yet she knew the Good Lord was the only one who knew the answers to most of them. Rose was in His hands. Laura prayed and prayed for her precious baby. She knew they would have to accept His will, but how could any of them go on without Rose? Why did she have to suffer so?

The doctor informed them that he had done all he could do. It was up to God from then on. They tried to keep her as comfortable as possible.

Ma would hold her often and tell her how much she and the others loved her. She would talk to her about how Jesus loved her more than any of them. She didn't want her to be afraid. "Fear is often worse than what is happening to a person," Ma would say. She told Rose and the others, "We must trust God, no matter what happens."

In spite of all their efforts, she didn't get any better. Soon, she couldn't get her breath at all. Rose Catharine Krigbaum passed away from this life at the age of two years. She was buried at Paint Rock Cemetery, close to her Grandparents, Elmira and William Krigbaum, and her great-grandparents, Phylander and Lucy Place Storts.

The whooping cough had been rough enough to stop her breathing at times, but when she developed pneumonia, there was not much anyone could do.

Ma explained to the children that Rose was in the arms of Jesus as he had taken the children in his arms when he walked on the earth in Jerusalem.

She could tell the children that, but she had a harder time accepting her own words. Though grieving more than anyone knew, she had to go on for her other children.

But how could she manage? The pain was greater than anything she had ever endured. She remembered losing her own mother when she was fifteen. She tried to find comfort in the thought that, somehow, they were together in heaven and knew one another. "Harley, get her crib out of here! I can't stand to see it."

Pa was hurting too, almost too much to stand, but his heart was breaking for Ma. How could he help her? They had to go on with life, but the sadness in that house was too much. No one laughed anymore. Ma put the food on the table as usual, but she didn't seem to be able to talk much to anyone.

They all understood because they loved and missed Rose, too. No one felt like playing music anymore. The fiddle and guitars just sat in their cases. It just wasn't the same without Rose dancing to the music.

Months passed, Ma saw the sadness in her children's eyes and realized they had to come to grips with what had been dealt them. "God knows what he is doing," she told her family as they sat quietly around the supper table. "Rose is happy now and never had to endure the heartache of losing someone she loved, like we all have. For that, I am thankful. God took her for a reason. He intends for the rest of us to keep on living. We are not living now; we just exist. There is a difference. We need to be thankful for what we have and the special memories we have with her."

After supper, we can read from the Good Book (Bible) for a little while. God always knows what we need. We are not the first ones to lose someone we love."

Pa was relieved to hear Ma speak at all. He mentioned that maybe they should look for another place to live so they would not be constantly reminded of the last terrible few weeks. The children had been having bad dreams almost every night. None of them could sleep well.

Pa would start looking for a place to move to as soon as he could. It would need to be someplace close to his job, if possible, because he wanted to come home at lunch to check on his family. He was working every day from daylight 'til dark with only an hour or so for lunch. Something had to turn up. They really needed to put their lives back together. They still had children to raise.

He had hoped that he could have bought the homestead back by now; however, that seemed to be out of the question. He was just glad to have his wife back and wanted to find some sort of normal again. The children had always been so happy that seeing their sadness was hard to endure. He would try to start playing his fiddle again. No music had been played since the death of their precious baby.

The next evening, he got out his fiddle. As he began to play, some of the children began to cry. He stopped and went to put his fiddle up, but Ma said it was good for them to cry. All of them had tried to be so strong for each other. She told them how proud she was of all of them, then asked them if they wanted Pa to play again.

They all said yes, they did want him to play. Cloyal opened up his case and got out his guitar to play with him. Thus, they began their healing time. Things would never be the same, but they would always have the memories of their baby sister, who loved to dance to the music.

Ma began to enjoy and treasure her time with the other children even more than ever. She had lost one baby without much warning. "I don't want to take anything for granted. Life is never sure." she thought and began trying to spend more quality time with each of them.

Chapter 36
Saving for a Home

Harley and Laura had been trying to save enough money to buy back the land, so anything they earned was spent very wisely, and they put just a little of any money they got into savings and refused to spend it unless it was an absolute emergency.

Harley would count it once in a while. Years had passed since his grandpa Storts lost the homestead, but he was not giving up and knew that it would take a long time to save enough to buy it back.

The owner of the Storts homestead had not even said that he would sell; however, they would need to purchase a home somewhere, sooner or later. He hoped it could be there.

Laura's brother was living on her family land. She and Harley had six children and really had no place to call home. Ma informed Pa that they were expecting yet another baby. Ma and Pa were glad that God knew their needs, and this was a special blessing to offset their terrible loss.

They might have been able to afford a smaller place, but Harley was quite set on getting his grandpa's farm back, whatever the cost. He worked on the homestead every day as if it was his land. The owner was amazed at his devotion to his work but wasn't fully aware of his wish to purchase it from him.

Many years were hard, but one was a little more difficult than others. Harley worked hard in the fields and was allowed to keep part of what he raised, but the land was not producing as they hoped for lack of rain, they figured.

Harley found that he could get paid for any extra work as a blacksmith and carpenter. So, he had to work somewhere else to get money to buy the necessary supplies. He was tempted to spend their savings but kept putting it off. Almost desperate, at times, they managed to keep most of their savings.

They made a small garden for their own use next to the house so Laura would have easy access to it. Most of Harley's time must be devoted to working the land as a sharecropper.

Everyone seemed to have a hard time that year. Crops didn't do as well as usual. The owner realized that he wasn't able to pay the taxes that were way past due. He tried and tried but soon saw that he was not going to be able to keep the land.

Feeling as bad for Harley and his family as he did for himself, he knew that they depended on his farmland as much as he did. He tried to find a good way to tell him but to no avail. He would have to tell him as soon as possible; the sooner, the better.

One evening after supper, he went over to see Harley and asked to speak with him alone. They went outside and took a little walk. "Harley, I don't know how to tell you this, but this has not been a good year at all for me. I can't even pay the taxes on my land. I am going to lose the farm just like your grandpa did. Is there any way you could buy it? I know you've always wanted it."

"I wish I could, you know I don't have that kind of money. We have been saving very little at a time, hoping to buy it from you someday. I doubt we could even pay the taxes on it. I am sorry."

"Well, that might be a thought; I am losing it anyway. Just wanted to let you know in time for you to make arrangements to care for your family, but if you have some saved, you might get it just by paying the taxes. That's how I bought it. You have put a lot into this farm also, and if you can't buy it, I hope you can find work before spring. I hate this for both of us. If you can come up with the money before it is taken from me, I will let you have it for the price of the taxes. If not, maybe it will be a little while before it is gone. You will need to see Judge White."

Harley stopped and stood in silence, not knowing what to say. He had been saving to try to buy that land for years, but he felt very sad for his friend who was losing his land and knew how he felt. He finally spoke after a long period of silence. "What are you going to do?"

The man just shook his head as if to say he did not know, and they walked back to the house, and he left.

That night, Harley didn't talk much, and he didn't play his fiddle. Laura knew he was deeply troubled; He would tell her what was bothering him in due time. She could imagine all sorts of things but waited for him to speak when he was ready.

He did not say anything about it that night. Early the next morning, he asked, "How much money do you think we might have saved?"

She was totally surprised. "I'm not sure, but it is not enough to buy the land from him. Does he want to sell?"

No, he doesn't want to, but he doesn't have the money for the taxes and says he is going to lose it soon. He already received notice to evacuate. It could be that all we have to do is pay the taxes to get it. "Do you think we have enough?"

"I don't know. We've been saving a little each year for a long time now. Remember, we have had to use a little of it a few times. But there might be enough just for taxes. Why don't you count it while I get breakfast? You won't be able to think of much else 'till you do."

"Think I will. I will get the fire going for you first." We may not have a home yet. The cabin is too small to stay in for long, but we can start building in the early spring."

"That sounds fine, Harley, but aren't you forgetting something? You don't own the land yet. After you see how much money we have, go see what you can do at the tax office. The kids and I can take care of things here today. They are real helpers these days. We are very blessed."

Harley thought of his grandpa and wished he could be here to help as he got ready to go into town. Not really knowing what steps to take, he went to the tax office first. His heart was pounding, and he realized that he was short of what he needed for money to pay the taxes; however, he still had pay coming from two jobs he had done. He would have to wait a little while longer and hope that no one bought it first.

He went to Judge White and told him that it would be a little while before he could come up with the money but that he had a large portion of it, explaining that his grandfather had lost it once, and he had been saving to get it back and that he lived on the property.

He was willing to give Harley a little time to get the money he needed before selling to anyone else if he paid him what he had in faith that the rest would come. He was also allowed to live there for a few more weeks while trying to come up with the rest.

Harley was truly relieved and grateful. In due time, it might be their land and crops. They might finally have a home after all.

Harley and Laura Krigbaum

Chapter 37

Redeeming the Homestead

A few loose ends had to be taken care of, but in a few weeks, he was able to pay off the taxes and became the proud owner of 80 acres of good farm and timber land. It was in 1929 that they actually gained ownership of the land during a depression, at a time when they could sure use the money. The timing was God's. They realized that only He could have worked that out.

Without wasting any time, he headed back home with the deed in his hands, anxious to share the news with his family, who would be just as happy as he was. On the way, he thought of where he would build the new house.

The cabin was getting way too small for so many growing children. No one would mind sleeping on the floor or in the barn for a little while longer when they needed to. They had become good workers, and they could build the house together. There was much excitement about the plans for the new house. The family had learned what it was to be happy again.

By that time, Laura was officially called Ma, and Harley was called Pa by almost everyone who knew them. It is funny how those names grew on them. From now on, I will refer to them as Ma and Pa.

Uncle Madison called them Ma and Pa because he was talking to the children so much. Ma and Pa were thankful to have him close by.

Just west of the cabin, the same distance from the creek, was the place chosen to build the new house. Pa would first build a very large room with huge logs, much larger than the cabin they were living in. Neighbors and family came to help whenever they had time. It took a lot to get the huge logs in place. Uncle Madison was always standing by to do what he could, and Ma and Pa had brothers and sisters close by who were ready to help.

The neighbors helped when anyone was building a house, as Pa had helped many others. That was the custom in those days. Raising a house or barn was a community effort.

Neighbors would come to help. The older children knew the importance of working together. Cloyal was sixteen, and he and his friends were willing workers. All the children helped with anything they could. They had learned to work as soon as they were old enough to do anything.

Their jobs were whatever they were big enough to do: gather wood, carry water, work in the garden, or care for younger children. But they must learn to work for their own good. There was much to do and not enough daylight hours.

Their uncomplaining hard work was rewarded by a shorter work day and more time to relax in the evenings when they could sit and listen to Pa play his fiddle or join in with whatever instrument they played. Or they could play games of checkers, marbles, or whatever they chose to do. Ma insisted they had some time that belonged to them. They could meditate on the activities of the day or whatever they wanted. It was their time.

Ma told them that everyone would rest better and be able to do more the next day. And even with all the summer work, they were not to neglect their studies. Especially the ones who didn't get to go to school. Ma taught them to read and write while they were very young.

They designed the first room so that it could be added on to later. It would be as long as they could find the timber, and sawing and skidding logs were the first chores. Harley and Madison were used to that. It required a lot of sawing and teamwork, and you had to be a real team to handle a crosscut saw properly, so it was important to be in rhythm with one another. Many had been sawing together since they were young boys, so they stayed together as a team. Others paired up as could best work together.

Soon, they were almost competing to make the sawing seem less burdensome, and time passed faster. They talked about when they had moved the church and things that had happened while they were cutting logs for other houses. This was no exception; a few close calls and saw blades and axes got a workout, but no one got seriously injured.

This was a good opportunity for the older boys of the community to fine-tune their crosscutting skills. Most of them were used to cutting wood, but it takes a lot of practice to sew together. Pulling and pushing needed to be in complete harmony.

As soon as a tree fell, someone else trimmed it with an axe, and then there was a horse or mule standing by to take it to the building site.

Before long, the logs were cut, and the building had begun. The framework was laid out with split logs. The younger children were to stay out of the way, but the bigger ones were expected to do their part. An idle mind was the devil's workshop, so everyone was to work without goofing off, or they were not allowed to help.

Losing concentration on a big heavy log could mean someone's life. No misbehavior would be tolerated! It would get them sent home, and they would not be able to live it down easily. The boys were expected to be responsible men for that job.

The walls were almost up. The top ones were the hardest. Ropes were tied around the logs and pulled up over the other logs to the top because they could no longer lift them up. On the very top ones, they often used horses to pull them up. The men carefully set the last logs in place so that the notches fit together before loosening the rope.

The windows were cut out, and the shutters were being made to fit. He was hoping to get the roof on before the next big rain, so he instructed some of the boys on how to start making wood shingles.

They had to have a skilled adult to supervise the work because one wrong swipe with the sharp blade could mean a lost finger or worse. It kept them all busy, and he would at least have a start on the roof. If they worked really hard, the walls might be done in another day.

Women were busy preparing food for them, so when it was lunchtime, they all ate outside under a shade tree. After a little rest and food, they were back at work.

Soon, it was time to put on the roof. Once they got the decking on, standing on the ladder, Pa started the first row of shingles. Then, with the second row offsetting the joints of each shingle so that the rain would not get in, one of the other men started the third row behind him.

After they got several rows of wood shingles on, Harley started the next row and then gave it to one of the boys to follow on across. The pattern had been set. The boys could learn how to roof a house and the value of helping each other. They worked hard and tried to please, knowing that they all would probably want to build a home someday, having total confidence that all would come together to help them.

Some were busy carrying shingles up the ladder while others were still making them. More would be needed for the other side. The race was on to keep up. Pa and some of the experienced men worked at both jobs to see that it was done right and carefully. Pa reminded them a bad shingle could be burned for firewood, but a foot, a hand, or even a finger cut off was a lot more difficult to live without and could not be replaced. If one got careless, he was asked to give his position to another.

Harley had waited a long time for this house. As he looked out the door one morning, he knew they were running out of time. The roof wasn't finished yet, and the doors and the shutters were not on. The doors were made, but they still needed to make a few more shutters, and it looked like it might rain in the west.

He told the children to eat quickly and come to help in any way they could. Ma and the girls had been helping when the other men could not be there. This time, everyone was needed. The ones that were too small were to stay in a safe place, with one older girl to watch them. Everyone else was to help get shingles up the ladder or whatever they could do. Clossie tried to keep up with Cloyal and did a good job.

The last of the roof was almost done when the rain came. Pa sent everyone off the roof, and he finished up. "No use in all of us getting wet." So, they went inside after hanging the last shutter and then closed the shutters and doors. Pa was soaked. Ma had dry clothes ready for him to put on.

The lanterns were lit, and they continued to work on the inside. They were finally done except for chinking the walls. The children could help with that. Learning to work together was being carried on to the next generation. It had doors on the south and north. A place for a door to the east would lead to the kitchen, which would be built later on. But for the time being, it was used as a chimney for the cook stove.

The doors in the north and south would give a nice cross breeze through the house during the hot summer. They also put a window in the south, north and in the west. The windows had shutters that opened to the outside but no glass in any of them, so if it rained, they would close the shutters. Then, it would be dark enough to need the lamps in the daytime. But it was a new home, and they were ready to move in.

Pa looked at it with warm thoughts of his grandpa and hoped that he could see that he had made good on his promise to him. He still missed his grandparents a lot. Although he was 36 years old, with a family of his own; he still wanted to please them.

Chapter 38
Home at Last

"Go pack your things, kids. It's been a long time coming, but we're going home! The first half of the house is finished."

The cheering and clapping could probably be heard for a mile. Heading for the cabin, they laughed and talked with excitement all the way. They would only need one day to move if everyone did his part.

The kids were all packed before bedtime that night, and the bedding was gathered up and ready just after they got up the next morning. It was not so far from the cabin, so some of them put the clothes and bedding on their back and took them to the new house, coming back quickly because much had to be done.

The wood cook stove would be the hardest to move, but it would have to cool, so Ma only put a little fire in it to cook breakfast with wood that would burn up quickly.

Loading the table and chairs into the wagon was a job for all. The girls got the chairs while the boys carried the table. Ma and the girls packed the dishes carefully, even though they would only go a short distance. Ma was proud of the dishes she had and didn't want them broken. The cabinet was in two pieces and had to be handled with care. Ma helped with that. She reminded them that it was not heavy but very important and needed to be moved with care.

The beds were next. There were places in that one-room house to put three full-size beds; one for Ma and Pa, one for the girls, and one for the boys. If they had company like if Uncle Madison was there, there was a cot that could fit in either of two corners. Sometimes, the kids could make a pallet. Pa and Ma had planned for every inch of their new house.

It was an exciting day at the Krigbaum house, and they were all tired but happy. That evening, Pa got out his fiddle and began to play a cheerful song. Cloyal picked up the guitar and handed Loren the smaller one. They played together as they all joined in and sang along. Ma told them that they must all thank The Good Lord for their home.

The building was done for that year. Everyone was glad to have such a warm and dry place to sleep. To have a bed to sleep in was pure joy. It was much more than anyone had hoped. The gardens had been somewhat neglected, and the kids had not gone to school.

First things first, the garden had to be tended, or they would not have food for the winter. They could do their schoolwork by lantern light. In the winter, the kids could go to school if the weather was fit. If it was too bad, Ma was accustomed to teaching them at home anyway.

Her ma and pa had been schoolteachers. But it was almost harvest time, and they had missed a lot of school. Ma worried that some might get behind. She would spend time with each of them to be sure they understood their lessons.

Pa reminded her that most of their kids were willing learners, and he praised her for the way she taught them. Ma worked on making them want to learn instead of making them learn. She gave them reasons to learn what she felt they needed to know.

She wasn't sure why Matt could not seem to learn to read and write like the others. He could write his letters and write words if he copied them. They had not been able to send him to school much, but she tried to teach him at home.

She felt that he should be able to do anything with math that he wanted to. He was a good hand on the farm, but try as she would, she could not teach him to read or write much more than his name.

Pa said, "Well, you don't have to read to plow a field. He can do his part and is a good worker. He will be ok."

The winter was cold the first year they were in the log house, but it seemed quite warm and cozy inside. The stove put out more heat, or maybe it was staying inside instead of going out all the cracks and holes. The walls were freshly chinked, and the shutters were tight when closed. Ma put curtains between the beds.

At the first sign of spring, Pa started working on the new room. He would have to take out time to plow the gardens and fields, and they would get the early crops planted. The rest would have to wait until the building was done. His growing family needed another room.

He had been having lumber sawed at a nearby sawmill, a little at a time until he could get enough ahead to start building. The logs he took to the mill must have been huge. Some of the boards were twelve to fourteen inches wide. The wood would need to be seasoned, so he might need to buy or trade some out at the mill.

Tying into the room already there, he added a room the same size without putting a door between them at first. They needed the cook stove to stay usable. With no windows on that side, one wall was already complete. The building was easier and went faster with the flat lumber, covering a lot more area with fewer holes between them.

Pa had helped other people but had never built a house with lumber before. With both their families and friends working together, the room was finished in a few weeks, except, for putting a chimney in the kitchen. Then, they would need to take the one out of the other room and put a door in its place.

It would take a little while, and they needed to cook in the meantime. The boys didn't need a door inside to move their beds into the other room. It was no problem going to the outside to get to their room. Pa was getting a lot of practice building flews and chimneys. The one near the front door would stay there for the heating stove.

As soon as the new chimney was ready for the cook stove, Pa tore the one down in the middle of the house and opened up the doorway. The top was left and covered rather than patched the roof until later on.

With lots of help, Pa managed to move the stove into the kitchen. "I hope this is the last time we ever have to move this heavy stove. We are finally home, Laura!" It sat in the center of the east side wall, leaving room for any beds that might need to be made. With the table and cabinet moved into the south side of the kitchen, they had room to spare for a bed for some of the children, and guests were always welcome.

They had another baby that year in September of 1929. His name was Delmer Conrad. Pa brought the crib in from the barn loft, and the girls cleaned it up. "This is getting a little worn, but it should hold for a little while longer. Ma was almost her old self again. She seemed much happier because she had feared she would not have any more children after losing her little Rose.

The new baby was a special blessing. He eased the heartache of the whole family. He was growing up fine and getting a lot of attention. They started calling him Dale. It gave Ma a lot of comfort to have another baby to hold, and she didn't want to put him down. Wishing she could spend more time with him, she kept him as close as possible when she was cooking, sewing, or whatever she was working on. Ma didn't work in the fields as much because Pa said she needed to be with her babies more.

Dale was the delight of the family. He was the baby boy, and as he grew up, he was apt to get into mischief with older brothers to pick at him.

Whenever Ma or Pa tried to correct him for any reason, one of the girls would grab him and take him outside or anywhere to get his mind on something else or just run off with him and try to keep him out of trouble. He was their baby as much as Ma and Pa's. Alene and Clossie took care of him as they had the others. But somehow, he was special to them.

Ma thought it was good that they tried so hard to watch after him. It was hard to find the right way to discipline Dale because it made her laugh to see them try so hard to protect him. She was more than thankful for them. Her love for him grew each day, and she was determined to do everything possible to care for him. Somehow, there was still sadness in her eyes that she never talked about.

They all knew what she was remembering, so they would each try to find something good to talk with her about, as she had always taught them.

Chapter 39
Family Values

Madison stayed with Harley and Laura a lot and helped with the farming and whatever else. He wasn't married, so he lived with whoever needed him, or, in later years, each would take their turns of about six months at a time, allowing him to live with them. He had a home in any place he chose, and he was always welcome and tried to earn his keep.

Ma had brothers and sisters who lived nearby. Some worked for them and with them in cotton and other fields. They each had children, of course. So, they would take turns watching the babies. The older girls took their turns in the fields and caring for the babies or younger children, and whoever had babies to nurse had to take time out to go feed them?

One day, while Ma had gone to the house to nurse Delmer, her sister Mattie's baby, Johnny was getting hungry and fussy. The girls were trying to make him happy, but it wasn't working. Mattie was taking longer than usual to get back from the cotton field. "I wonder what is keeping Mattie," Laura spoke out loud as she watched the girls try to tend to him.

Finally, she couldn't stand to hear him cry any longer, so after putting Delmer down for a nap, she picked little Johnny up and nursed him, too. He didn't seem to mind. He soon was full and fell asleep in her arms. She put him to bed, went back to the field, and left the girls to watch the babies as they slept.

She met Mattie as she was going back to the field. Mattie stated that she had better go feed her baby. Ma told her not to bother; she had already fed him, and he was sleeping.

Mattie was quite surprised, as were others, but they could keep working. They laughed about it as they worked. It gave them something new to talk about. Then they teased each other about who was going to go nurse the babies next time.

Of course, it really never happened anymore. When a baby is hungry, the mother knows it as well. Mattie was not very comfortable the rest of that evening because of milk pressure. So, she went early to feed Johnny the next time. She woke him up for that feeding.

Ma and Pa had one more daughter in a couple of years. They named her Wanda Corine. The house was full but happy again, and they knew this was enough.

Ma began to deal with more of her grieving as she took care of her new baby girl. No one could take Rose's place, and she loved Wanda for who she was, but God was giving her healing through time spent with her new baby girl.

Though they really had not planned on having any more children, God had blessed them with the greatest blessing when He gave her to them. "Isn't it just like God to give us something we didn't even know we needed? She's such a sweet baby," Ma would often say.

Dale made sure he kept his place in the baby department for a while, but he was glad to have a little sister, too. "We must be careful to watch after him and not make him jealous of the new baby," Ma would tell the girls.

They had a big two-room house with everything they needed to make life good for them, and best of all; it was theirs. Ma really enjoyed the cook stove with the water reservoir and warming closet that had belonged to Pa's Mama and then Grandma Lucy. They had a real home at last. It was good to have such a pleasant place to raise their Children.

Within just a short time, Cloyal was married and would start a family of his own. There was room on their land, and a third house was built on the Storts' homestead. He stayed close for a while to help Pa with the farming. Later, he would buy some land and build a house for his new family.

Pa didn't get to see many of his family often. They kept in touch by letters and knew a lot about each other's lives. His Uncle John Sheridan was not far away. They visited each other. His cousins, Willie and Jack, were living near each other in Oklahoma. When they came to visit, they traveled together to make the trip more affordable, and they just enjoyed traveling together.

It was a big event for everyone. Ma would make sure that beds were arranged to meet the needs. It was so much easier in the big two-room house. The children didn't mind giving up their beds. Uncle Jack and Uncle Willie and his wife had great stories to tell. They enjoyed time together with cousins as well, going fishing, taking a walk in the woods, or swinging on a grapevine across the creek. It didn't matter what they did; it was a chance to be together that they enjoyed so much.

Fighting seldom interred anyone's mind. Their time together was too short and only happened about once a year at best. On Sunday afternoons, there might be a game or two of marbles or horseshoes, sometimes both. The neighbors often came down to play.

Marbles all look alike to most people, but Cloyal, Loren, Matt, Dale, and their cousins and neighbor, Joe, saw it differently. They chose the one they played with very carefully; trading marbles was serious.

Often, there was a full circle of onlookers as they played. Relaxing with a cool glass of lemonade or orange aide as they watched was a very rare and delightful treat.

One by one, the children grew up and most of them got married, and the family began once again to grow. Ma would begin helping raise her grandchildren. Their oldest grandchildren were not much younger than their youngest children. So, even the youngest had someone to play with.

Delmer didn't go to school as most of the older children had. The whole country was struggling, and it was all they could do to put food on the table.

Paint Rock School had consolidated with Driggs by then, and it was too far to try to get them to school. Ma had decided that she could teach Dale and Wanda at home what they could teach them at school.

(They both did well. My dad, Dale, could out-read, out-spell, and out-figure any of us going to school. I'm sure Aunt Wanda was the same way. She later went to school some, but he never went a day in his life. Ma was an excellent teacher. Home School is not a new thing.)

It was a very busy life. They were a close-knit family who stayed close by, helped each other and shared whatever they had, especially food from the gardens and fields.

Whatever season it was, those who were available worked planting fields of corn, peas, beans, and popcorn or making a garden. Harvest was just as much a family affair.

It was canning time. Shelling peas or beans, peeling apples or peaches, or shucking corn or whatever else of the many jobs was a lot of work and must be done before the food would spoil.

Buying food at the store was limited to flour, lard, sugar, rice, or cornmeal. Maybe a few other things, but most everything else must be raised or bought from peddlers or sometimes from an orchard. It really didn't matter what the task was; it was the family time and values that were the most important things to all of them. If they had any extra, they would, in turn, take it to market; however, that was a rare thing with such a large family.

Chapter 40

The Unforgettable Noon Meal

Alene and Cloyal were married and soon had children of their own. Cloyal had a daughter, Louis, and a son, Darrell.

Alene had sons James and Freddie (Boots). Clossie had one son. His name was Harold, and Lathy had a son named Billy Earl. Neither of them had other children.

As the grandchildren began to grow and learn their places, Ma was helping to raise another generation. She found the grandbabies as much joy as her own children. They all wanted their time with Ma. She would read to them and talk to them as if they were the most important things in the whole world. Teaching them was very important to her. She loved all her grandchildren as she had her own.

The mid-day meal was always at 12:00 noon. Ma made it a rule to have it ready on time, for there was much work to be done in the fields in the summertime. Whoever was left to do the cooking was expected to have it on time. With the two gardens and truck patches, there was no time to waste. "To work hard, you have to eat well," Ma often said.

She or another of the women or the girls would leave the fields or garden about an hour before the others and have lunch on the table. No one had to call them for lunch. Pa would look at his pocket watch and announce, "It's noon; let's eat." All work stopped, and they went to the house.

My cousin, James, stayed there a lot, as did most of the grandkids over time. He liked to sit in the open window by the table to eat his meals where it was cooler. One hot summer day, he was sitting in his usual window seat eating his lunch; he was tired and very hungry. Concentrating on the fresh hot biscuits and delicious bowl of beans that had been cooked all morning on the wood cook stove, he lost his balance and fell backwards, out the window and onto the ground!

This caused quite a stir for the whole family. Everyone ran outside to see if he was okay, fearing that he was badly injured because the window was the one highest from the ground. It was high enough that one could not look in from the outside if standing on the ground beneath.

His mother was the first one to reach him, finding him lying on his back, not moving. For fear that something might be broken, they didn't try to move him, giving him a few minutes to see how badly he was hurt.

Ma and Alene began to talk to him and observed his response. They soon discovered that he had hit so hard as to lose his breath for a little while, but nothing seemed to be broken, and he was soon ok. Alene fixed him another plate of food, and he sat at the table to finish his lunch that day; however, he soon was over his shock and back to himself.

Their fear was worse than his fall. They all went back and finished their meal in silence for a little while, and then someone started to tease James about falling asleep while he was eating.

They couldn't get the best of him because he laughed right along with them. He told them it wasn't just anybody who could fall out a window like that and live to talk about it. They all had to agree. In a few days, he went back to sitting in his window seat to eat his noon and evening meals, but he was a lot more careful after that!

Chapter 41

Pa's Special Mule

I got stories from different family members, I think this one was from my cousin, James Fitzjurls. Sharing stories was a fun way to spend time together, and they were glad I was writing about the times with the family we all treasured. I can see Pa in this setting. He was a hard worker and expected his horses or mules to do what he needed them to do and he took good care of them.

Sometime in the 40's, times were again, really hard for lots of people. Pa got a government loan to purchase a pair of mules. He named them Jake and Pat.

Pat would balk while she was plowing or pulling. Instead of whipping Pat, Pa would hit old Jake and make him pull harder. He had figured out that it would not do any good to whip Pat. But Jake would make her work.

Jake did not understand Pa's reasoning. He often jumped the fence and got out. Not long after Pa got them, he started jumping the fence and running off every time he got a chance. Pa could not find a way to keep him at home. One time, he ran off and swam across the Arkansas River and went back to his previous owner.

Pa went after him and brought him home. After that, he was Pa's mule. Jake would do anything for Pa. He would follow him everywhere he went and would come to him whenever Pa went into the field.

When it was time to plow, all Pa had to do was go to the barn and call Jake, and he would come right into the barn to have the harness put on. Pat would follow Jake every time, anywhere.

They were good mules, and Pa wanted to keep them. They worked well together; however, the money was scarce, and he was not able to pay off the loan and was forced into selling the mules in order to pay his debt. He just couldn't come up with the money, even though they worked hard for him.

Finding what he thought was a good home for them, Pa told the man he would have to watch Jake to keep him at his new home. He didn't realize just how true that was.

The problem was that Jake was so attached to Pa that no fence could keep him in. He would jump it and come straight back home.

Pa would take him back, or his new owner would come to get him. Sometimes, Jake would beat Pa back to the house. It seemed as though he would just have to buy them back, which he would love to do, but he didn't have the money because he had paid it on the loan.

He told the new owner that they were good working mules if he would show Jake who was the boss. Pat would follow him anywhere. It took several tries before the new owner could manage to keep Jake from getting out and coming home to Pa.

They missed each other. Jake didn't understand that Pa hated to see them go just as much as they hated to leave. In time, they would both be ok, but it was hard on both of them for a while.

Chapter 42

The New Horses

Later that year, Pa was able to get a team of horses at a fair price. It was good to actually find a team of fairly young but well-trained horses. He had seen them work together and knew them to be a well-mannered team. He would not have to work so hard to train them.

He had worked with a few oxen and sometimes mules, for a lot of his life. He had always preferred horses because he said they had better horse sense and were easier to handle, and they understood things better. He had used mules because they were stronger, but they were more stubborn most of the time, as well.

Shorty and Lady became Pa's new team. Shorty got his name because he was so very tall. Lady was bigger than him but was as gentle as could be. They were huge horses, but that didn't bother Pa. They were strong enough to pull wagons full of hay, sometimes rock, logs, and whatever else. He had chosen them because he felt that they could handle anything he required of them.

Ma liked them better also. The ride into town or to see friends or family was much more pleasant because Pa didn't have to spend his time yelling at them as he did the mules.

She worried about him a little because they were so big, about the size of a Clydesdale, though I am not sure what they were. He assured her that he could handle them, and that was good enough for her. They earned their keep and stayed with Pa and Ma for a very long time.

In the late 40s, a major storm came through the Paint Rock community. Pa decided he had put off the cellar way too long. So, he dug a big hole for it as deep as he could into the side of a hill just north of the well. Making it about the size of a large room, he took the horses and skidded up big logs, placing them across and overlapping the top of the whole cellar as close together as possible. Soon, the door was put over the slanted opening. They had a place to go when it stormed.

With all the leaks, he had to put rocks on the floor to step on in order to stay out of the water, and they always had to check for snakes if the weather was bad before going in, but they had a cellar that would be there for many generations.

Everyone rested easier about the storms. It had no windows, just a kerosene lantern, and someone was always looking for snakes or other critters, but it felt safe.

Their son, Matt, was one of the family members who learned to plow with the horses. For whatever reason, he didn't seem to learn well in school. He never really learned to read and write like the others, though Ma had tried hard to teach him.

Matt never married and stayed with them and helped with the plowing and hauling things, and whatever work there was, so Shorty and Lady also became Matt's horses. Pa was a good teacher, and Matt was a willing learner with the horses.

Pa thought maybe this would offset his lack of interest in school. He seemed to learn anything with numbers and helped with the farm work. He and Pa took turns plowing, hauling wood, or doing whatever needed to be done.

Ma felt a little better but did not understand why he could not learn to read. He could write and recite the alphabet but couldn't put words or sentences together on paper or read very well. She was glad that at least he could figure out and had a concept of money and could manage to calculate what he should get for the wood he sold.

No one needed to know he couldn't read lest they try to take advantage of him. He could write his name well; maybe that was enough. The horses gave Matt a sense of accomplishment.

As it was with the family, not many of the other children ever got workhorses of their own. This close-knit family depended on each other. If one had something, it was just assumed that it was available for all.

Pa had horses, and it was just expected that either he or Matt would plow their gardens. Those horses got a workout, as had the mules before them; however, they were always allowed to rest on Sundays.

The families, in turn, still came over and helped with the big field of corn, beans, peas, and anything else that Pa and Ma had planted. When it was time to dig potatoes, it was a family affair for sure.

Every child or grandchild was expected to help pick up potatoes as fast as they were plowed up. They all shared the harvest, so all were to do their fair share of the work without complaint.

The Good Book says if a man doesn't work, he should not eat. Ma and Pa stressed this to their children and grandchildren. To be lazy was to be teased by the others, but the thing that kept them working was Ma. They wanted to please her because she was so kind to them. She didn't make them work; she made them want to work, giving them a reason that they could understand.

By that time, they had several grandchildren; Harold, Bill, Darrel, Louis, James, William (Cowboy), and Freddie (Boots). Matt never married or had children.

The family was growing. Pa and Ma tried to make the land work for all of them. He tried to do what his grandpa had not been able to. In hopes that his legacy would live on, and the next generations would live in harmony as they had. He stopped to thank God for the chance to get back Grandpa's land and for the house they lived in.

Within a few years, their number of grandchildren was increasing. Loren and his wife would have a son, Carroll, Cloyal would have Coy, and Alene would have Troy. They were almost the same age. They worked and played together any time they got a chance. They knew Ma loved them all.

Chapter 43

Ma and the Horses

I just heard a story that surprised me a little, well, maybe a lot. My cousin, Louis, shared a story that her dad, Cloyal, had told her.

One day, the sheriff's wife and daughter came to visit and wanted to borrow their team and wagon. Their custom was to lend anything that anyone needed to borrow, as the Bible taught.

Ma was there with the children. She asked the older children to watch the younger ones and then went to catch and hitch the horses to the wagon. "I sure wish Harley was here, but a body's got to do what a body's got to do. I really would hate for someone to get hurt," she said to herself.

Ma refused to let them take the team until she had driven them first. She feared they would be too much for the lady to handle, so she drove them around the fields, even made them run a little until the horses were settled down, tired, and a little easier to handle.

In about thirty minutes or so, she came back to the house; then she got down and let the lady take the wagon and team. Ma warned her that they were pretty hard to handle, but they were good horses and that she should keep a tight rein on them, putting as much stress on them as she dared.

This kind, sweet little woman never met a job she couldn't handle. If she saw the need to do it, she probably could have helped with the plowing also; however, Pa saw to it that she didn't have to. His wife was not going to have to plow if he could help it. They borrowed the team and brought them back later that evening.

The sheriff was driving this time. He said that those horses were a little much for his wife to handle.

Harley was quite surprised to see them coming home with his team and wagon. He had never seen Laura drive them either, which made for an interesting conversation at the supper table. He wanted to know how she managed to harness them.

She reminded him that she had only been fifteen when her parents died, and besides that, she had watched him many times. She said that she wasn't about to let the sheriff's wife do it. They really needed the wagon, or they would not have asked. She just said, "A body's got to do what a body's got to do."

Pa left it at that, however amazed he was. He wouldn't worry about her so much after that. He figured she could take care of herself and about anything that came her way.

They finished with supper, and the girls did the dishes as they told Ma that she needed to rest. She had done more than her share for that day. Pa agreed. They went to bed that night, still laughing and talking about how Ma ran those horses to slow them down for someone else. This was a story to pass down to the grandchildren.

Chapter 44

War Time Again

It was not often that I heard stories of any war from Ma or Pa. I had to ask first. Then, the conversation was short-lived and brought on more pleasant topics.

However, in the early forties, World War II changed the lives of many. Even though Pa was forty-eight years old, he and Madison signed up for the old man draft. Some of their brothers and cousins were already in the army. Sheridan and his son Utah, as well as several others in their immediate family, were in the Army during this war.

Again, the American people came to the fore. Pa had nephews and cousins who were in the Military. I hate to try to name them because I would miss so many. I tried to learn all I could about our family and the war.

Within the Krigbaum name, I found several casualties, three prisoners of war, many injured, and others missing in action, fighting for our country.

Once again, they had been reminded that freedom is not free. Many stopped to pray often for their families and all of our soldiers.

I don't wish to dwell on this topic; I just want to say thank you to all our military, not just my family. This just happens to be Memorial Day, that I am writing.

I now have two sons who have served in the Army for several years and are planning to make it their career. Having spent three years with one or the other of them on the other side of the world in a battle, I am thankful for all our soldiers who watch out for each other.

My heart goes out to those who have lost sons, fathers, or other family members. WW II was a terrible war with many casualties, our family included. Many times, it was prayers that brought them home.

Chapter 45

The Surprise Wedding

In July 1951, Delmar (Dale), the youngest son of Harley and Laura, was 21 years old and still at home. He had not mentioned getting married, though he had dated a little. Ma was glad to still have him at home all these years but figured it would come to an end sooner or later.

One day he met a young girl, Peggy Hicks, near the square in Paris, while on a usual Saturday trip to town. He stopped and talked to her. As he asked her different questions, he found out that she would have no place there to live in a few weeks.

Her family would be moving. After meeting him, she didn't want to move with them. They needed more time to get to know one another, but there didn't seem to be any more time. They had two weeks to decide something.

He was twenty-one years old and had never married. She was only fourteen. To everyone's surprise, just a few days later, he announced that he was going to marry Peggy. Ma was a little concerned but knew it was useless to tell him he needed to wait a while. He explained to Ma that Peggy needed a place to go, and he thought they could be happy together. If there was love at first sight, he thought he loved her. His mind was made up.

He had waited so long that Ma wondered if he would ever marry; now, he was ready to marry a young girl whom he had just met! Ma had taught him to make wise decisions and care about others. Without trying to talk him out of it, she accepted Peggy as one of her own.

Peggy stated that she fell in love with Dale before he ever said a word to her. When their eyes met, she knew, but when he spoke to her, he captured her heart forever. Moving away after meeting him was unthinkable. She wanted nothing more than to spend the rest of her life with him.

Two weeks, two days, and two hours after they met, they were married on July 29, 1951. His sister Clara Alene and her family lived close by on the Shirley place, near Paint Rock. They had a small cot, and they allowed them to put it out in her front yard by a big oak tree. They slept under the stars on the first night of their marriage.

And then, living with Ma and Pa for a while, they moved from one rented house to another, but Dale had to come to visit Ma every day, so, they never moved far away. He had stayed pretty close to her his whole life. He wasn't going to change now, though he was twenty-one when they married.

Ma and Pa needed him to help with the big farm, and he needed them, so he built a little one-room house up on the hill just northeast of their house. It was called the little house because it had one very small room.

Laura was a very special Grandma, with plenty of love and patience to share with everyone. Most everyone called her Ma. She and Pa had raised eight children and helped raise several grandchildren before I was born.

About a year and a half after they married, their first baby girl was born. They were living in the little house. Peggy was only fifteen and not feeling well.

Ma said, "Peggy, it looks as if you're about ready to have this baby. I better go see if I can find Dale. It's time you went to see the doctor."

He soon brought the truck close to the door and took her to the hospital in Paris, a big change from when Ma and Pa were having their babies, all of whom were born at home; however, they'd have a hospital bill of $25. He wondered how they could come up with that much money as they entered the hospital. He would pay for it somehow.

On September 18, 1952, their baby girl was born, five days after Dale's birthday. They named her Charlotte Gale. Peggy was fifteen and glad to have Ma nearby. Having been the oldest girl in her own family, she had helped care for younger siblings. But having a baby of her own brought back memories of the baby sister that she had lost at only two years old. It scared her a little. Like Rose Catherine, her sister, Nelly Christine, had died from whooping cough and Pneumonia.

Missing her family, who had moved away to Fort Smith, and wishing for guidance from her own mother, who had a six-month-old daughter of her own, Peggy gladly accepted any advice and help that Ma might offer.

She had married into a family that changed her life forever, but was always happy to see any of her family when they came to visit. They wrote letters to each other to keep in touch, so she was never really homesick. She and Dale were very happy together.

Dale was their baby boy of nine children. He had one little sister younger than him. Her name was Wanda.

Ma had helped to raise several grandchildren by then and understanding that Peggy was young and might need a little guidance, she invited them to stay with them for a few days until Peggy was on her feet a little.

They could stay for as long as Dr. John had told her to stay in bed, about nine days. Of course, she didn't, but that was a normal recommendation for new mothers at that time.

Ma had to keep reminding her to stay off her feet; however, she was young and felt fine and could not spend her days in bed.

They soon went back home. It was only a short walk away, but it was up a hill, so Dale brought the truck to take them home. Ma would go every day to see if Peggy or the baby needed anything or just to watch the baby and let Peggy get some rest. Not that she really needed to since the baby slept almost all the time.

Ma just wanted to make sure Peggy was ready to care for a new baby. Soon, the new mama would be up and about again and able to care for her family. Meanwhile, she could rest easy knowing Ma was nearby.

About two weeks later, they were at Ma's for a daily visit. It was time to go home, and Charlotte was asleep. Ma said, "She's already asleep. Why don't you just let her stay the night?"

Dale could never tell his mama no; Peggy didn't get a chance to answer. At two weeks old, she stayed the night with Ma. That was just the beginning. Peggy had to come back very early in the morning to nurse her baby.

Chapter 46
The Little House

When Dale and Peggy moved into the little one-room house, it seemed to have plenty of space. With not a lot of furniture, there was enough room for the two of them. As he would have time off from work, Dale would continue to build as they lived in it. He would add a room later. Peggy would help him as much as she could.

She was fourteen when they married, and fourteen months later, their baby was born. The house still wasn't finished, but the one room was livable. They could have asked for help, but they seemed to want to do it themselves.

With a growing family, they started adding another room, which they would work on as they got the time. It was a cozy little house, and they were building it together, and it would keep them warm and dry.

One Saturday, when the baby was only a few months old, Dale was working on the ceiling while she was sleeping on their bed as if she didn't even hear the hammering.

In a little while, Peggy yelled at him over the noise, "Dale, a sanifee!" (centipede). It was about eight inches long, bigger than any she had ever seen. It had fallen from the ceiling and landed beside the sleeping baby.

Grabbing her up, Peggy held her while Dale attacked the centipede and took it outside, making sure it was dead. "This house is not big enough for us and a creature that size; I have to get this room sealed off better," he exclaimed. "It appears that I better get some help before the weather turns and all the little creatures try to get in."

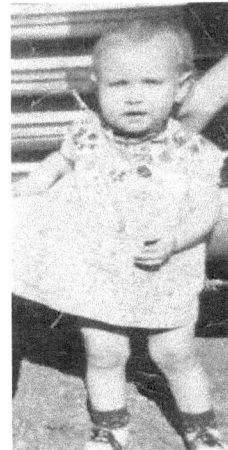

Pa and some of his family came the next week to help get the ceiling finished and the cracks sealed off. They put a good door between the rooms, stopped work on the other room and concentrated on making one safe from unwanted little creatures. Working together, as they had been taught, the little room was finished in no time at all. They could take their time in the new room; the one was big enough for the time being.

They would later need to move to a rented house closer to a job that Dale had found, but wherever they were, it seemed that for one reason or another, there was a need to go see Ma almost every day.

Moving to Havana once, he worked in a sawmill until he could find something closer to home. Peggy didn't like being there by herself while he worked, and Dale worried about Ma and Pa working the farm without enough help.

So, he quit his job there, and they moved back to the little house. The kitchen still needed work, but it was closer to being finished. They decided to finish the add-on, and with help from family, they would soon have two rooms.

Dale might give up many things, but music was never one of them. That was something the whole family enjoyed together at some point every week.

After all the chores were done and supper was over, we could count on hearing Daddy play his guitar and sing for about an hour before bedtime, even if no one else was there.

I tried to sing with him, and he tried to teach us many songs, maybe so our minds would be free of the stress of the days as we went to sleep. As I think back on those days, I think he wanted to instill the music in us, so that we would always want to stay together as his family had done.

Chapter 47
Going to Ma's for Breakfast

It was a beautiful spring morning in 1955. The birds were singing already, welcoming the warm sunrise, and the chickens were out clucking and scratching the earth briskly to find the juicy worms before the birds did.

Charlotte could see from the window of the little house that smoke was coming from Ma's chimney. She knew it was from her cook stove, and she really needed to be there to help her fix breakfast.

Quietly, she sat looking out the window. Her parents could see that she was in deep thought, so Daddy kept an eye on her while Mama started breakfast. Neither said anything to her; they just waited to see what she would do.

They had said it was too cold for her to go outside every time she asked. So, she was sure they wouldn't mind that morning because the sun was very warm coming through the window; just in case, maybe she should not ask. After all, they had told her she was a big girl now that she was two. The door latch had a pull string and was not hard to open. Daddy had gone out earlier, so it wasn't locked.

Charlotte waited until he was busy helping Mama with something; then made a beeline for the front door, without a word. She had never gone by herself before. It was a little scary. She didn't know if she was more scared of going by herself or what her parents were going to say when they caught her.

The hard part was getting off the steps fast enough. She had to turn around and climb off backwards. As soon as her feet hit the ground, either fear of going by herself or getting stopped, made her run as fast as her little legs could carry her, falling every few feet because it was all downhill and rough.

To go around by way of the road didn't occur to her since the house was straight in front of her. The sun was shining, but the ground was still wet from the spring rains they had the day before. It was also colder than she thought.

Mama and Daddy were both watching from the window, surprised and amazed. Mama started to stop her, but Daddy said just let her go. We can go get her in a few minutes. You know she will go straight into the kitchen. We can watch her until Ma opens the door for her.

They could not help but laugh as the full-circle little dress tail flopped up and down in the air as she ran as fast as she could, trying to stay on her feet, but fell several times. A few times, Mama was afraid she was hurt, but she would get up and keep running, looking back often.

Meanwhile, not aware of the little girl's presence, Ma was in the kitchen making a pan of biscuits as she did every morning. With flour on her hands, she stopped her work and listened to the faint pecking on wood.

She said, "Harley, did you hear something?" He had not heard anything. She went on with her bread making; then heard it again. This time, she could pinpoint it at the door, wondering if a woodpecker was pecking on the door, she opened it to find a two-year-old girl, small for her age, who was scared to death and almost crying by that time.

Aside from being worn out from the run, and scratches here and there from falling several times, her dress was muddy. At the sight of Ma, tears began to fall down her cheeks and dress as she sobbed, not sure why she was crying.

Ma opened the door wider, looking around for her parents, and then picked her up, getting as much flour on Charlotte as she had on herself. The mud and flour mixed onto both of them. She stood there and hugged her tightly, "You're alright, don't cry."

With a pretty good idea of what had happened, she asked, "What in Heaven's name are you doing coming down here by yourself? Where is your mama?"

She began to cry even harder. Ma had never scolded her. She always told her she was a good girl. "I dis wanna watch you make bickits."

Unable to hide her laughter, Ma tried to analyze the situation. Somehow, finding it a little humorous; she pretty much had it figured out. "Did your mama tell you it was ok for you to come by yourself?"

"No, but it's warm outside. Dey always say it's too cold." She cried harder and asked, "Are you mad at me?"

"No, baby, I'm not mad at you. But you should never leave the house without Mama or Daddy's permission. They may be really worried and looking for you." As she began to cry louder,

Ma continued, "I'm sure it will be ok and they will be here shortly. Why don't we wash some of the mud off of us, and you can help me finish breakfast?" That was just what she wanted to hear.

Mama and Daddy gave Ma a little time to talk with her, knowing that she had wisdom of years and this was their first child. They finished their breakfast after seeing her go inside the house.

When they came to the door, they called out frantically, "Ma! Pa! The baby's gone, something may have happened to her. Wanting to make this the last time she did this, they seemed very sad and worried. Mama pretended to cry.

Ma opened the door and let them in as Charlotte stood behind Ma's dress tail, not knowing what was going to happen. She started crying all over again.

Ma said, "She is ok. She just wanted to help me make breakfast. We had a long talk, and she said she won't do it again."

Daddy picked her up and said, "You better not do that again, you scared Mama and Daddy really bad."

"It is warm outside. I help Ma cook." They all sat down at the table and had a hard time keeping a straight face, finding the whole thing quite amusing. But they all agreed that she must never come by herself again unless someone was watching from both doors.

Her solution for that was, "Maybe I dis need a stay da night." They couldn't hide their laughter any longer.

That evening, the work on the other part of the house stopped, and while Charlotte was taking a nap, they decided the front porch needed a fence around it. It wasn't exactly what they had in mind, but they had chicken wire available and enough lumber to make it safe and secure. So, soon, it was fenced off, and the gate could be built the next day.

They were both tired, and Charlotte was awake by that time, so they stopped working and decided to go down to Ma and Pa's for a while. When they returned, they thought they should rest and spend some quiet time together. "We have a big puzzle. I have wanted to put it together but not by myself," Peggy stated.

"Well, go get it, and I will clear the table." It had over 1000 pieces. "This is going to take a while, but it will make a beautiful picture when it is done," chided Peggy.

"Can I help?" Charlotte tried to climb into the chair. "This is a really big puzzle; how would you like to work a smaller one with bigger pieces?" Mama went and got a twenty-five-piece one for her. She was happy with that one. "I need some help, Daddy."

"Ok, let's see what you got." They worked the rest of the evening on the puzzles. Daddy finally said that the puzzle was more tiring and harder than working all day, but it was becoming a pretty picture and covered half the table as the edges were finished. It had been a long and exciting day and created lasting memories for all.

With a huge bag of cheese puffs to eat while they worked, Charlotte had never tasted them before. They said she could have all she wanted, but all she wanted was too many. She ate until she almost got sick and did not want any the next night. Mama had to find her some crackers instead.

The next morning, when they got up, she wanted to go outside but had no intention of going to Ma's by herself. When she and Mama went out, she was quite surprised to see the fence.

"We gonna put chickens on the porch?" She asked.

"No, we just want to make it safer for you, so you don't fall off and so animals can't get in the house," Mama replied.

OH." She was ok with the fence, but the gate was another story. She didn't like having a lock on it.

Chapter 48

Learning to Cook with Ma

This is where my memories begin. I am Charlotte. Dale and Peggy lived in a little house, a short distance from Ma and Pa when I was born. However, we were at Ma's most days, and I was there many nights. Mama and Daddy had to watch me closely, or I would be at Ma's house in a flash.

I was convinced that she was the best grandma in the whole world, and I wanted to be like her. I loved my parents a lot, but I would willingly have lived with Ma. I was very small when my first memories of her began.

Many times, I remember pretending to be asleep when I thought it might be time to go home. I just wanted to hear Ma say, "Why don't you just leave her? She's already asleep." I wonder if they ever knew I was faking.

If I was there in the morning, I wanted to watch Ma make biscuits, she would leave a little piece of dough to flatten on top of the stove until it was nice and brown on both sides. I, or any kids who happened to be there, just loved to eat that hop bread lightly floured, just right, it seemed strange that she only had extra when we were there.

I loved getting up early and watching Ma as she cooked breakfast, as Pa was out milking the cows or something else. Time was a blessing and not to be wasted.

The table was in a corner by the south window. I was allowed to help or sit there and talk with her as she was preparing the food. I could learn by just watching. I will never forget the smell of that kitchen. The wood stove was full of delightful aromas of bacon, eggs, gravy, and biscuits, and she always had jelly and canned fruit.

If I was there when Ma made biscuits, she would leave a little piece of dough to flatten and cook on top of the stove until it was nice and brown on both sides. I, or any other kid who happened to be there, just loved to eat that hot bread lightly floured, just right. It seemed strange that she only had extra when we were there.

I think the best part of the day was watching Ma in the kitchen and talking to her while she worked. She was always cheerful and never made us think we were in her way. We were helping just by keeping her company.

With more patience than anyone I ever knew; she never used harsh language or told us to get out of her way but would talk to us as if we were as important as any adult.

As I sat at the table, she reminded me, ever so kindly, "We must always be careful not to get close when the bread comes out of the oven. It is very hot!"

That is when it was best, steaming hot. As soon as the biscuits came out of the oven, she would put one on a saucer and give it to me or any other child that was there. I would eat the middle first and save the crust for last. Who would want to sleep in? Any left-over biscuits were put in the warming closet on the stove for later. If we didn't need them for lunch, they made an awesome bread pudding for supper. Never was any left for the next day.

As soon as there was room on the stove, Ma put her dishpan of water on to heat so she could wash her pans as she cooked. By then, the water in the wood cook stove reservoir was very hot, if more hot water was needed. Pa made sure that all she had to do was pull down the spout to get hot water. It was always kept full.

Breakfast was often over, and dishes were washed by sun-up. It only took her a few minutes to finish because she had washed the pots and pans as she finished cooking in them.

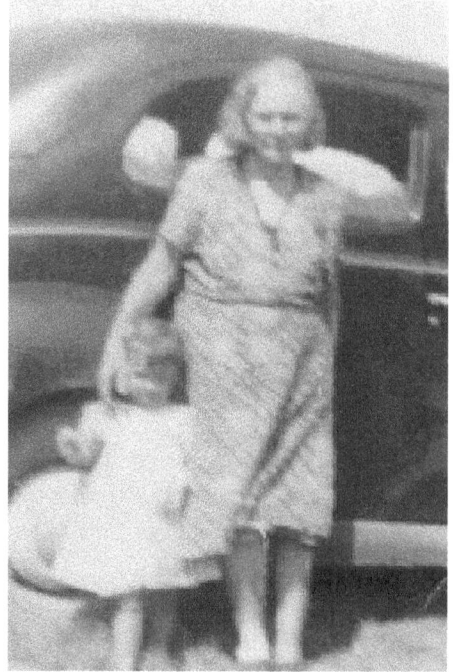

I could never forget the feeling of security and happy times there. After breakfast, the men were off to work, and Ma would start the daily household chores. And I was, as a small child, allowed to help clear the table. She would give me a wet cloth to wash off the table and chairs, making me feel important.

I wanted to help wherever I could, so as I sat at the table and watched, Ma would wash each dish in hot, soapy water, then, in the other pan, pour boiling water over them to rinse them in order to kill all the germs.

As soon as the dishes were done, floors swept, and beds made, as far back as I can remember, Ma would take the time to communicate with the children. Every child should be so blessed.

Even as a baby, whining or being impatient had not been an option. Ma would encourage me by saying, "We must get the house cleaned first, then I will (nuss) you for a little while," which meant she would hold and rock me in her rocking chair.

But first, the beds must be made and floors swept or mopped. I soon learned to watch the clock and wait for my special grandma time.

Her words of praise and guidance made me feel safe and confident. Words like I like you. You're a sweet girl. I'm proud of you. We must always be kind to each other. We must always treat everyone fairly, or we must treat all the kids equally. Ma's routine was very good for teaching children.

They might have a split log floor, but that was no excuse for untidiness. She said, "Cleanliness is next to Godliness."

Pa and Ma's eighty-acre farm was used by anyone who wanted to help farm it. Everything was shared. It was a family farm. The main goal was to make sure we all had enough food and that we let nothing go to waste. Lots of canning was done every year.

Above all, the babies were to be tended. Ma was there for all of us, and we lived near them; she was a lifesaver for us.

Daddy wanted to be sure they had whatever help they needed. It didn't matter what age we were, we all wanted to be with Ma because she always made time for us.

Chapter 49

Precious Years with Ma

For the first several years of my life, if all the beds were full, I slept between Ma and Pa, the most secure place in the world. The next was Ma's kitchen. I don't remember ever waking up in the morning to find Ma still in bed. She was always up very early with a warm fire going in the wood cook stove.

Their fairly large, two-room log house was always filled with warmth and sweet aromas. One room had two full beds, and the kitchen also had beds. I don't know how they fit all of them in there, but Ma would make room for anyone who needed a place to sleep.

There was a small couch, and they had two small rockers and dining chairs. The house was full but had plenty of room, with a pot-bellied stove in the northwest corner.

It seemed a fold-up cot could be found when needed or kitchen chairs put together for young children to sleep on. With so much work to be done, there was no time for lagging.

When the men and boys left for the fields or other jobs, our day started. It had a routine like school, except it was never boring. There was just something special about being in the log house they had built with their own hands.

The stories of how the family and neighbors all worked together to get the big logs in place would be told for generations. God had protected them all as they worked, and Ma was very thankful for her home and family.

In years to come, we would enjoy many evenings of stories and music in what I thought was a big two-room log house. We might have popcorn popped on top of the stove.

Pa was always chinking the walls or repairing the roof. It was just a part of life, as I saw it. The wood shingles had to be replaced at times, and the chinking was an ongoing job. He soon learned that if anything was brought in a cardboard box, they were doubly blessed. He would take the box apart and find a place on the wall where wind and rain might come in, and he would chink it first and then tack the cardboard over it to hold it in place.

Eventually, he had most of it covered. As years passed, he managed to purchase some cardboard paneling, nailing it up over existing cardboard. It looked like wood panels.

It did seem warmer after he put the cardboard paneling on the inside. Maybe it kept the mud from falling out from between the logs.

I don't suppose Ma ever made us do anything. However, she tried to patiently teach with everything she did. The beds were made, and the floors swept as soon as the kitchen was cleaned. I would sometimes get to wash the chairs while she was cleaning.

For the first few years of my life, a little past sun-up, the housework was finished, and she would sit in her rocking chair and say, "Come here and let me nuss you a little while." I never heard that term anywhere else. It was her special word for us.

To Ma and me, it meant more than just being rocked. It meant letting me know that, even though she had lots of work to do, she still had time for me. To Ma, children were the most important things in life. They were to be cared for, comforted, loved, and praised when they did something good or lovingly corrected if needed.

Sometime during our rest time, Ma would ask one of us to go get the Good Book so she could read to us for a little while. John was a very familiar book in the bible by the time we could read. It must have been her favorite book.

Ma would welcome any child who was allowed to stay and made us feel like we were no bother but a blessing. She would never say no if we asked.

Our parents probably had second thoughts, but Ma always made sure to let them know she was glad to have us there. Even our parents could not argue with Ma.

Sometimes, I would go to sleep while Ma was rocking me and wake up on her bed to find that she was working on a quilt or something else. Whatever she was doing, she found a way to include any child who was there. There was always something the kids could do to feel useful.

In due time, Ma would do the garden work or whatever else. But children were not to be neglected. They all worked together. Mama did a lot of Ma's chores while she watched me or any of the other children. Each one just did what they could. There was always a job to do.

The house was close to the cellar and the well, which made wash day easier. They had finally got electricity, so Pa bought an electric wringer washer. No more washing on the rub board, the washer was set up at the west end of the house, under a big walnut tree.

Someone got her an electric iron that didn't have to be heated on the stove. Ma had not asked for, nor even thought about, an electric iron. She had two irons; so, she could keep one on the cook stove getting hot while she ironed with the other one. That really made a difference when ironing the sheets.

Wash day was Monday, and ironing was on Tuesday. I will not forget wash day there under that tree. I was allowed to help as long as I was careful. I didn't see what could be dangerous about washing clothes, but I soon found out the hard way. I wanted to help put clothes through the wringer and was doing just fine. Ma thought I had it down.

I did until one sheet did not go straight; I reached up to smooth it. Before Ma could stop me, my whole arm was in the wringer up to my shoulder. I could not reach any higher.

Ma turned the washer off as fast as she could and released the ringer. It was no use. My arm was stuck. She had to call for Pa to bring some tools and take the ringer apart to get my arm free. I know she feared it was broken.

Meanwhile, she talked to me and kept me calm and still, as if it was no big thing, so I wouldn't pull against the ringer and for sure break my arm. Pa had to take the whole thing apart. Finally, after about twenty minutes, I was free and ok.

As soon as I was free, we went right back to washing. I wanted to stop, but Ma wanted me to not be afraid but to learn from my mistakes. "You'll be okay. You learned your lesson."

Chapter 50

Learning as We Grow

I was thankful for the electricity they finally got, especially when it rained and they had to close the window shutters since they only had screens but no glass windows.

The lamps were ok, but we didn't have to go to bed so early with the electric lights.

Ma and Pa's house was always very simple, but warm and inviting. The sign that Pa had made (No Place Like Home) hung over the front door, and they were truly thankful to have a home.

It didn't compare to the homes in town that either of their sisters and brothers enjoyed, but it was pleasant, and they were content.

One of my favorite jobs at Ma's house was cleaning out her cabinet. She had a flour bin in the top left, with a sifter behind the bottom door. All she had to do to get flour was to open the bottom door and turn the handle; Slide out the metal workspace and make the biscuits. Cornmeal, sugar, and other baking items were behind the sliding door, dishes at the top, and cooking pans at the bottom. The three drawers held silverware and dish towels. I loved to spend any night with them.

The garden by the house was used for vegetables like tomatoes, onions, and okra; things that must be picked daily. A few peach trees and apple trees were along the north side of that garden. Those were for eating any time we wanted.

If several were ripe at the same time, we would need to can them. However, much of the canning was done from the old garden and the truck patches of fruit or vegetables that were purchased from peddlers who came by. We seemed to be canning something most of the time in the summer. It was easy to wash them by the well near the cellar.

Life was busy at Ma and Pa's, and wherever we visited, I was always glad to be back home with them. It was as much home to me as our house.

I realized later that this was her teaching time. Ma's famous words, "We must always be kind to one another," or, "We must help one another." I think "we must" really were her favorite words. Ma was trying to form our character and make us fair and honest citizens who could make our country a peaceful place in which to live.

Some of her childhood stories had been of the Civil War. She never shared many of those with us. The Good Book said to think about the good things. That is what she tried to instill in us.

I am so thankful! If we came to her saying bad things about another child, she stopped us, "If you can't say something nice, it's best not to say anything at all."

Catching lightning bugs was something we never seemed to tire of as we sat out in the yard in the evening. Sometimes, we put them in a jar so we could take them into the house when we went inside. First, we had to put holes in the lid so they could get air. Then, we would have a light by our bed since the kerosene lamps couldn't be lit at bedtime.

We soon learned that the only thing we could see with them was the bugs themselves. We had to let them go the next morning.

Chapter 51
The Fireplace

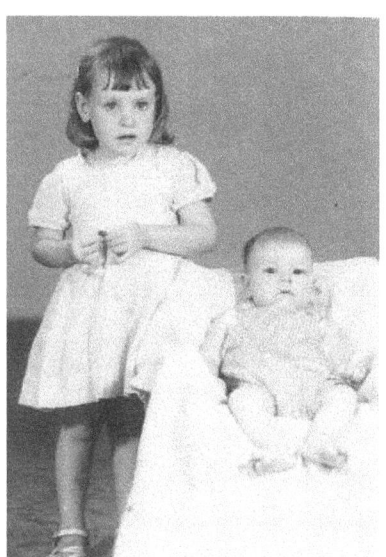

After my brother Jimmy was born in June of 1955, we found a little bigger house for rent, just a few miles up the mountain. Daddy was working in Driggs at the time. It was getting a little crowded in the little house.

It was a good place, but away from almost everyone. It did not matter how far away they lived; Dale had to come to see his Ma every day anyway, so Peggy knew that if they moved away, they would be back in the little house in a short while.

He didn't remember Rose, but he still sensed that Ma needed him and was not going to desert them with the farm work. Peggy didn't mind because she soon knew that Ma loved her as much as anyone ever had. She soon would do anything to please her also.

They moved on top of Brushy Mountain, above Ma and Pa, still within walking distance but up a mountain road. Ma and Pa came often to visit. Most of the time, when they left, I was with them in the wagon or even if they walked; though, they knew I would be carried most of the way. I was three at the time and would promise to walk, but I seldom did; therefore, much of the time, they brought the wagon.

The house on the mountain was different than any house I had ever seen. The bathroom was right inside the house. It had a fireplace to keep us warm. I think that was the general idea. I loved to watch the flames flicker, but compared to the big potbellied stove that Pa had, it was always cold in that house. We had to stay close to the fireplace to stay warm and wore warm clothes, even inside.

Mama was still young but very capable of taking care of my brother and me while Daddy worked. With only six diapers, she had to wash them every day, some days more than once. She would hang them on a line that she had made over the fireplace. This was a daily practice, so it should be no problem.

Well, one day, as she was cleaning the house, she swept the floor and picked up the trash in a dustpan. As she tossed it into the fireplace, flames shot up and caught one of the diapers on fire.

If she had just thought to toss that one into the fire, all might have been well. However, she thought of fire and babies in the same house, and they were up on the mountain alone. No one else lived up there to ask for help.

Turning immediately and picking up the baby, and grabbing me by the arm, she took us outside and away from the house. Jimmy was a rambunctious six-month-old, and I was only three and could not really hold him.

So, Mama sat me in a hole in the ground to make it easier to hold on to him. "Sit there and do not move, and don't let go of him!" I was scared and did not want Mama to go by the fire, but I did what I was told.

Holding an active baby boy was a big job for a little girl, but I didn't let him out of my death grip. He was getting angrier by the minute. My arms were hurting by the time Mama came back, probably much less than an hour later.

It was such a relief when she reappeared and picked up that squalling baby. "Are you ok?" Mama asked.

"Yes, I'm ok, but I think he ate a bug. He was grabbing everything and getting mad if I took it away."

They stayed outside for a while before going back into the house, waiting for the smoke to clear. The fire had burned all the diapers and a piece of material that Mama had washed to make Jimmy a shirt. I didn't think much about the diapers, though it left him with the one he had on and one more. But I remember crying for days over that little piece of material for his shirt.

When Daddy came home from work, and they talked about the fire, he decided that little house or not, Peggy and the babies didn't need to be up on the mountain away from any help if we needed it while he was away at work for eight hours a day, at least.

From the new house, I could only go to Ma's when we all went, so I was thankful we were moving back to the little house, especially after the fire.

It shouldn't really matter much since we saw each other almost every day anyway. We were a family who helped each other. My mama was a willing and hard worker, and glad to be a part of such a family. Daddy's brothers and sisters treated her as one of their own sisters. They were glad we moved back to the little house, and we were glad to be home.

Charlotte Krigbaum, Tucker, Rowlett

Chapter 52

Gathering Wood with Ma

This is Ma's youngest daughter, Wanda. They were often there to visit. These are her children, Ronald and Carolyn, and I think the baby is Roy, Jimmy, and me. Just up the hill is our little house.

Ma was always glad to see them. The grandkids all would stay as long as their parents would allow. The family often worked together on the farm because the food was shared by all who needed or wanted it. No one should go hungry.

Ma helped with the farm work until it was time to get a meal ready. You could count on it being on time, whether she had wood for a fire or not, at 6:00 am, 12 noon and 6 pm.

Most of the time, Pa kept wood to cook with, though, she often helped him cut and carry it; yet, there was never a word said about not having wood to cook with.

When she didn't have wood, and it was close to time to cook supper or lunch, she just went to a brush pile or on the edge of the woods and found enough wood to cook with.

Pa would have wood there as soon as he could find the time to get it. Just in case, he left brush piles nearby for Ma to get a fire started.

Of course, if I was there by myself, she needed my help. We would drag up the biggest dead branch that we could find. My little branch was just as important as hers. I was willing to help and really thought I was. I would get a branch as big as I could drag, and Ma would drag a much larger branch back.

She would get the bowsaw and cut the wood into small enough pieces to build a fire in the cook stove, patiently letting me help her carry it into the house.

I know now that it would have been so much easier to do it by herself, but she took her responsibilities very seriously. She must get dinner on time, the workers would be in at 12:00; however, teaching me was just as important.

She would do both. Mealtime was to be pleasant with a conversation about whatever, often about what they were doing that day. Any unpleasant problem could be discussed later, so as not to disrupt a meal time. That was quiet family time.

Pa always sat at the head of the table at his house. It was his honored place. Ma made sure that everyone had enough to eat and something they liked. No one left her table hungry.

I have seen her cook as many as three eggs, trying to get it just right for me. I would have eaten it anyway, but she wanted me to enjoy it, not just eat it.

As I got older and realized what she was doing, I noticed that she had busted the yolk of my egg. She sat it aside for someone who would like it better. I said, "Ma, it's ok. Just cook it. If I'm hungry, I'll eat it."

I may as well not have said a word. She would do it again and again. Her heart was so full of love for us all.

Everyone was tired and usually rested for a little while after dinner(lunch). Pa seemed to think they could get more work done if they rested for a few minutes. But we sat in chairs to rest; we would not disturb the neatly made beds unless one was sick.

Chapter 53

Picking Cotton in Oklahoma

Life seemed difficult at times. Daddy worked at several jobs, but picking cotton was something we all could do. One summer, Uncle Loren and Daddy decided to go to Oklahoma and pick cotton for a few weeks. So, we went together and rented a house that had a rock building beside it. Daddy, Mama, Jimmy, and I slept in that rock building. We had never been away from Ma that long. I missed her.

Loren's family was much larger, so they stayed in the big house. They had Carroll, Linda, Connie, Wilma, and Freda, and their uncle Archie. We shared the kitchen, ate our meals together every day, and found time for music.

While the women were cooking supper, their Uncle Archie often sat at the kitchen table and asked me to sit in his lap and sing to him.

The only song I remember singing was He Set Me Free. I knew all four verses by the time we got back to Arkansas. I don't know about the others, but I had a lot of fun that summer.

One day, Freda was sick, and Linda was going to stay home with her. I asked if I could stay, too. Mama said yes, if we'd keep Jimmy. With both babies, we might need more help, so Connie stayed, too. After all, I was still only five. We had lots of fun that day playing hospital. We were doctors and nurses, and Frieda was our patient. I am sure Linda was just trying to keep us all busy so we didn't get into something. She carried a heavy load that day.

The cockleburs were all over the yard. Jimmy had lost his shoe on the cotton wagon, so we had to carry him when he went outside, and he refused to stay inside if we went out.

We also had fun playing restaurant with egg cartons cut apart to make cups. Our water became whatever we ordered. We had a great time as far as the kids knew. I always enjoyed time with all of my cousins. But those days with Linda and Connie were really special.

No matter where we were, there was music. Daddy and Loren never went anywhere without their guitars, at least. Much of the time, some of the kids would sing or try to play something. The evenings were filled with music, as always.

That was a fun but hard month. It was the longest any of us had been away from Ma and Pa. We were all ready to go home. Soon, we went back home, living in the same little house where we lived when I was born.

Chapter 54
Back to the Little House

It was good to be home, and I could not wait to go see Ma and Pa. They were waiting with open arms. They had worried about us and were glad to see us. That was the longest we had ever been away from them.

It was the best place we had ever lived! I thought it was just right. It didn't matter much; anyway, as soon as I woke up, I wanted to go to Ma's.

Very early in life I had learned to get up early and go straight to Ma and Pa's house. The first memories of crawling out of bed and going out the door and down to watch Ma cook breakfast on her wood cook stove were just too much to forget. I didn't understand why I had to wait for Mama or Daddy to go with me. I could see the house.

We only lived a short way away, but my parents had thought two years old was a little young to go by myself. So, they built a wire fence on the porch with a gate that would lock. I couldn't go to Ma's until they opened it.

When we moved back to the little house the second time, I was bigger and thought of ways to open it. I was almost four. I was sure I could open the gate, and I really needed to get to Ma's house. One morning, I realized I could reach the lock. I tried and tried, but it took several tries to learn how to open that gate. I never gave up.

She had lots of visits with all her grandchildren from time to time. They all helped one another on the farms. Now that I think about it, it was probably mostly helping with the children. Ma's house was always full of them. It was too inviting. The aroma in the kitchen, the fresh line-dried linen on the beds, and Ma's open arms were waiting for any of us. We all felt so loved.

Since I was five, I was allowed to go as long as Ma watched for me from her door, and Mama watched me from the other until I got there. There was no certain time. I just had to wait for it to get really light outside. Ma knew to watch for me. I had to see her standing in the doorway.

It wasn't that I didn't like being home. That little house had great memories. Some of the fondest ones are listening to Daddy play his guitar and singing along with him. He would play every night. I would read his lips and listen carefully, singing just behind him. He never said anything, but he just let me learn the songs and encouraged me to sing.

It would have annoyed me, I think. He was patient, like his Ma, as I thought I had to learn every song he sang.

I also remember the family time of putting puzzles together and drinking orange aide, a very rare treat. I was glad to be back in the little house and never wanted to leave again. It was home.

Just outside was a perfectly round well that had been drilled, much smaller than the dug well at Pa and Ma's house. I could not see how anyone could get down in it to clean it out. The bucket was long and just fit down into the well. Yet I was glad because it scared me when anyone went down into Pa's well to clean it. I never understood.

Next to the little house stood an oak tree with branches that were low enough that Daddy built a nest in it for the chickens so they might lay their eggs closer to the house. I was sure I was big enough to check for eggs, even though I couldn't see into the nest. Daddy or Momma would often lift me up so I could get the eggs from the nest.

One day, I decided to check for eggs by myself. Though I stretched and stretched, I wasn't tall enough to see any eggs. Finally, I managed to climb just high enough to reach the nest.

Unable to see the eggs, I attempted to pick one up. The nest was full, alright, but not with what I expected. I was not so eager to gather eggs after that because what I actually put my hand around was a big chicken snake! I let go of the snake quickly and tried to get down, hoping the snake didn't follow me, screaming at the top of my lungs.

Before I could get to the ground, Mama and Daddy were both there. Mama helped me down, and they looked closely for a bite. With all the commotion that I made; they thought I must surely have been bitten.

The snake was more scared than I was, it seemed, it went out the other side of the nest and down the tree. Daddy tried to find it for a while, then gave up. I don't remember being scolded, but I didn't try to gather any more eggs without help, either, unless I could see everything in the nest. Daddy said that I must have scared the snake away. He never did find it. We didn't see it again for a long time.

A third baby was born in December of the next year, her name was Laura Mae; after both grandmas, the little house was just getting too small; even though it had two small rooms.

Mama and Daddy finally decided that such a small house could only hold so many people, and we could not keep moving back. We stayed there until the next summer, then moved a mile or so up Paint Rock Road to another larger house.

The chicken coop was loaded into the trunk of Daddy's car. It was a real surprise to us when we opened the trunk and out crawled a huge black chicken snake! We had no idea how it could have gotten in the trunk of the car.

This time, he didn't let it get away. Daddy said that was enough, that snake had to go! We needed the eggs worse than he did. He got rid of it once and for all.

Once again, we had moved from our home. I was sad and wanted to go back. I don't know why really, the new house had three bedrooms, a kitchen and a living room. I think it was too much house for me. It even had a bathroom inside with hot water in the bathtub.

But I wanted to go home because we seemed so far from Ma and Pa, though it was on the same road, and we walked to visit each other often. Memories of the little house flooded my mind and my dreams. The other house was too far to walk to Ma's by myself. That little house had been my home, and I saw no reason to move, but we never moved back.

Daddy said it was just too small, and the school bus would not come that far. I would be glad to wear the dress Ma got for me, but I was not looking forward to starting school.

All I really knew was that I loved Ma, felt safe and happy with her, and tried to please her, but I had lots to learn.

That was the last time we moved out, and Alene moved into it so someone would be near Ma and Pa. She didn't have a car, but it was a short walk to their house.

I really don't know what any of us could have done without Aunt Alene. She had a heart to serve others, just like Ma. She took care of Ma and Pa much of the time, and she was here for all of us, it seemed.

I enjoyed visiting her there. It always felt like home, and I loved my time with her too. She was one that any of our family could count on for anything.

All my aunts were special, but somehow, Alene was more like Ma. I could talk to her about anything. Maybe it was because I spent more time with her, and she spent more time helping Ma. I also enjoyed going back to my first home. It always made me sad to leave, but I was glad my aunt lived there close to Ma.

That little house held such fond memories. It was never painted, so the color aged quickly, but we didn't notice. It had been our home, and I never wanted to leave it. However, we never moved back.

Aunt Alene lived in the little house for quite some time after that, and I got to visit her often.

It worked fine for her since all but one of her children were married.

Eventually, it got torn down, maybe so we couldn't move back. I was very sad to see it go. Daddy said he didn't want to be tempted to move back. It was too small, but we all loved living there.

My parents were happy to have such a luxurious house with a full bathroom and hot water, but I would go to Ma or Alene's any chance I got.

In the new house, Mama could give Laura a bath in the kitchen sink with running water that was already heated.

I loved watching her play with her bath toys and calling her Cutie Pie. She was so cute with her blond curly hair. When I called her that as she got older, she would get angry and say, "I'm not Cutie Pie, I'm Laura."

I thought it was funny, so I continued for some time. She was five years younger than me, and I was a proud big sister and thought it was my job to take care of her.

I didn't mind watching Laura, except in the cotton fields. But where I could make maybe fifty cents, Mama could make five dollars if I watched Laura. During the summer, the family picked cotton almost every day.

I wanted to pick cotton so I could make a little money myself, especially since Ma had made me a little cotton sack of my very own, I tried to work harder than ever.

She had a way of making any child feel important. Kids could help if parents would let them. I wanted her to be proud of me.

Chapter 55

Saturday Trip in the Wagon

As far back as I can remember, Pa would hitch up the team every Saturday if the weather was fit. Ma would pack lunch, put a stack of quilts in the wagon, and off to town we would go. I was not sure what we needed. The only groceries we bought were flour, lard, corn meal, salt, and sugar; maybe, if we were lucky, a bag of dry beans or rice, as if we didn't have beans from the garden. That was my fault, I liked "town beans" better than "garden beans".

Of course, many times I was eating some they had dried themselves. But I had seen beans in a store bag and was sure that was what I wanted. Glad I wasn't spoiled. They did what they had to and just didn't care to argue with me about it. Ma's wisdom never ceased to amaze me.

The ride was slow and relaxed. Pa had a firm hand on Shorty and Lady, the big, strong horses. We noticed every animal and bird along the way. It was only a few miles, but it felt like an adventure, and we never knew who or what we might see.

The idea of the picnic pleased everyone. Ma always packed extra in case someone came along hungry at lunchtime. On very rare occasions, we might even go to Wiggins' grocery store and buy some lunchmeat and readymade sliced bread. The light bread was too much for me to take in. I wondered how anyone could make bread so light and fluffy. Ma's biscuits were light and fluffy, but not like that. You could hardly tell you were eating it.

Pa would unhitch the team behind Wiggins' Hardware, under a big oak tree, and then tie them to the hitching post after taking them over to the water trough that sat just by the side of the street. Hitching posts were all along the side of the road in front of most of the stores. The wagon sat there until we had visited with what seemed like everyone in town, buying very little but everything we needed.

At noon, we would come to the wagon to rest and eat. Usually, someone would be there to visit with us. The whole town seemed to be a family who had not seen each other for a while.

The men would discuss their farming needs or share something they had learned, often making plans to help one another the next week.

As we climbed down out of the wagon, we were looking around for family and friends that we might see. This was a town day for the Krigbaum family and many others who worked all week.

Some brought goods to sell or trade; others came to buy a few items for the week and to socialize with friends and family.

One Saturday, as we were on our way to Paris, Ma stated that I would be old enough to start school in the fall. "You'll need a coat for school. Yours is way too small and pretty worn."

Ma and I went to a store on the south side of the square; she had me try on different coats. I felt like a princess. Never before had I remembered getting a new coat, especially a store-bought one! I didn't know what to think, and I wondered how badly she needed the money.

Apparently, Ma had been planning this for some time. She had enough money to buy not only the grey wool long coat that cost $6.00, but a $2.00 new dress, also. It was a beautiful dress with a red sash around the waist. I couldn't have felt any better if I had won a pageant. I wouldn't be so scared to go to school. I never told her that I was scared. Ma seemed to know our needs.

Visiting Ma's brothers and sisters was fun for all of us. Those special memories will linger forever in my heart. Ma and Pa usually saw friends and family in Paris. That was the real reason for the trips to town.

The town was full of people who were there for the same reason. They loved one another and helped each other when needed. If someone needed help, they would ask. Telephones had not been thought of in our families.

Before the day was over, we would go to see Aunt Bessie and Uncle Joe, or Aunt Ollie and Uncle Matthey, or maybe Uncle Boyd and Aunt Lieler.

They all lived in town and could not see the need to go to town every Saturday except for Mattie. It was time to have company for them. We chose one each week to visit. We would spend the whole afternoon and eat supper with them if we still had time to get home before dark.

Occasionally, we would visit Aunt Mattie, but she was usually in town visiting everybody there. Seldom alone, Mattie sometimes came to eat lunch with us. Her granddaughter, Linda Kaye, and her brothers were often with her. Linda and I were about the same age. I would later be in her class at school. She must have stayed with Mattie as much as I stayed with Ma.

An evening with different family members who lived in town was a part of every trip. Each Saturday held different adventures with one family or another. Life was never dull.

Ma loved her time with her sisters and brothers. It was always a joy to be at their houses. At Aunt Bessie's house, we could always count on playing a game, or sometimes Ma would help her comb her ankle-length hair. It was put up in a bun, and watching it come down was amazing. Ma's hair was long, way below her knees, but not as long as Aunt Bessie's.

She needed a little extra help, Ma said, because she was in a wheelchair and had been for years after a fall that left her more afraid of another fall than crippled. She could get up with Uncle Joe's help but did her cooking from the wheelchair.

I watched her as she made cornbread and placed it in the oven, and then she took it out again, refusing Ma's help. She said she was not crippled, just in a wheelchair. Her arms were strong, and she could take care of herself. So, she gave Ma another job of setting the table or something to make her feel useful.

They both laughed as they worked. Ma and Bessie were such a joy to watch, they loved their time together. Their love for each other seemed special somehow as they talked about the days of their childhood.

I could either help in the kitchen or play a checker or board game with Uncle Joe. Sometimes I would look at picture books. I learned that they had three children instead of just one. A boy and girl that were no longer living at that time.

Uncle Joe was baptized at Bethel Church in his later years. I was glad I got to be there to see it. He was an awesome person, and I was so thankful to know that he loved the Lord.

When we visited Aunt Ollie and Uncle Matthey, life was very different. Every evening, they would gather eggs. Ollie would stay in the house and fix supper, and Ma would help. Ma and Aunt Ollie were equally happy to be together. They missed each other and talked non-stop while they cooked and set the table. They could never run out of words.

Aunt Ollie would show me her picture albums, and she and Ma would explain who was in the picture.

They were thankful for their grandchildren, Patsey and Johnny, who seemed to keep in close contact with them. Johnny was sometimes at their house when we visited. They spoke of Patsey often. I think I only met her a couple of times.

Though they only had one living son, they seemed always cheerful when we came to visit. Ma and Aunt Ollie had many good times together, both knowing what it felt like to lose a child.

It seemed they tried to think about the good times instead of the painful memories. I loved going to Aunt Ollie's house on Saturday and just watching them as they worked on something or just visited.

If I was the only kid there, I wanted to help with something. I stayed inside with them most of the time. The first time I saw the chicken house from the inside, it almost scared me. It was miles long, it seemed. If they had company, the eggs still had to be gathered. So, the visitors either helped or waited until they were done. Pa always grabbed a basket and went to help without an invitation.

I was about six years old before I was allowed to help. The nests were a little high, and there were so many eggs that it took several baskets to gather them all. I wondered why anyone would need so many eggs.

Later, I realized that they only had a small garden, not the fields of grain and other things. The eggs were how they made a living by selling them, to be distributed to stores.

Dinner with them was nice; there were lots of fresh vegetables and other things, and there was almost always a dessert. But no matter how late it got, no one dared to touch a bite of food until Uncle Matthey got there. He would always ask God to bless the food before we ate. It seemed to give me a strange but wonderful feeling when he prayed. On Sunday, he would be in a church somewhere, and the world had to wait until the church was over at the Johnson house.

Uncle Boyd and his wife Lieler lived in Paris. Sometimes, we went to see them. It was a little different with Ma and him. They were close but not like the girls. They didn't have as much to talk about. She spent her time with his wife as women do, mostly in the kitchen. Southern hospitality requires a lot of cooking.

Life had dealt them some hard blows, and Ma understood and tried to encourage them whenever she could. They had twin sons in California and had lost one son in the war. Their other son, Darrell, was blind from childhood. The only light he remembered seeing was through a keyhole once.

Yet he worked as a dispatcher for the police department for many years. Darrell could walk anywhere in town that he wanted to with his cane. He was not handicapped, just blind.

He could tell them that, but it didn't stop them from worrying about him when he was gone. Often, one of his many friends would pick him up and give him a ride. He had to be one of the happiest and kindest people around.

In later years, I would be privileged to give him rides myself. He knew everyone by the sound of their voice. If you spoke to him, he would call your name. I was quite honored when he knew my voice when he had not seen or heard me speak for months at a time. He never had a complaint that I heard.

Darrell's blind wife was the piano player for the church across the street. She loved the Lord and used her talent well. He and his wife raised one daughter and helped raise two grandsons with the help of his parents, who always lived across the road from them.

Ma's older brother, A.J., lived at Driggs. Usually, we would see him and his family on Sunday evenings when they would get together to play music. It was not. Are we going to play? It was "Where are we going to play?"

Uncle A.J. loved the music as much as Pa's family. His house was interesting to me. It had a breezeway between the rooms. It must have been like living in two houses. Going outside to go to the bedroom fascinated me.

Sunday evenings of music were fun with Uncle A.J. as he would get together with (my daddy) Dale, Uncles Loren and Cloyal, and anyone else who wanted to join them. We all looked forward to music with him at either of our houses.

Our families often worked together. Uncle Ray and his family were usually wherever the music was. I'm not sure how it happened, but I got the chance to ride with Ray's wife in the hay field one day. It was probably to keep me out of the way while Daddy helped Ray load the hay. I did enjoy the time spent with their daughters, Ruth Ann and Patsey. Our families were together a lot. They all seemed to help one another.

They really didn't have hers or his family. It was theirs. Holland lived in their home place, at Barn Hill. We would sometimes see him in town with his family, but we didn't go to his house often. He had a car and would come to see Ma and Pa once in a while. Ma was always glad to see her brother. It was hard to find time on a weekday, but they all tried to stay in touch somehow and help one another when needed. It was a part of their family values.

No book is big enough for all of them, but any place we went to visit, the stories would never grow old. I probably wore out my welcome, but I always wanted to go with them. I loved just listening to them share the adventures of their lives.

They sometimes laughed as they talked about the snow coming through the roof when Aunt Alene was born. Pa said, "There was no time to fix it then or even to move Laura. The baby was coming."

Talking about fixing the roof brought joy and sadness because Pa's grandpa was not able to help, yet would have it no other way. He would always want to do his part of any work. It gave Cloyal memories and stories to pass on to his children of his life with Grandpa.

Sometimes, they might talk about Rosie and Lula, whom I never met. They had passed away years before, but they spoke so kindly of them as if they had only left yesterday. We were reminded to appreciate our families while we have them. Ma would always get rather quiet when Daniel was mentioned.

Uncle Daniel was sometimes spoken of but had been gone for a while. Ma would never forget his love and kindness to her. He had been so young when he lost his parents, and it made her sad that his son had to be raised without a father.

As they realized the sadness in the conversation, one of them would change the subject to a more pleasant one. The Good Book says to think about good things.

I could listen all day, no matter which house we went to. It was apparent they treasured every moment together. In all our visits, I don't ever remember a television or even a radio coming on. Families just enjoyed being together. However, as the sun began to go toward the west, Pa would say, "Well, it's been fun, but we better be getting toward home if we're to make it before dark."

Our visits ended, and we said our goodbyes; climbing into the wagon, we started for home. Pa was pleased with these horses he'd had for so long, and I was thankful they were gentle because they were very large.

Shorty and Lady appreciated the rest and were ready to return home, also knowing Pa would have a treat for them of some grain or something.

The well was right by their log house, so we didn't have to carry water very far. That was good because we always wanted some fresh water when we got home.

The creek was just a short way from the house, so Shorty and Lady never gave Pa any trouble, but they were glad to be turned loose to go to it and drink. He gave them extra grain on those evenings; he thought they had earned it.

Within a few years, the road was paved, so they could no longer take the wagon and team. If anyone went to town, they had to go in a car. We could stay longer, but Ma hated to ride in a car. She said it made her sore, and it took days to get over the ride, so she didn't go as often.

Mattie moved to Driggs, so Ma would occasionally visit her and Johnny's family, who lived next to her.

Chapter 56

Ma's Memories of Her Family

Often, someone would ask Ma about her life and family. Everything stopped, and we would sit down and listen.

Sometimes, it made her sad, but she would tell us anyway, over periods of time. The few pictures she could find were precious.

The youngest in this picture are Dan, Holland, and Laura. Most of them went to school at Barn Hill when they were young. Ma's memories of her family as she grew up lingered in her heart. They were always very close. She talked of them often as we sewed or did other chores.

Her parents, John Slater Graham and Amanda Louise Anderson Graham, must have been diligent in teaching them to love one another because they all still loved to spend time together.

Both had been schoolteachers at Barn Hill School and then at Driggs, and they had taught them a lot at home when school was out.

Laura's grandparents, Robert Anderson, was born on January 6, 1829, in Edwards County, Illinois, and Cynthia Perkins-Lyon was born on August 17, 1833, in Scott County, Arkansas. Amanda was the fifth of their ten children.

Her father, John Slater, was born February 15, 1848; the second son of Abraham and Caroline (Elkins) Graham. Caroline was the daughter of Thorit Elkins.

Barn Hill School holds a lot of memories for Ma since she was raised at Barn Hill Community. But it was torn down many years ago.

Later, she attended school at Driggs. Their parents taught in both schools.

Ma's oldest brother, A.J. Andrew Jackson, born April 18, 1883, went to college in Taylor, Texas, and became a teacher like his parents.

He came back to Arkansas and taught school at several places, including Liberty and Driggs. He married Oma Coleman in 1906. They had five children: Lennie, Loren (Jack), Lyndall, Ray, and Marie.

Ollie was born in July 1884. She and Laura were very close. Now I see why. She was nine years older than Laura, yet stayed there to help Laura care for her ailing parents. I didn't remember hearing that when I wrote my first book. I did know that she was always there if Laura or her brothers needed her.

Ollie and Laura took care of their mother as she was dealing with cancer until she died on May 17, 1908. Laura was only fifteen.

Their dad was not doing so well after she passed. They worried about him and tried to encourage and take care of him. However, he became ill soon after losing his wife. I think I put six months into my first book, but as I understand, it was closer to a year and nine months. It seemed like a much shorter time, according to Laura's stories. She missed them both.

John Slater Graham passed away on February 27, 1910, at 62. He was buried beside his wife at Paint Rock cemetery.

Ollie married Mathew Johnson soon after their father died. They had a farm in Driggs for several years; Laura was glad they were close by because Laura was left with the two younger brothers, Holland and Daniel, who were always out working. The house became very quiet.

Ollie and Matthew later moved to Paris, where they had a chicken farm, selling eggs from their huge chicken house. Their first two daughters, Ruby and Winnie, died as infants. God blessed them with two other children; Carl was born in 1913, and Mathew was born in 1916.

In 1957, Ollie and Mathey dealt with another tragedy. They grieved the loss of their son Matthew, who died at thirty-one years old due to a car wreck, as I was told.

Their sister, Rosie, taught at Driggs school for several years and was married to Kiefer Wilson. They had one daughter; her name was Clara.

Ma was proud of her and missed her, she had named one of her babies after her. Rose Catherine was her namesake.

That made speaking of her even harder because Rose Catherine died at only two years old. A mother never gets over losing a child, I could see.

I never got to meet Rose or Lula because they both died before I was born. Ma missed her sisters, Lula and Rose, and talked about them sometimes, though I don't remember what she said happened to them.

I'd heard Pa mention Everett and Lula Jones' family many times but didn't put two and two together. Ma's sister, Lula, married Everett Jones; their children were Vollie, Mattie, Otha, Victor, and two who died as babies.

I met some of these and never knew we were family. So many people we were around seemed like family. I guess they just assumed I knew. It didn't seem to matter; family and friends were all welcomed just the same.

We all looked forward to more stories about her life and family, but she said we had to wait for another time. Our time together was precious, too, and we had work to do. In time, she would tell us more. Any chance we got, we would gather around for some more family stories from Ma.

Holland married Arlie May Storts and lived in their family homeplace. Their children were Lila, Vera, Vonda, Lacy, and Anita.

Mattie married John Lee Phillips and had eight children: Lura, Laverna, Lora, Johnny, Julius, Fred, Bobby, and Betty.

Some of them lived near Driggs most of their lives. I went to school with their children. We were cousins and friends. Johnny and his family also went to Bethel church. Sunday was family time, it seemed.

Their daughter, Betty, married Granville Fairbanks, who would take many of us to Church for years, in the back of his pickup.

Boyd married Leila Jones. They had twin boys, Daniel Ray, Walter Fay, Darrell Dean, and Voy Gene. Their twins lived in California, and I didn't see them for many years; I eventually learned that Voy Gene was a soldier who was killed in Korea. This made them sad, but they came to grips with it, I guess. What choice did they have?

Their son, Darrell, was known by everyone in town as the police dispatcher and as a friend to many. He and his wife were both blind. They raised one daughter and helped raise two grandsons.

Ma's other sister, Bessie, married Joe Foeshee. They lived in Paris all the years that I knew them. Going to their house on Saturdays was a real treat. I never saw her out of her wheelchair, but it seemed she was always active.

Their son Herman, who lived in McGee, Arkansas, kept in close contact with them. I learned they also had a girl and a boy, who were no longer living.

It was a sad day when Andrew Jackson (A. J.) died in 1959. It was hard for Ma to lose another brother. He was her oldest brother and had always been one they all could depend on for almost anything. They loved to spend time together and would miss the music at his house. She tried to be strong for all her family, but she was hurting a lot. We all would miss him.

Her memories went back to her little brother Daniel. She loved and missed him so much! He had married Zelpha Ashlee Fairbanks, and they had one son, Nathan Daniel. Ma was always a little sad when she talked of him. They had a special bond between them because she had tried to take care of him after their parents passed away. Then he died at such a young age, in his early twenties. I heard from others that he died in an accident with a horse. She loved and missed him so much more than most realized. Family time was very important to Ma (Laura).

Harley and Laura had known each other for years, but she hadn't thought of him as anything but her brother's friend, who gave her another person to cook for.

Soon after she turned eighteen, they began to think differently. Within a year, they were married. Life began to have a different kind of meaning to Laura, and it seemed she was happy for the first time in years.

Laura had planned to teach at one time, but the sadness and responsibility at home were just too great. Taking care of her parents, and then her brothers, and the house kept her busy. When she and Harley got together, she gave up the teaching idea, feeling confident that she could teach her children if need be.

They would go through many battles together, but they had each other and the Good Lord to help them for the rest of their lives. They would become known as Ma and Pa to many.

Chapter 57

The Blacksmith Shop

Two buildings on their farm that were very important. They were Pa's Black Smith shop and Ma's Chicken House. The Chicken House was a two-room building made of wood slabs from the sawmill. One room had nests for the chickens to lay in; the other had places for them to roost.

Ma wanted her chickens to have a happy home, with enough nests that they didn't have to wait long for each other and plenty of room for hens to sit on the nests. Outside the house was a little house that looked like a dog house with a fence around it. This was for the setting hens to raise their baby chicks safely away from the others.

It made it safer for children also; a setting hen would protect her chicks at all costs. She didn't like her babies bothered and was sure to let anyone know if they came near.

Then there were the Martin houses that Pa kept in good shape and on high poles. He always had at least one high on a pole with six to nine individual nests.

Pa's shop was a whole different setting. We loved hearing about how he had built it. He explained how he had much work to do on his harnesses and making horseshoes. He had needed a blacksmith shop but could not afford to build one. As time went by, he accumulated so many tools out of necessity that he had no place to go with them. They either took up space in the barn or in the house.

He was always getting jobs making wagon wheels or fixing axles. Often, he was asked to build something of wood or repair someone's shoes. He thought about it for a while until Uncle Madison asked, "What are we saving all these rocks for?"

Pa said he felt a little foolish. Why had he not thought of that? That was the answer he had been looking for, but he had no comment. There were three, possibly four, huge stacks of rocks of all sizes. Soon, the two of them, with the help of others, were hauling rocks by the wagon loads to the place he chose for his shop.

Without cement to put them together, they would have to stack them just right to keep them straight, but Pa was sure it could be done. It was not what he had in mind, but "you do the best you can with what you have," he remembered hearing his grandpa say. With no money to buy mortar, he put the rocks together with red clay. It would hold until they were stacked tightly between poles.

"Poppy, I don't see how you can build a rock wall with no cement and make it stand." Matt tried to tell him. "But I'll help you haul the rocks."

"Maybe if I stack them right, I won't have to have mortar. I can use posts and mud to hold it while it's going up. It will hold long enough to stabilize them between the poles." He used mud in places to make it hold, but in some places, he just stacked the stones together to make the walls, making it wide enough to stand, mixing the sizes, and putting corner posts and a pole wherever he thought it was needed to tie in the roof.

Cutting extra-long poles to tie the sides together at the top, he would have something to fasten the roof to, and then, with poles that he cut from trees growing on the place, Pa began to build the roof. When the frame was done, he put a tin roof on the top. I have no idea where he got the tin.

Before long, he realized he needed more room to have a place for everything. "This will hold as good as any wood building, maybe better," he said to Madison. "If we put more walls, it will just make it even stronger."

"Looks like we better gather more rocks," Madison remarked. There was no need to argue the fact. He had already seen Harley's satisfaction with his work. "We can start in the morning gathering rocks from huge piles and fields." No need to worry about a shortage of stones either; he knew there were enough rocks on that place to build several buildings that size. "Glad we found a use for the rocks we have piled all through the years. Grandpa would be proud."

The next day, they started the room on the West side. When it was finished, a few days later, they built the one on the east, making sure to set poles close enough together for support for the walls and the windows and a door in each room, they would have it finished in a few weeks, well maybe several weeks.

The walls on the east and west would only be about five feet high to make it safer and stronger. It would not have a ceiling, so the pitched roof would give plenty of room on the inside. By the time it was finished, it was sturdy and had three rooms. The divided rooms would make it stronger and support the roof better. After many years, the rocks that had been pulled out of the gardens and from the fields since they were kids had a real purpose. Pa was glad they had piled them.

He made the walls and roof as low as possible because it would be needed many times, like for drying peanuts or other things. Nothing was wasted on that farm if he could help it.

Pa was very pleased with the shop and began to put his blacksmith tools in place. His anvil and large vice were attached to a big, heavy split log workbench that he made on the east wall of the big middle room.

Along the walls, he placed all the tools that he would need to work on wagon wheels and make horseshoes. Just outside the middle door, he built his fire pit. The hand bellows were just inside the door, within easy reach.

Pa's leather work moved from the barn to the shop. Any harness that needed work was brought to the shop where he had his hand tools and vice.

The really dangerous stuff was put in the back part of the east room; another little room with a lock on the door. He had things hanging on the walls from a rod of some sort sticking in a crack. A brace & bit, hand saws, bow saws, crosscut saws, sledgehammers, tools of all kinds, and a lot of leather.

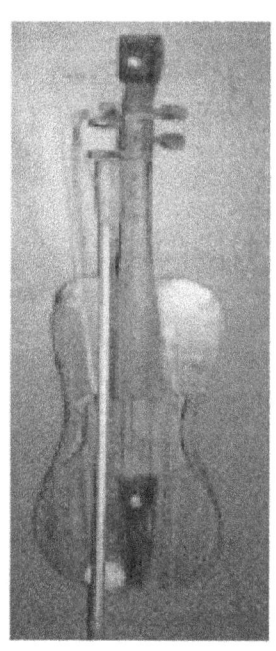

Where he had kept all this stuff until then is still a mystery. Pa was a new man with his new shop, made out of stone and ready for any job. Everything had its place. The east room was for leather and parts that he might need to make or repair harnesses or saddles.

The west room held the shoe lasts and tools for woodworking and repairing smaller things. If we had a need, he knew right where to get the things to fix it. To get a new pair of shoes was not thought of if they still fit. Just take them to Pa. He would have them re-soled and as wearable as possible in no time, just as he did any pot or pan that Ma needed to be repaired.

People soon heard about his new workshop, and he had more work than he could do. He had his own work to do, also. Pa was really happy with his shop; in his spare time, or even just while he was resting, he might make something for the kids.

He even made a fiddle once of some leftover wood. Nothing was ever wasted. His horse-hair bow with rosin from the pine trees would prove whether it would play or not. It wasn't like his other fiddle, but it played, and they had fun with it.

This was not the first nor the last instrument that he made or helped his boys make. They all loved music, and with not enough money to buy instruments, they sometimes made whatever they could think of or found something to make it out of. Every child needed his own.

My cousin, James Fitzjurls, still has this one hanging on his wall. Life was always full and busy with fun or work. Idleness was not usually a problem.

I would not have understood what he was saying had it not been that I could see the shop, and it all made sense. It was used for many things and for many years.

We pulled peanut plants and put them in bundles and then put them on top of the shop roof to dry in the sun for many days. Pa would check them periodically to see if they were drying well, turning them whenever needed.

When they were ready, we all had the fun of taking them off the roots one by one. In the winter, we would put them in a pan to parch on top of the stove. We felt more fortunate than the town children because we could have popcorn or peanuts anytime, we wanted and with the sorghum from the mill, we could have taffy as well, and we got to help make it ourselves.

The Krigbaum family raised anything that might be needed if the ground would produce it. The shop with the tin roof proved to be useful in many ways. It was not very high on the sides, so it was perfect when we harvested the large patch of peanuts or popcorn.

That shop holds many memories of watching Pa as he made horseshoes or fixed a wagon wheel. If we were careful, we could push the bellows for him to keep the fire going so he could heat the iron as he shaped the horseshoes or whatever else, but we had to stay back when he took his work to the anvil. It was very hot, and he had to work fast while it was hot. When it cooled off, Pa would bring it back to the fire; and then back to the anvil to shape his work just right.

Pa's shop had three rooms; He could build anything we needed. If we had a need, he could fix it in his shop, be it shoes, pans for Ma, or toys. He was always fixing something for someone. For whatever reason, I don't remember ever being told we could not play in his shop. We spent hours in awe of the walls of rock with no cement to hold them together.

My favorite thing that he made was a shelf he made for our toy set of dishes. And there were always harnesses to work on or horseshoes to make.

Work on the farm was never-ending. They were always ready to help anyone they could. Pa sometimes took his team of horses to Driggs and plow gardens for his children and their families.

Chapter 58
The New House

Cloyal had bought some land and built a new house for his family, about two miles from Ma and Pa, if we walked through the trails. It had four rooms. They weren't as big as either of Pa's rooms, but they were lined with sheet rock and painted.

He had been married for several years and had three children, Darrell, Louis, and Coy. We would often walk there when we went to pick berries or muscadines. Sometimes, we would share with them, or they would share with us. Ma was glad they lived close.

They all were glad to have such a home. His wife, Ida, was happy to have a nice home for her children. Cloyal built another small building just outside the back door for her to wash clothes in. He even had a heater inside, so it wasn't so cold in the winter. She tried to only take a few at a time to hang on the lines with Louis to help they didn't get so cold.

They were happy and had no way to prepare for what was coming. The two oldest ones were almost grown, but Coy was in his early teens when they learned that Ida had lung cancer. It didn't make any sense to anyone; she had never smoked.

This was a sad time for all of us. Cloyal would raise Coy alone. The last time I saw Aunt Ida was about a week before she died. She was lying on her bed, still with a kind voice, she told me bye.

I didn't know it was forever. I cried for a while when Mama told me that she had passed away. She told me that she had gone to heaven, and we would see her again. That was comforting, but I felt so bad for Uncle Cloyal and his kids. I was six years old but would never forget her.

He was sad but didn't want to just think of himself. About a year later, he decided to help Pa build a new house. I think he hated to have something so much nicer than his parents. He wanted to help Pa build a new house that would not have to be chinked every year, and that had glass windows.

Ma was quite satisfied with the house they had and saw no reason for glass windows. They had screens over all the windows in the house to keep out the flies and mosquitoes, and they had good shutters. It was large enough for a body to clean. The living room could hold two beds and a cot if needed, and there was room in the kitchen for beds. They were not ready to give up the house they had worked so hard to build and had raised many of their children in.

With all the memories of that house where they had finally had a place to call home; Ma and Pa were happy where they were. They had worked so hard to keep it up because they were so thankful for it.

One by one, the boys talked to them about building a board house with boxed-in walls painted inside. Pa finally gave in. He said if you want to build one, have at it.

Cloyal was the engineer and designer. He was the only one with a house, anything close, and knew what to do.

It was decided they would build up on the hill on the same level as the shop, away from the creek a little, because it did flood from time to time. The mosquitoes would not be so bad. However, this meant they would have to carry water up a steep hill, and they would have to go down the hill to the cellar. It had been right in the yard. There was a lot to consider.

Anyway, the work began; everyone brought their handsaws and hammers, nails and tacks along with anything else they might could use. That house was completely framed with sawed lumber from a mill, but the only saw they used in building it was hand saws.

It had a 2" by 6" floor joist instead of split logs, two feet apart. A floor would go on top. The walls went up as fast as their handsaws could get the boards cut. The nailing was the easy part. The nails were round and smooth, not like the square ones in the other house.

Pa didn't even have to make shingles; everybody pitched in and bought tar paper and rolled roofing. Pa liked it so well that he put it on the outside of the house as Cloyal had done his. He decided it would be better than keeping it painted.

A light hung down from the middle of each room, with a switch on the wall to turn them on. The four rooms were finished; the roof was on, and glass windows with screens, as they had promised.

The chimney was put in the middle of the house to be used with both the heating stove in the living room and the cook stove in the kitchen. Cloyal had to do some thinking on that one to make it work. It turned out great, with only one chimney to build. The stoves were back-to-back, in opposite rooms.

They asked Ma if she wanted an electric stove since she had electricity. It took her all of one second to answer. "Why, No! We need to be able to eat the food we cook."

Aunt Alene was there to help every Monday. Wash day never changed for Ma. Ironing was done on Tuesday. With the electric iron, she only needed one. The old irons worked as door stops. My mom and Lathy helped often, also. It was a fun day for me when I wasn't in school.

Sometimes, I found it hard to comprehend that Ma was once a child herself because it seemed she knew the answers to any question we asked. The love and warmth in her home were unexplainable.

Ma planted flowers across the front and north sides of the new house. She planted touch–me–nots, which we could not leave alone, of course, because if we touched them, they would pop open. Maybe she planted them for the kids.

She also planted beautiful flowers, like pretty blue forget-me-nots, among others, with many colors, like four o'clocks, that bloomed every evening right about four o'clock. I wondered how they knew what time it was. And Morning Glories would bloom early every morning. I am still amazed when I think about those four flowers.

Ma's parents must have taught her well because it seemed her flowers were raised with love. I wondered if she was thinking of her mother when she planted them. She talked of her often and told us stories of her as she was growing up.

I loved to sit outside in the evenings and talk with Ma as we watched the four-o-clocks bloom. We didn't seem to have time to watch the Morning Glories. Life was too busy in the mornings. However, they were pretty throughout the day until evening. Her goal was to teach us things that would help us as we got older.

We didn't go to the cellar as often after they moved to the house on the hill. However, if it was a dangerous storm, we usually went to be with Ma and Pa. We were together in case anything severe happened.

We were always thankful for the rain; it only took Pa a short time to figure out a way to catch rainwater for washing clothes by putting barrels and tubs below the roof to collect rainwater, and then the water was right outside the back door, saving a lot of steps up and down the hill, carrying buckets of water. "Where there is a will, there is a way," it was often said.

I liked drawing the water and feeling useful, at least for the first couple of small buckets. But that uphill walk was about too much for me. I was glad Pa thought of catching the rainwater to wash laundry.

Visiting while we washed things from the garden or peeling apples, peaches, or other things outside had been a lot more fun under that big tree by the log house.

A few times, we still washed and peeled them there near the well, if we had a lot. By the new house, there was not as much shade. But we all got used to it, and we liked the four-room house, with the lean-to across the back for doing laundry and storing grain. Pa even started putting wood there to keep it dry and make it easy to get to in the winter.

Wash day was almost fun after Pa, and Ma moved to the new house. But somehow, I missed the time with Ma near the log house, underneath that walnut tree, remembering our talks as we worked. I am sure she did most of the work, but I was proud to be allowed to help. Getting my arm in the wringer taught me a valuable lesson. I was much more careful after that, and I'm glad my arm was small.

Eventually, years later when she was not able to do much of anything, they did get an electric stove, but she never let them take out her wood cook stove; it was still used often, especially on laundry day.

Ma still had to do her laundry outside. But the lines were on level ground and much easier to get to. Those sheets smelled so fresh and clean when we brought them in. I never wanted to miss laundry day or ironing day. If I was there, I was allowed to iron the handkerchiefs and pillowcases. I liked the electric iron. It stayed hot until you unplugged it.

A while later, Pa built a lean-to across the west end of the house with a dirt floor because it would be Ma's laundry room on one side and a place to keep wood dry on the other. She could wash inside the house for the first time ever. In the winter, it would be a real treat she had never dreamed of.

From then on, in the wintertime, Alene, Lathy and my mama sometimes brought their clothes to Ma's to wash them in the warm indoors.

I didn't understand why we had to sweep that dirt floor. I would ask her over and over. She just said if God gave us a dirt floor, it is our job to keep it clean. It was a room, and I had to sweep it every time I swept the rest of the house, sometimes more often.

There was no logic in it for me, but Ma said it must be done; so, I swept that piece of dirt until it passed her inspection; because she was Ma and she would not ask anything unreasonable even if I couldn't see it.

Within a year that room became as useful as Pa's shop. We would fill the one side full of popcorn, or field corn for the animals. Then in the winter when we had nothing to do, we could make our hands bleed by twisting the corn off the cob. It wasn't so bad taking off the popcorn but we didn't get much out of the field corn. Sometimes Pa would just feed them to the animals, cob and all, that was fine by me.

When peddlers would come by, Ma and Pa bought bushels of tomatoes, peaches, apples or any other fruit or vegetable they might have.

That room was standing ready. Money wasn't abundant but Ma always calculated what they might need that didn't grow well or they did not raise, so she always had a little put back for the peddlers.

It was a race to get it all peeled and canned before anything could spoil. We could count on about six bushels of something to can, because that is about what Ma thought we could put up if we all worked hard.

We never had much money, but never a time in Ma's house could anyone go hungry. Peas, beans, corn, popcorn and peanuts were planted in large fields and that little lean-to became so very important that they wondered what they ever did without it.

The peanuts were pulled up by the roots and laid on the shop roof to dry, and later brought into the lean-to so we could separate them from the vine.

Then in the old garden were lots of potatoes and in the new one was okra, tomatoes, onions, and many other things. I don't know which was more important, Ma's lean-to with the dirt floor or Pa's shop. They both were blessings and put to good use.

Whenever it was harvesting time or planting time, the whole family, it seemed, would come to help. Very little of the food they harvested was sold; only if it was extra. It was distributed to everyone who helped and anyone who just came to visit. It was not to be wasted. If anyone asked why we raise so much food, the answer was, "because somebody might need it."

Mostly what they had to buy was a few jars and lots of lids to can the food. The jars were used over and over. Two big gardens and a huge truck patch. Someone would ask are you going to sell some of your crops this year. The reply would be maybe, but it seldom happened.

Ma had such a giving heart and a very large family. They were feeding half the world and considered poor by many people. You could never do more for Ma and Pa than they would do for you. It was like trying to out give God, to do for them. As a little girl I remember that because I worked without complaint, Ma got me a little set of dishes with stamps she had saved. I was so proud of them that Pa built me a little cabinet to put them in and hung it on the wall in the lean-to.

They wanted us to learn to work for our own good; so careful to teach us values along the way. I would not have traded places with anyone even in the fanciest castle filled with many kinds of riches. Pa's plaque over the door that said, "No place like home," was embedded in my heart and my heart was with them because they made me feel so loved and needed.

The Easters at their new house were wild and wonderful. We could have as many as fifty or more people sometimes. Too many to fit in the four-room house but no one noticed or cared. There was room somewhere. There was all outdoors, a huge amount of food, cobblers or bread pudding was a favorite. We always had enough, many brought food already fixed. It was a surprise to see the different dishes.

After a big egg hunt over the very large field, of about five hundred or more eggs, we had eggs in many ways; deviled eggs, salads, and new dishes that people dreamed up. It was wrong to waste the eggs, but we could eat all we wanted just as they were. The main thing is we had fun together.

At some point in the evening, they would bring out their instruments. The yard would be hopping with children, running, jumping rope, playing jacks, or we might get a ball game started. If that happened the music waited until the game was over.

Christmas was the same way. We all went to Ma and Pa's for Christmas, at some point. It was not about getting presents, it was about appreciating each other. Whatever we did get was shared with the other children or left at home. We could not take a toy we didn't wish to share. Ma's unspoken rule. She never said so, we just thought that was her wishes. We all had the same opinion.

That new house became a welcomed treasure for Ma and Pa over the years. Never an electric saw touched it, but it looked just fine. The family was proud to do something so nice for them and the music just got bigger and better in that front yard.

Chapter 59

Daddy's Model T

There was always another story if any of us wanted to listen. I found this one very interesting. The stories were too many to share them all. I have to share this one.

Ma and Pa never did travel much by car; however, Daddy always managed to have one of some kind. The first one he had was a Model T Ford. A trip to town was always a challenge in a wagon because of Doug Mountain Road. The hill was so steep that logs were kept nearby to put in the spokes of the wheels to help hold the weight of the wagon off the horses.

He couldn't really do that with the truck, so he would put it in low gear and try not to get the brakes hot. One day as he was driving down that big hill, the steering wheel came off in his hands from pulling so hard, he supposed. Looking up in surprise at a friend who was riding with him, he handed it to him and said, "Here, you drive a while."

"I don't want it! Get it back on!" Trying to get stopped was an issue on such a slope. He managed to put the wheel back on the shaft enough to get to the bottom of the hill. They would get the tools from the back and fix it when they got to the bottom.

I heard stories about that steep hill but never had to go down it. I am thankful for the road that eventually got built around that mountain. It had a sharp curve, but it wasn't so steep. I also missed out on the Model T.

It seemed to Daddy that he always had some kind of trouble with the Model T and wanted to trade it for something they could fit in a little better. We eventually had a car that had two bench seats; but most of the time it was a flatbed truck the he could use to haul wood and hay.

The few times we did have a car was exciting to us but Daddy thought it was a waste to have something that could not earn its keep. But as the children got older, he had to have both. We wouldn't all fit in the truck.

Eventually Matt and the others got vehicles of their own, but Pa never got a driver's license. In later years, he bought a Hudson car for $25; however, he would never drive it anywhere but on his own fields. If he wanted to go anywhere, Matt or Daddy took him or he drove the team and wagon.

Ma still didn't like to ride in a car, as she said that it always made her sore for days afterwards. Most of the time she would walk if she wanted to visit neighbors and then would pick berries on the way back to spell herself for the rest of the walk.

I loved walking with her. We had found a patch of wild blueberries that were delicious, about a quarter mile from the house but up a steep hill! One summer day we went just to pick blue berries, came back with two buckets full, and she made a fresh blueberry pie that I could hardly wait to eat. I had a difficult time waiting until supper.

Needing a rest, we sat and talked for the rest of the evening. I found that I would rather talk to Ma than do anything else that I could think of. She had advice that I could learn from.

Chapter 60

The Big Change

In the early to mid to late 50s was a time of great change for Pa. He never owned a car, though some of his children did. Cloyal had an A Model and Dale had a Model T.

Pa had spent his life making sure the wagon wheels and spokes were in good shape. Never had he seen a problem that he couldn't fix.

Good news, they were paving the roads. Bad news was, the wood and iron wheels would never survive the pavement. The streets in town had been paved for a while, but they could avoid them with the wagon. Someone told Pa he would just have to learn to drive a car.

He had a better idea and Ma would not want to ride in a car. He would change the axles on the wagon and put on rubber tires. That is just what he did. His shop took on a new task. He would figure it out one way or another. It took him a while, but we never doubted him. He put car tires and axles on the wagon.

The next Saturday trip to town was amazingly smooth and quiet. Ma sat beside Pa, wearing her bonnet, as usual. "I believe this is a bit nicer ride today. A body could get used to it."

The wagon was a little heavier, but I think the horses liked it also. They eventually needed to wear rubber shoes for the pavement. But how could he change for the dirt road and for the farm work?

This went on for a while; then, more and more people started driving cars. Not many would put rubber tires on their wagon. The wooden wheels wouldn't hold up and it seemed that he was forever making new horseshoes.

One Saturday I was at town with my parents and noticed they had taken the hitching posts down in a lot of places around the square. Matt, Cloyal, Loren, and my dad all had cars by then.

A few weeks later I noticed that the water troughs were missing and I almost panicked! The horses needed water after the long drive to town.

It was then that I realized we were in for a big change. It scared me, somehow. No one had discussed it with me. I'm not sure they knew what was taking place, either.

Ma and Pa stopped going to town on Saturday for the most part. Ma never did like to ride in a car. She would walk for miles to visit anyone, or ride in the wagon; but she said it made her sore to ride in a car.

She would go on rare occasions but said that it took her two days to get over the trip, so visits to her siblings became less often. Usually, she would go see several on the same day. The ride in the car or truck was more like taking away her blessing. She thought she might get used to it, but never did.

I didn't doubt her word; because, Ma would not tell a lie. I just never understood what she was saying. Someone else did most of her shopping after that. We were on our way to a faster paced world going nowhere, as Pa saw it. They would have to learn to cope and make changes.

A few people still rode horses at times, just not usually to town. On a rare summer day, we might see Johnny Phillips and several of his children riding horses across the field, coming to visit for a while. Ma was always glad to see any of them. Johnny had always been special to Ma, as she and Mattie had worked the gardens and cotton fields together when he was a baby.

Since they could no longer take the wagon, Ma wanted to see Ollie, Bessie, and Boyd all on the same day, and most of them didn't have a car either.

Their visits were shorter and less often. They missed each other a lot. It seemed she would never learn to enjoy riding in a car or truck because it took the fun out of the trip for her.

Chapter 61

Life's exciting Moments

Daddy cut and bailed hay during the summer. When Jimmy was four, he put the truck in compound gear and taught him to drive in the hayfield. After hitting a few bales of hay, he Kind of got the hang of it.

That made him feel important I suppose, and too smart for his own good; because he got the idea that he could drive anything. One day as we were sitting in Ma's house, a car went by the front door.

Daddy thought it had jumped out of gear, so he ran out to stop it but couldn't; it kept going down the hill and rolled right into the creek. Several of us ran after it.

Jimmy was sitting in the seat, unharmed but a little shaken up. He had gotten it out of gear, though I am not sure how he reached the clutch to do it. Daddy started teaching him a little more about driving cars after that.

Ma was worried about him driving so young, but Daddy was certain it was ok. He always put the truck in compound and stayed close by until he was sure he could do it. He tried to assure Ma that he would be ok.

We moved again and shared a house with Aunt Alene and her son. They had two rooms and we had two, and we shared the large kitchen. Alene could ride with Daddy to go to see Ma and Pa. We all were there very often, trying to help with the farm when we could.

Aunt Alene had moved from the little house because it was too small for her with all her grandkids. She had a new grandbaby also. Her name was Brenda. When she moved out, Daddy decided to tear it down to keep us from being tempted to move back into it. It was just too small. I got a baby doll that year and I named her Brenda.

Then there was Delmar. He was number four. Mama had a hard time with him, maybe because she worked so hard in the gardens and reached up too high or something. He was born feet first; because the cord was wrapped around his neck, he could not turn.

Then her milk supply was very low, so he had to drink canned milk because they had not enough money for formula. Nursing him all she could, she thought it was better than giving him fresh cow's milk.

We all loved being together, and although it was getting a little crowded, we were glad Alene was there for us while Mama was in the hospital.

We often went to Paint Rock church when Delmar was a baby. The music and the services were usually exciting one way or another.

During one service, we heard a noise in the attic; soon we saw flames. The squirrels had built a nest near the stove pipe. Mama handed the men Delmar's blanket to put it out, then took her coat off and wrapped him in it. I was upset about his blanket, but they got the fire out.

Delmar was giving before he was old enough to share. Over the years, there would never be a sweeter baby or kinder person. He had Ma's or Daddy's personality and would do anything for anyone and ask nothing in return.

In later years, if someone brought only three pieces of candy for us to share, he didn't want one. Delmar was beyond kind. Never would he fight for anything that anyone else wanted. God must have a special calling for him. This is Delmar and Mama.

I remember another service that someone just felt led to check the attic and found that a rafter was split and needed repair. God must have put it on his heart.

The men got together and found some nails and another board and fixed it that night. They would not neglect the building God had blessed us with.

I started school that year and we spent a lot of time at Paint Rock Church. We had lots of good music and good preaching there. The church always seemed to be full. I got to sing in the quire even if I didn't know the songs. Clyda and Lorna and several others played instruments and the music, and the preaching was awesome.

Much has been done to make it what it is today. A new roof and new siding. I can't help but miss the windows that once were on each side. But two were put in the front.

Adding the porch helped a lot also. I don't know when they removed the steeple; maybe when the new roof was put on. Over the many years, it has held a special place in the hearts and lives of the community.

Families have worked together through the years, to keep the building usable, remembering that many have attended school in this building, including my grandpa and his brothers and children. The heart of a community makes a difference in anything.

Chapter 62
Berry Picking with Ma

It was a hot summer morning. Ma wanted to pick some black berries. Pa told her of a full patch across the creek. This was an important job that helped provide much needed food for the winter, like delicious cobblers and jams. We could eat all we wanted raw, but everything comes at a price. Watching for tiny spiders and insects was a must.

I needed to learn to watch and listen for snakes while we picked. There were three kinds on the side of the mountain that we had to watch for, copper heads, rattle snakes, and cotton mouth water moccasins because it was near the creek.

Teaching us was important to my grandma. Our lives might depend on what we learned. Ma put on a pair of Pa's overalls, since she didn't have pants of her own. A dress was just not practical in the berry patch.

I wore a pair of pants also, with a pair of high-top boots. We gathered our pails and walked across the creek and down a little trail, just to the end of the pasture. We found a large patch of juicy sweet berries.

Ma reminded me to watch for snakes and listen for rattlers as she began to fill her pail then pour it into a larger one sitting nearby. Picking as fast as I could, the briars were getting the best of me. Ma had emptied two pails before I could get one.

We were not to eat them until we got back to the house and washed them in case there were spiders and bugs on them. I was getting very tired and hungry about midmorning, but we could not stop until our pails were filled. The big one was full. Ma filled her two-gallon buckets, and then helped me with my two; we had to have them all full, if possible. We had walked a long way to get them.

Finally, just as we had managed to get most of the pails filled, I heard a rustling in the patch. I asked Ma, "what was that?"

Ma had not heard it, but stopped to listen, then in a few minutes we heard another sound. I didn't know what it was, but Ma said, "I think we better take what we have and head to the house, that sounded a lot like a rattler."

We never did see the rattlesnake, if that is what it was, but I was glad we were done. I was scared and ready to go to the house.

At last, we started toward home! She had a large bucket in one hand and two smaller ones in the other. I was on my own with my two smaller ones. We got to the creek and started to cross. As I started to step on the rocks at the crossing, Ma told me to stop and not to cross. She saw a large snake stick his head up out of the water just in front of me. It was a cotton mouth water moccasin!

He decided that he was not going to allow us to go across the creek! Ma didn't want to try to kill him in the water. Yet, he just held his head up out of the water and watched us. Ma said, "Maybe he saw the berries. "But we were not about to share them with him. He could get his own.

Staying in the water, he waited, knowing we wanted to cross. We thought since he was there, we would just walk, what seemed like half a mile to the other crossing. It would come out just below the house anyway.

Well, little good that did. That snake stayed right with us as we walked. We just watched each other! If we stopped, he stopped. He knew we were no threat to him as long as he was in the water. We knew we had to get him to come out in order to kill him and he would not let us go past him. This was one day that lunch was a little late! Pa new full well that something was wrong when Lunch was not ready, so he soon came to see what the problem was.

That snake wouldn't come out of the water so Pa started throwing rocks at him from the other side to get his attention, as he walked noisily, down the creek on the other side. It followed Pa back down the creek, but it was smart enough not to come out on the bank where Pa was. It would have been the last time anyone had to deal with him.

When Ma felt he was a safe distance away, we quickly crossed over the rocks and started up the long hill to the house, and then Pa followed.

"You must have been in his berry patch," he said. "I knew something was wrong. I would never have guessed a standoff with a snake in the creek. Are you both all right? Here, let me carry some of those berries. No wonder he's upset! You girls must have cleaned out the patch!"

"I wish we had, so we wouldn't have to go back!" I complained with a shaky voice. "I thought he was going to try to take them back. And we may have heard a rattlesnake in the berry patch."

Ma managed to laugh a little. "I had lots of help today." Tomorrow we can make some nice jam. I bet she can help with that also." Ma was trying to get our minds off the snake, knowing I was still scared at that point.

We didn't have a hot meal for lunch that day. We were all too tired and excited. Pa told Ma that some cold biscuits and a few leftovers were just fine and Ma didn't argue. She went to the kitchen and got the biscuits out of the warming closet on the stove and ham from the ice box and jelly; we had a cold lunch, but before we ate, Ma said that we had to get out of our clothes that would be covered with chiggers.

We changed and washed off any area exposed to chiggers or ticks and hung our clothes on the line outside so they wouldn't get in the house.

After lunch that day I was ready for a nap. I had not really understood why we had to rest for an hour after lunch, but that day I understood well. If you work hard, you need rest. I was still shaking from fear that we would not be able to get home with the black berries we had picked.

Chapter 63

Quilting Experience

Mama made some of my dresses from the flour sacks that her dad brought to her from the feed mill where he worked. He had also bought her a sewing machine. So, we had clothes, they just faded out quickly, it seemed, but if she used good material, we always saved the scraps for quilts. No piece of any size was wasted.

Our families were together almost daily. In the evenings, the men and boys sometimes got into a game of marbles in the front yard, which usually brought the neighbors.

Easter was a time of family togetherness with lots of good food and a huge egg hunt. Several games might be played, but we could count on a time of music. Every corner was full I'm sure, but no one noticed. Not everyone was in the house at the same time.

It didn't have to be a holiday. Pa played his fiddle every evening, others came often to play with him, especially in the summer. We sat outside while it cooled off in the house and many children were together often. We were never alone for long. We always wanted to stay the night.

A child could never have felt more loved. The memories of Ma and Pa go on and on. Ma always stopped to explain why I should or should not do something. She was quietly teaching me how to love my own children by caring for me.

I always loved my time with her because it was just that, my time. If I was patient, she would let me know she was proud of that. We talked until I got sleepy then closed my eyes and listened to the squeaks of the old rocking chair. The squeaks soon became a song in my mind. So, I guess you could say, the rocker sang me to sleep. As I got older, she would have to wake me to get on the bed, she couldn't pick me up, but still kept on rocking me until I was about eight.

While I slept, she got busy doing something. Many times, it was sewing or quilting by hand. Nothing was ever wasted; the smallest piece of material could fit into a quilt of some design and with an ever-growing family another one was always needed.

If I woke up while she was still sewing, Ma was prepared with a fairly large needle, so that I would not be apt to lose it.

She would give me a piece of material, some small scissors, and a pattern she had made for me, along with a thimble that was too small for her, yet too big for me. It was easier to sew without it. She had bought the smallest she could find, telling me that I would grow into it soon enough and until then I must work slowly and carefully so as not to prick my fingers, knowing that I would, many times. Quilting was something we needed to learn.

We all enjoyed the wintertime when the women would get together and put a quilt in the frame. My aunts and cousins often come to help and just be together.

Those days are embedded in my mind forever. I was working hard to get a quilt top ready, but it would be a very long time before it would be ready to put in the frame.

Though many patchwork quilts were made, a sewing machine never touched them. It is hard to work together on something with only one sewing machine. Making quilts was a family affair. Ma's solid stitches would usually hold for as long as the material did.

When I had cut enough pieces to make a block she said, "Now, get your needle and sew them together." The words (I can't) never entered my mind, because she always encouraged me. It took years to finish my quilt top, but that was ok. It was our time together that was important.

When I started putting my first top together, I was about six. But I had tried making several blocks since I was about four. Somehow it took forever to make it to quilt top stage. But I was not to give up, Ma told me I could do it; it just takes a lot of practice. It didn't seem to matter that Ma finished dozens of tops and I was still working on one.

When she got one or two ready to quilt, she would hang the frames from the ceiling and spread the domestic and fasten it to the sides evenly with strong twine.

Cotton was spread out in a neat layer then the top was pinned on. Whenever she got time, between the farm work of milking the cows, taking care of the chickens or any other jobs that needed done, she would let the quilting frame down from the ceiling and start sewing.

It was mostly in the winter that she quilted. The summer was too busy with crops, canning and other work. Time was a precious gift from God, and it was wrong to waste it. "We must never be lazy," she would say.

Ma's stitches were even and straight, but whoever was there worked on the quilts. Quilting time was like mother daughter banquet time. It was time to sit and visit with one another. When Alene or Lathy lived nearby, they would come often to help with the quilting, along with Clossie, Wanda or my mom, Peggy. It was nothing to have six to eight people working at the same time.

Grandkids were always encouraged, but never forced, it was meant to be a fun event. I could not wait to get started. I had to grow enough to reach the quilt and the thimble must fit my finger before I could quilt on a quilt in the frame. Eventually I was big enough. My spot was left for me to quilt on Ma's Quilt.

I wanted to be able to know which part I had done when it was finished. That was really no problem. Try as I would, my stitches were not close together nor were any two the same.

I worked for hours on one block, taking out more stitches than I put in. No one would do it for me. If I took them out, myself, I would learn faster.

I lost interest and went on to play and my fingers hurt from pricking them so much. Ma never mentioned that I got blood on the quilt, though I did many times. I didn't want to disappoint her, so I would come back and try again. Only if the rest was finished would someone finish my block.

If anyone else had a top ready, in turn each quilt was put into the frame and quilted until all was done. Finally, after several years and I was more coordinated with my sewing, my top was almost done. It would only be for a small bed. It was getting too hard for me to handle the top. I was getting discouraged and didn't want to make it bigger.

So, Ma checked my stitches and tightened up any loose places so that it would hold up better, telling me what a great job I had done. She said that she just had to fix a few places on each block. She probably re-sewed most of the top, but I was proud as could be.

My nine-patch top was put in the frame as if it was the most important one ever done. I quilted on it with pride and since it was mine, I would not stop until everyone else did. They talked about what a good job I had done. It was great being a part of such a special family event. I worked with pride, finally.

By that time, I was nine years old and glad it was finished. At that point I did not want to make another for a long time. I would help Ma or Mama make blocks but if I started my own, I would have to finish it myself.

Ma encouraged us in our endeavors; if we failed, she would say, "It's ok, just try again. You haven't failed until you quit trying."

However, if we started something, we must finish it. Ma let us know that she loved all her grandchildren equally, but whoever was there felt special.

Chapter 64

Going to Church in the Snow

I spy was a favorite when we went to Aunt Sara's house; She let us use her thimble. Why? I am not sure, but we never did lose it. She trusted us with it, outside and in the dark; except for the light that shined from the windows and distant streetlights.

Her granddaughter, Linda was usually there and helped watch after the little ones and played with us, making an effort not to lose the thimble, knowing that her grandma used it often.

We all loved Aunt Sarah, Pa's brother, Sheridan's wife. He had been gone for several years but we still visited her.

She was a noticeably short, small built lady, and quiet most of the time; but, in a church service, it was a different story. Aunt Sarah could play a tambourine like no other! She gave real life to the music and her love for the Lord was unquestionable. The smallest musician with the smallest instrument made the biggest impact on the music part of the service. I can't remember who was playing the piano or the guitars and other instruments; however, I will never forget her tambourine.

You never knew where she was going to be, if the spirit moved, Sarah moved with Him. We missed her when she went home to be with The Lord. Heaven's music must be sweeter now.

Raising their children to love the Lord was her greatest goal. Some of the fondest memories of my childhood were with their daughters, my cousins Clyda and Lorena. Clyda and her husband Tom Phillips were preachers and often held services at Paint Rock.

When I was about eight, we still lived in the same house, about three miles away and down a dirt road. It was in the wintertime; we had a big snow that year; so deep that a car couldn't get down our rough road and we could not get out.

Clyda and Lorena knew that I loved to go to church. Most anyone would have just said the weather is too bad and not made such an effort to get a small child to church.

Not them; together, they carefully drove to the end of the road in the snow, left the car and walked about half a mile to my house to see if I could go. I know they had on dresses; they never wore anything else. Surely, they had long coats and boots. I didn't notice. I probably did also. I really wanted to go.

Mama and Daddy were a little surprised to see them but said I could go if they wanted to bring me back. They left it up to me. Not a doubt in my mind. I had been sad because I thought I was going to miss church; it was the highlight of my life.

That walk in the snow was cold and difficult, but I had on boots and they both held my hands to keep them warm, and to keep me from falling. I didn't have gloves, but they kept my hands warm with theirs, making sure to check my fingers often and to cover my hands.

My heart was warmed that they came to get me, even more during the service. The love of God flowed through those two women, just as it did their mother.

Lorena played the guitar and Clyda played either guitar or mandolin and they sang, The Sun's Coming up in the Morning. The congregation sang several other songs. I was only seven, but I remember that service and will always remember their kindness and sweet spirits.

Lorna's daughter, Linda sang a song I could not get out of my mind, I Prayed Through. I eventually had to learn and sing it myself. The sermon was just as heart rending. I thought my heart would jump out of my chest that night! I didn't want to leave. And then after a power packed sermon of God's love and Salvation, they sang, Let the Spirit Descend, as the alter filled with people praying one for another.

We came back home the same way; parked the car and walked the same half mile or so to my house. I hadn't thought of the darkness after the service, but I am sure they had. They could tell I was a little scared to walk in the dark.

Clyda assured me that the Light of the World was walking with us. "He can see the way." Lorna told me how that Jesus loved us and would take care of us, even in the cold.

Then, I wondered why they went to such great lengths to get a seven-year-old child to church on a cold winter night, with several inches of snow on the ground. I did know that I wanted to know the Lord that they served.

Now, I realize that they were following the leadership of the Holy Spirit. I have to smile when I think of how much they must have had to wrestle with the Spirit that night, as they tried to use human reasoning.

I can almost hear them trying to tell God that with all the snow, I probably couldn't go anyway, and the car would not make it down the road. "Lord, show us what you want us to do."

God gave the command and they obeyed with a joyful heart. He doesn't always ask us to do things that are easy or convenient. Sisters came together, just for a little girl to get to church. My cousins were just the same in church as they were anywhere else, always happy and praising God. I never saw either of them without a smile.

Wow! They went beyond the call of duty. The time we spent together that night was beyond a blessing. They used the time to talk to me about the love of God and how I must love him too, so I could go to heaven someday. I will always be thankful for any time I spend with them or at Paint Rock Church.

We often went to church at Paint Rock. I will never forget that night when my cousins walked through the snow to get me to church because they knew I wanted to go.

They're both in Heaven now. I can't remember thanking them, properly. I do hope they knew what a difference they made and wish I had told them. I had lots of opportunities, but I just didn't realize it at the time.

Chapter 65

Revival at Paint Rock

I always wanted to go to church any chance I got. When revival services were held at Paint Rock, years later, Pa went and took his fiddle. It was a community building and several churches held services there from time to time, if no church was having regular services.

Brother Barns and Bethel Baptist church was holding a weeklong revival at Paint Rock one year. He had personally gone to Pa's house to invite them to the services that week and asked Pa to bring his fiddle.

"I ain't never played in a Baptist service before, but I figure I could play along with about anyone."

Bro. Barns replied, "Well, Baptist folks enjoy good music too. When God gives someone a special talent, He expects them to use it for him, don't you think?"

There wasn't much he could say to top that. Pa went almost every night. The music was great, and the services were awesome and Spirit filled. Pa was playing along with the music in one service. The bugs were flying everywhere because of the open door to let in as much cool air as possible; he finally stopped for a second, "think I swallowed a bug."

Someone commented, "You're supposed to chew 'um up first." Everyone laughed and the service went on. He kept playing. It would take more than a few bugs to stop the music or the service.

We had a wonderful revival that week at Paint Rock. For that week it was a Baptist church. Brother Lester Barns was a powerful preacher because he reached out to a community that others could not. Because of him some have been saved and many uplifted and others challenged to be better Christians. The pews were hard but no one noticed. Most didn't want the week to end.

Someone from Driggs asked if he would hold services there. He said he would pray about it and get back to them. A few weeks later He preached a revival at Driggs Community center also, with another good turnout and great services.

Bethel Baptist Church grew and gained a lot of country people after that. I loved to go there because their love for God was evident and shared. I began to have a better hope and understanding of God's word.

Many, over the years, from both communities have given their hearts to the Lord, thanks to one preacher who didn't mind stepping outside the box to reach lost souls. I shall never forget Brother Lester Barns and others who started going miles out in the country and picking up as many as would fit into their cars, sometimes two trips. He lived next door to the church.

I guess he did more for my grandparents than any other preacher ever could have. They always welcomed him.

I wanted Ma to go but she couldn't bring herself to. I didn't understand at the time, but it was because of Rose. She always made roses of different colored crape paper and sent them by someone else to decoration services. She could not stand the pain of visiting her baby in a grave or going to funerals

She believed in and taught us about God and His love and salvation by the blood of Jesus. Ma often read to us from the book of John or the other Gospels; yet, seldom went to church, though, she had gone all the time when she was growing up.

Ma said that going to church was a good thing, if we could go. But it was not what would get us to heaven. She would often give us offerings. She didn't go anywhere unless she had to, in a car or truck.

Later on, as I was in church, I was worried that they might not be saved, because church was so important to me. I kept asking prayer for them. I didn't understand, but I knew she spent a lot of time praying.

If ever there ever was a Christian, it was my grandma. She was the first one to ever tell me about Jesus. She often said to me, "Bring me the Good Book and let me read to us a little while."

Almost always it was about the life, death and resurrection of Jesus or Jesus taking time for the children. In general, she read about the love God has for his children, wanting us to know and feel God's love.

Pa was getting up in years and I was reasonably sure he was a Christian. He read the Bible a lot but I still worried because he read from so many different religions, then one night he made a profession of faith in Christ, while sitting out in his front yard.

I was at Bro. Carters house; it was my night to stay with the children as the church went out to visit people, not even aware they were going to see him. They told me, as they walked through the door, that my grandpa had been saved that night. I was so happy I was speechless. In God's time–victory will come!

One of the many times that a preacher had come to visit and pray with them, Pa invited Jesus into his heart as Bro. Carter, my pastor, and a visiting evangelist, Bro. Kinsey were praying with him. This was years after Brother Barns had planted the seeds of faith and visited and prayed with and for Pa many times.

One sewed, another planted, and God gave the increase!

The schoolhouse still stands today, as a church and community building. My brother, Delmar preached there for a few years, until he went on to be with the Lord.

He had the cross with the sign, Old Country Church, put up and they renamed it The Old Country Church. It sure has a lot of memories for many people. There are still church services held there and the community still gathers there from time to time.

Chapter 66
Summer Evenings with Pa and Ma

Of all the memories that flood my mind are the summer evenings when we sat outside in the front yard and listened to Pa play his fiddle; usually, there would be someone with a guitar. Often it was my dad or uncles. This day it was my cousin Billy Earl.

By this time some of Ma and Pa's grandchildren were married. Alene's son, James, had married Anna and Clossie's son, Harold married Helen. They all went to California for a while.

I was too young to remember much about any of them, but when they came back to visit. Helen painted my fingernails. I had never heard of such a thing!

James and Anna later moved to Oklahoma to make their home. Harold and Helen came back to Arkansas and stayed. Uncle Madison stayed with them many times when he didn't have work in other places.

When Uncle Loren would come, we had the best time. His daughters, Linda and Connie were his oldest girls and helped me watch after the children or we sang together.

We would enjoy whatever cool breeze there was. If no one was there to play with Pa, he still would play for hours, but when he stopped, someone would always remember a song he didn't play and would ask for just one more.

The soft sounds of the night creatures were soothing as we would sit and talk until the house cooled off enough that we might be able to sleep. Just talking to either one of them was pure pleasure. We didn't need anything important to talk about.

Ma and Pa taught us not to take the little things for granted. My daddy often said, "It's the little things that count." They taught him well. Spending time together gave us strength and courage to do whatever came our way the next day.

Noticing and appreciating God's creation was important to Ma. She reminded us to always

 remember to thank Him for such a beautiful place to live and for each other. I often thanked Him for her kind, gentle spirit.

We tried to learn to appreciate the little creatures of many kinds, so we tried to find their purpose; however, it was not easy to find any use for the ever-plentiful flies, wasps, and mosquitoes. Ma couldn't tell us that one.

Trying to do our homework, we found it was easy to get sidetracked. The clouds were fascinating as they moved and it was interesting to see how they could turn into elephants or sheep or whatever form they took. Ma allowed if God took the time to make it, we should take the time to appreciate it.

This was such a special quiet time of the day; and relaxing to use our imagination and compete with each other to find the most shapes. Sometimes, we would lie on the soft, cool grass and watched them for hours.

We had learned a rhyme in school that made the clouds look like ice cream or cotton candy; Though, I don't remember ever eating cotton candy. I saw some onetime.

The rhyme went like this; If I had a spoon as tall as the sky, I'd dish up the clouds as they go sailing by. I marveled at the way God made things work.

"Wow, the stars are pretty tonight, aren't they Ma?" I observed as we rested one evening. Ma was careful to point out the different stars and explained how to find them. There was the North Star, the Little Dipper, the Big Dipper, and on and on.

She told us how the earth was turning all the time and explained how the sun went around the earth that gave us day and night.

Ma, forever the teacher; we had a science lesson without knowing it. "What does your science book say about the stars and planets," she asked. She encouraged us to discuss what we had learned and took time to listen to anything we wanted to talk about. Often, she would remind our parents to talk with us. The Good Book says to talk with your children.

As I was older with smaller brothers and sisters, I was needed at home more and I had to go to school. I could go to Ma and Pa's on the weekend. It was Friday night and we did not have school the next day.

I couldn't wait to get there to spend the night and wanted to go as soon as I got off the bus, but I had chores to do. It was my job to do dishes and help with housework. Mama had her hands full with gardening, canning and many other jobs, not to mention the younger children.

We sometimes had to take turns by that time. It wouldn't really matter; Ma could make beds out of anything and anywhere. It would always be clean, fresh and comfortable. But I was the oldest, so I had more to do at home.

All I knew was that it was my night to go. I loved to talk about the day or just sit and listen to Ma and Pa tell stories of their earlier years or something that had recently happened.

Much of the time we would just watch the stars and talk about the events of the day or listen to stories about something that happened as they were growing up. Many of which I wrote about earlier in this book.

One evening as we were sitting outside, after supper, as seemed to be a custom for us. Pa played his fiddle as we all listened for a while; asking him to play different songs. We never did name anything he couldn't play.

After he put it up, we were trying to see who could find the star groups and name them first. This was a very important part of many days. It must have had something to do with being relaxed before going to bed. I always thought it was just too hot to sleep. I know better now. It was family time.

(These days it would be called TV, computer, or video game time; or maybe, Facebook or cell phone time.) I am so thankful that we grew up without the luxury of TV.

The days were so filled with work that we didn't have time to just enjoy being together, that is what made being at Ma and Pa's so special. They took time, every day, just to communicate with each other and with us. Ma never told us to stop talking, just to listen as others talked. We got the idea it was rude to interrupt as others were talking.

Then on another evening just after dark, while sitting in the front yard, we began to see falling stars, one right after another. Ma, Pa and I watched along with one other kid, who was staying the night with them. I don't remember who that was. I think it was Laura. We would watch each one in awe as they traveled across the sky until they burned out, trying to keep count of them.

Then, there was one that fell for the longest time. It got closer and closer until it actually was still burning as it landed right in the yard, only a few feet from Pa's chair! How exciting! I think we must have forgotten about the rest of them. This one came right to where we were sitting! We all got up and went closer to look as Pa leaned his chair over and moved his fiddle.

The light went out soon after hitting the ground, but there was a small pile of warm ashes. We could feel the heat from it as we held our hands closer. We were allowed to bring a lantern closer to look at the neat little mound of ashes that had actually fallen from the sky.

Ma said that we shouldn't touch it because it might be radioactive or something. "I think we might need to go inside. That one was a little close for comfort." You can watch from the window.

It was not cool enough to sleep yet. We would just have to make the best of the night. We were up as soon as it was light before the sun was up and went outside to see if this little piece of the star was still there.

We found a little pile of ashes, more than enough to fill a teacup if we had picked it up. However, Ma so kindly made us promise not to touch it. So, we didn't.

In later years I wondered why we didn't touch it anyway. Was it just ashes? Would it have felt different? If our parents had said don't touch, one of us would have had to do it anyway.

What magic did Ma have that made us want to obey her? I wanted so much to be like her when I grew up. Her patience, love and gentle spirit is something most of us could only dream of.

If I stop to count my blessings, she is still at the top of the list. Maybe I would have to count her twice. I wouldn't be half the person that I am had it not been for her love and patience.

The most devastating feeling in the whole world for me was to have her say, "Shame, shame. We mustn't do that." I tried hard to please her and avoided those words at all costs. In my whole life, she never raised her voice to me or any of us that I heard. "How did she manage?" I wondered.

Chapter 67
Ma's Lessons

Often, Ma or Pa would tell us stories of life as they were growing up or while raising their children or older grandchildren. We could listen forever and never get bored.

Ma had to have been the kindest person I ever knew. I loved the time we spent just talking, while we worked on either a quilt, canning, or resting from the day's work. I would ask her about her family.

It was not until I was older that I realized the reason she was so gentle and full of love and compassion was that she and God had been through a lot of trials together. He gave her peace in spite of the storms. She taught me that it is not who we are or who we are around that makes us happy. We have to take life as it comes and come to grips with it the best that we can, with God's help.

Most of the time, her stories were happy, funny, or at least educational; However, sometimes, the sadness would creep into the conversation. One such case was when she lost her mother at only 15 to breast cancer. Not long after that, her father died.

She was left at home with Ollie and her two younger brothers. One of which died when he was in his early twenties. Ma loved her family very much and still missed them.

Both her parents were teachers, so even though they had to miss a lot of school, they got a good education. She graduated 8th grade and thought a lot about becoming a teacher. Her older sister, Rose, and her brother, Andrew Jackson did become teachers.

Feeling such a loss, her parents didn't need her anymore. The two boys, Daniel Boone and Holland, were almost grown. She soon turned her attention elsewhere.

Leaving her home in Barn Hill and everything, including her pump organ, she decided to marry Harley. I doubt she ever told him she played. I feel honored that she told me. She only did when I asked her if she ever played anything.

One horrible story that she would never talk about was of her great-grandparent's war with Indians. She didn't share it with Harley on their trip to Oklahoma because they both had Indian backgrounds. They make it a point not to talk much about the really bad things. She told us that the Bible says whatsoever things are pure, good, and holy, think on those things.

Sometimes, in the quiet of one on one, the sad stories might come alive. Ma's father's grandparents had endured more than their share. She didn't understand many things but knew that God loved the Indians as much as he did the white people.

Her great-grandfather had been captured by Indians at the very young age of six, made to sleep outside and chop wood for the family who owned him at the time. He was cold, hungry, and weak. Trying to run away just got him beaten more.

Seeing he was severely mistreated, his brother, who belonged to someone else, tried to help him, but to no avail. His brother was treated much better by a different owner, who tried to help the young child as well. Trying to help just caused him more trouble, so they stopped trying to interfere.

Later, after about three years, someone else owned him, and he was treated a little better and was allowed inside the TP. Somehow, he managed to stay alive for eighteen years; and then they finally let him and his brother go.

So, the story goes, their mother had been captured and released. Before their capture, she had watched her three-year-old son thrown into her burning house.

Ma's sad stories were mostly kept to herself. She is not the one who told me this one. But I checked some records and found it written.

I have to wonder how she can be so full of love when life has dealt so much pain. There is only one answer to that. God is love beyond measure. His Mercy endures forever.

Her brother, Holland, ended up with the home place, everything on it, right down to the family organ; though, she had been the one who had played it. She missed playing and singing with her family; even though she had not played since their deaths, she never mentioned it to Harley.

"We must think about good things," she would always say to us. She loved her brother and was really glad he stayed there. It was just that she had very little that had belonged to her mother or father but memories. However, that was her fault; she could have gotten anything she wanted. She did have their picture that she treasured so much. As she thought about that, she realized that was enough. They had loved them all and had made the home for all of them.

Ma would never mention this topic unless asked; and she was always kind to her brother, Holland, when he would come to visit. It was easy to tell that she loved him. They were always glad to see each other, and she never told him how she felt. He was the last one living in the place. No one challenged him. Her home was with Harley and the children.

What Ma did do was teach her children and grandchildren, from the time they could talk, to always treat everyone equally and be fair to one another. Her favorite words, "WE MUST," still ring in my ears. We must always be kind to everyone, and we must treat all the children equally. We must give over to the little ones. We must share whatever we have if there is a need or if others come. Everyone must get a fair share. We must never take anything that doesn't belong to us. We must always do as the Good Book says, and we must read it to know what it says. We must help others who are in need, and we must not say bad things to hurt others.

Somehow, when Ma said, "we must," I don't think we knew we had a choice. We just wanted so much to please her. If we were doing something bad, she would say, "Shame, shame." and then walk away. I would rather have a whipping any day. She never raised her hand or her voice to any of us, yet she had more control over what we did than any strict parent around. What did she have that made all of us want her to be proud of us? It must have been because she practiced, to the letter, what she was telling us. Now, I see that Ma wanted to make sure that she taught us by example.

That is what her parents and the Good Book (Bible)had taught her. It said to talk to your children when you rise up, while walking in the daytime, and when you lie down. She carried this on to the second and third generations, telling us that the country could only be as strong as the families in it. She always told our parents that if they talked to us right; we would be good kids.

Ma also taught us that an idle mind is the devil's workshop. She told us that the Good Book teaches that if we don't work, we should not eat. Any child of any age could do work in the gardens, cotton fields, in the house, or yard. Whatever the job, we should do our best at it. If there were babies, someone had to care for them, and that was just as important.

I often got to watch them. It was a good job that grew with time. Our families worked together many times on one farm or another, or in the cotton fields, which meant more babies and required more hands. I found it fun to have one or more of my cousins helping me.

It was family time. With a big family and lots of cousins, in work or music was the only way we knew.

Through Windows of Time   *(God's Grace in Midst of the Storms)*

Chapter 68

The Grandchildren

No matter the time or the reason, our family always seemed to try to get together for work or play. Any one of their grandchildren would live there if they could. Work didn't seem like work, and the music and games were fun.

James, Harold, and Billy Earl grew up together like brothers, yet they were cousins. Ma and Pa's need to teach the grandchildren was just as important as it was to teach their own. The Bible said to train up a child in the way he should go. Ma thought it was important to train them while they were young.

I remember Ma telling a story of carrying Bill across the creek, walking on a log. He wanted to walk by himself, but she thought he was too little. "Let me carry you across so you won't fall in the water."

He let her carry him; but kept telling her they were going to fall in. Every few careful steps she took, he would say it again. "Ma, we're gonna' fall in! We're gonna' fall in the water." The way he said it caused her to get tickled. Before they got to the end, she started laughing so hard that they fell in. He just said, "See, Ma, I told you we were gonna' fall in, you should let me walk!"

They were just wet, not hurt. It was a creek that she carried him across almost every day. Bill just thought he had grown since the day before and was getting too big to be carried. From then on, she did let him walk.

I would like to mention all of their grandchildren if I could. All have their stories. We were always together by age group and watching out for the little ones. Never do I remember an argument. No adult would listen anyway. It was our job to work it out with kindness if we wanted to continue to play together.

There were too many children for adults to keep an eye on their own. It was the responsibility of the older kids to watch all the younger ones.

Cloyal had three; Louis, Darrel, and Coy. Clossie had Harold, and Lathy's son was Billy Earl. Clara Alene had four boys; James, Freddie Lee (Boots), William Harley (Cowboy), and Troy.

Except for Troy and Coy, these were the older ones and grew up together. Troy and Coy were a little closer to the age of Carroll, so they fit in a little more with the rest of us.

Loren was very musically inclined and passed it on too many of his eleven children. Their names are Carroll, Linda, Connie, Wilma, Freda, Charlie, Glen, Janie, Carla, Decena, and Pete, not necessarily in that order. Matt never married and lived in their home place his whole life.

Delmer (Dale), the baby boy, had six children, Charlotte, Jimmy, Laura, Delmar, Thomas, and Sandra.

Almost every week, we got together to play music at someone's house. Pa was always there with his fiddle and Cloyal, Loren and his wife, Ella, and Dale played music together, at least once or twice a week, with as many of the neighbors as would.

It was nothing to have thirty-plus people in one house. The kids learned to do their own thing; play music, sing, play games, or whatever, as long as someone watched after the little ones.

Wanda, the baby girl, had four children; Ronald, Carolyn, Roy, and Ricky. As I count, they had twenty-nine grandchildren.

By the time all these grandkids were very small, Cloyal had six grandkids that were close to our ages. It was nothing to have fifteen to twenty playing together.

Sometimes we listened to the music or sang with them. We stayed pretty close when they were making homemade ice cream and wanted to crank it before it got too hard to turn. One of the men would take over then to check to see if it was done. The women would make sure that everyone got a bowl.

There were instruments of every kind; guitars, fiddles, mandolins, steel guitars, a banjo once in a while, anything with strings, and lots of listeners. They sat in a circle big enough for everyone with an instrument to have room to play. Then, if someone wanted to quit, he put his instrument down against the chair. It was there for anyone to play.

When he was ready to come back and play, it was not always to his own instrument. He played whatever was available, whether he knew how to play it or not. He would know how within a few songs and maybe a pointer from someone else. They learned that music is what you make it on any instrument.

The fun night at our house was when we moved the table, and everything out of the kitchen, and Pa would call a square dance. It looked like so much fun! We all wanted to try. Some of us were not brave enough.

I, for one, just watched most of the time. I just thought it was beautiful when everyone was in step together. It seemed as if Pa was telling them what to do, and they all obeyed. I still wonder how they knew which moves to make.

I never heard Pa sing, but he could call a square dance as good as anyone else I knew, and he had that country fiddle mastered!

When his bow hair would get thin, he would just go find the horses and pull some hair from one of their tails, come straightway and get his bow, and put some hair in it like there was nothing to it.

(As one who has re-haired bows in my music store for the public, I can tell you it is not that easy! I wish I had watched him. I need to know his secret. It takes me hours sometimes! Where was I when my grandparents were teaching me these things?)

Music was a big part of our lives. If we didn't have a musical on Friday or Saturday night, we listened to the Grand Ole Opry on the radio. Even then, Pa would play his fiddle for a little while in the evening. The kids sat around him while he played and called out songs for him to play. He would play any tune we asked for.

During the weeknights at our house, we went to sleep with country or gospel music playing on the record player or radio. Dad just listened and learned a song in a short time. I, on the other hand, would listen to a part, then write it in portions, then go back and learn it.

Being together often, no one noticed that we didn't fit into a particular house. Much of the time was spent outside. We found games that could include even the smallest ones, like black spider, red rover, seven up, I spy, or anything else the older kids had learned at school.

Never was it said to anyone, "you are too young to play." Ma would have been ashamed of us. "We must always give over to the little ones," we heard her say as we thought of ways to include everyone.

Sometimes, we would sit in a circle and take turns telling stories or guessing games. It didn't really matter what we did; just being together was the fun part. Linda, Connie, and I were the oldest girls, and we took it upon ourselves to be the main ones to keep the little ones safe and happy. If the babies aren't happy, nobody's happy! So, basically, they became our dolls or our babies, and we had fun with them.

On occasions, only the older children were at Pa and Ma's house. Then, it was a different kind of adventure. We sometimes looked for arrow heads, which were all over the place, of many different sizes. Most of them had basically the same shape.

The thing to have done would have been to collect them, I guess, but we didn't. We found the straightest sticks we could and made arrows out of them. Pa showed us how to make a good bow, tighten and tie a good string on it just right, and how to shoot the arrows, reminding us not to shoot toward each other. "These arrows are designed to kill; they are not actually toys, so always be careful."

We didn't realize at the time how much Pa knew about the Indians. As a child, he had lived in Oklahoma, in the Choctaw Nation, for a while. We just thought he was smart and knew everything, and we wanted to learn from him. He had always told us he was part Cherokee and that some Indians had lived there once, on that very place.

Then, it was a constant challenge to make a better bow. The arrow heads were abundant; some were lost, and more were found. Eventually, we lost them all or outgrew the desire to play with them; but we never outgrew the interest in the cowboys and Indians. Many times, when we got together, that's what we played.

Those days were action-packed, and we were tired by night fall. I'm thankful that we didn't have a toy box because we didn't have to pick up toys before bed.

One small toy each year was received at Christmas. Mine was a doll; I kept it with me at night, and the boys got a gun or truck. My first doll was a baby doll, Brenda; and then a little rubber doll, Tommy; small twin babies when I was seven; a hard plastic, Indian lady with a baby on her back at eight; and a bride doll at nine, because it would be my last doll. Those were special to me, and I will remember them always.

When I got the twin dolls, I played as if they were real babies and I was to take care of them. I started thinking how wonderful it would be to have twins or triplets. I knew I wanted to be a mama someday.

(Now that I have children of my own, I realize that keeping children busy with whatever work they could do was a way of keeping them safe and where they could be watched.)

Chapter 69
Thomas Dean

We lived in so many places I could not name them all. However, about three years later, we lived between Paint Rock and Driggs in a house with several rooms.

Uncle Loren had lived there before us. I was almost twelve, and Mom was expecting another baby. We were all excited about the new house and the new baby.

Loren's wife played guitar and sang with the others, so it was our job to keep the little ones safe. They had several siblings also, so we understood each other.

The best times at that house were when he and his family would come to visit. We were together a lot, it seemed, because their parents and Daddy played music together at least weekly, with Uncle Cloyal and Pa.

We went to their houses, or they came to ours. This house was big enough that they could play inside if they chose. Although much of the time, we would go to Pa and Ma's, so Pa could play fiddle with them since he did not drive a car. Matt would bring them any time, but Ma didn't like to ride in a car.

By then, the wagon was not practical, so Saturdays were almost sad without that ride to town. Ma visited most of her family on the same day, maybe once every month or twice, since she had to ride in a car instead of once each week. It took her days to get over the trip.

We all appreciated the music, but we liked being together more. So often, we just went to her house. I missed the times when we had lived on the same dirt road so Pa could bring the wagon, or sometimes, she preferred to walk to our house so we could pick huckleberries on the way back home. It was about a half-mile walk. I could walk if she was with me.

In our new home, we had no animals except for one milk cow, so we could play in the barn. Childhood was fun for all of us at that time. When school was out, we still had lots of kids to play and work with, as long as the work came first. Each one had to do our part, which made playtime special, and the work go faster.

One February morning, Mama woke us up because she had to go to the hospital. It was time for the new baby to be born. So, we all got up and quickly got in the car and went to the hospital. We were sleepy but excited, at least for the first time.

Several hours later, her labor stopped, and we went back home and did the very same thing the next night.

We stayed a long time. I thought surely this would be the night we would see our new brother or sister. It wasn't happening. This baby was going to be a lot of trouble, it seemed. He was already getting a good start.

Back home, we went to get a little sleep. Again, the next night or early morning, Daddy woke me and said, "Get the others up and get in the car. We have to go back to the hospital. Maybe this will be the last time, I hope."

So, as tired as we could be, I asked, "Can't we just stay here? I can watch the kids." I was twelve years old and helped with them all the time anyway. But we had no phone and we lived out in the country, and he didn't want to leave her to come to check on us. I don't think he even listened.

Well, we got to the hospital for the third time; I prayed it would be the last. God is so good. Thankfully, it was. We had another little brother. I had hoped for a sister but figured it must be a boy; he was already causing a lot of trouble. But maybe he would watch and learn from Delmar, who was an awesome brother and child.

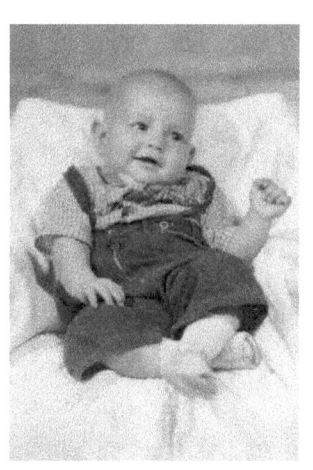

Mama let me help name him. She and Daddy chose Thomas as his first name and let me choose his middle. I said, "how about Thomas Dean?"

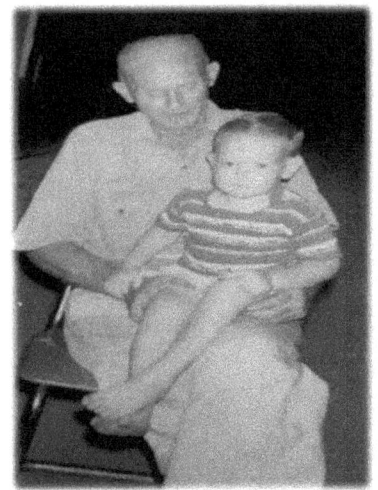

I thought of our cousin William Dean, who was a very sweet one-year-old. I hoped Thomas would be like him and Delmar.

We finally got to go to Ma's to stay for a few days until Mama and Thomas got out of the hospital. He was fine, and we were glad it was over.

Any excuse to be with Ma was ok with us. She let me help her make breakfast on her wood stove, and we all got to spend a few nights with her until Mama and Thomas came home. Then, I would need to go home to help Mama.

Within a year, Thomas was as active as the others, trying to keep up with them. He also wanted his one-on-one time with Pa any time he could get it.

Pa was more patient with children than I realized. He was usually working on something or playing his fiddle. Seldom did I see him holding babies, although he was always kind to them. The only time he would get on to any child was if they were going to get hurt.

If we messed up something of his, he would just fix it or use something else. We thought he just liked spending time in his shop.

As Thomas was growing up, it became harder and harder to get everyone in the car to go anywhere. I was twelve, Jimmy was nine, Laura was seven, Delmar was five, and Thomas was one. But we could not wait to get to Ma and Pa's on any weekend.

Thomas Dean was pretty occupied playing with the other children, Delmar, Laura, and Jimmy, and it was pretty obvious that he would play guitar someday. No instruments were ever kept from children. They were encouraged to play if they could. He liked to be outdoors anytime he could and they all enjoyed the warm sunshine and summer breeze. I enjoyed them.

Whatever the other children did, Thomas wanted to be a part of it. He missed us when we went to school, I suppose, because he wanted Mama to hold him a lot when we were gone. Our house was getting full, but we always wanted to go to see Ma and Pa. Mama didn't drive, so we had to wait for Daddy to get home to take us. We went often. Daddy said they needed help with the farm because they always shared with us, and we must earn our keep.

   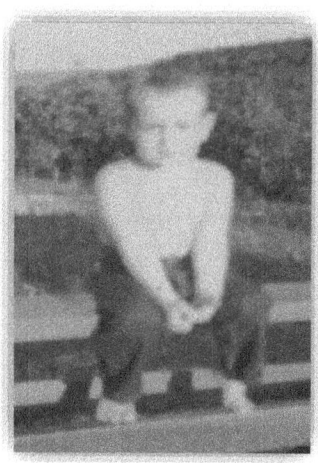

Chapter 70
Building a new Home

Daddy was working at the gas pump station in Driggs. He decided to buy a building they needed to get rid of because we had rented several houses since we'd moved out of the little house.

He and others would tear it down and bring the lumber to a place on the top of the hill, near where Cloyal had built his first house on Ma and Pa's land. We would soon have a new home of our own.

They took trucks to haul the lumber as they tore it down and brought it to the place Daddy wanted the house, nails and all. We would separate the lumber and pull the nails as needed. That gave Jimmy and me a job.

Many of the boards were already cut, so the walls went up fast. We all pulled nails and separated the lumber, enough to get started building, straightening any nails that could be saved and reused. Then, it was Jimmy's and my job to continue pulling nails as the others were building.

We almost got good at it. Trying to keep up with the builders was a challenge. Jimmy was so competitive that we both worked harder.

After work each evening, Daddy would grab a quick bite to eat and start building on the house. There was always someone there to help. He and his brothers helped one another. No carpenters were hired. On Friday or Saturday night, they would usually make time for music somewhere.

While Ma watched the little ones, Mama, Jimmy, and I pulled nails during the day and separated the lumber so it would be ready when Daddy got home. It is amazing how fast that house went up!

We were in it within a few weeks! Of course, it wasn't finished. It still needed a floor in one room and windows and doors, but it was our home. We at least had a roof to keep us dry. It would go up faster if we were living there.

Daddy told us that the walls were only six feet high, so consider that when we decide to get married. He was 5ft. 9 in. It would work for him, and it was our home, and maybe none of us would be taller than six ft. At least we would have no trouble changing light bulbs.

They finally got the floors finished, but living in and building at the same time was not easy. It needed a lot more work. Daddy and Mama got most of the windows put in, and we found boards for facings for a few of them.

I couldn't have been happier; we once again lived close to Ma. It seemed that we had moved every few months to a year. Thomas was a baby, so maybe this would be the first and only home he would ever know as a child.

I had not thought about the fact that we would have snakes to contend with. We just did what we could, and others helped as they could. I thought it was looking good until we came in from working in the garden one day and found a snake hanging over the window facing right above my bed.

At least we could see that one as we walked into the room. Laura found a baby copperhead in her shoe that was sitting in the closet. We had to seal the house off better, and soon.

It took years to finish that house while living in it. But eventually, it happened. Families came to visit often, and in the summer, music circles were out in the front yard. If the weather was cold or wet, they played in the small living and dining rooms.

People seemed to come from everywhere to play music. I am not sure who came for the music and who came for the homemade ice cream in the summer. We were thankful for our milk cow and the ice cream freezers that others brought. All the kids wanted to help. It was served until all was gone. Never was any saved.

Chapter 71
Laura's (Ma's) Birthday

For many years, the whole family had been together on many occasions. It was not unusual for all eight children and their children, grandchildren, and great-grandchildren to be at Harley and Laura's house at one time for music or working in the gardens or truck patches or something. Families worked together.

However, life had changed a lot; different jobs kept everyone busy, and most had several children of their own. Everyone visited often, but it was becoming harder to get there at the same time.

But this was a very special day, April 1, 1965. Lives were busy with work and school, but Ma was important also. We all decided that she had done more than was required of her for the family and she deserved a special day.

Sometimes, they tried to get group pictures. This is the only picture that I could find of Ma and Pa with all their children and maybe the only Krigbaum family photo with all of them. This may have been the last day that all their children and families were there together. It was a very special day.

Harley and Laura Krigbaum (Pa and Ma)
Ma's 72nd birthday. April 1, 1965.
Front row: Cloyal, Harley (Pa), Laura (Ma), Alene and Wanda.
Behind them; Loren, Dale, Lathy, Matt and Clossie

The house was more than full that day, and so was the yard, but no-one noticed or cared. We were just glad to be together.

Many brought food and desserts of all kinds as if it was easter or something. Ma had two birthday cakes because there were so many of us. She was not allowed to even help in the kitchen that day. It was her special day. I don't remember another party that compared to that one, before or after.

She got to spend her time visiting and opening gifts. The many grandchildren were playing games outside, whatever games we chose. The majority vote ruled with no arguments. I think baseball was played that day, but music was a favorite. It would only be a few minutes before someone would get out the instruments.

Our family was growing on every side. We loved to play together, but we must always watch after the smaller children.

It would soon be time to get the gardens prepared for planting, but this was just a fun family day together. Pa would not even go to his shop that day. Any work had to wait until another time.

In a few weeks, Pa would need to hitch up the team and head for the garden near the house. The old garden would be next. The days of rest would be over in a few weeks.

Some of Ma's flowers would be blooming soon. It would not be long before we could spend the evenings watching them again. That was always such a special time with Ma. She was so proud of her flowers.

Chapter 72
Finding Time for Prayer

It was wonderful living near Ma and Pa, but life was not getting easier as I was growing up. I had given my heart to God when I was nine, and I prayed often and tried to read my bible. It was just hard to find the time.

Daddy quit his job after buying twenty-one milk cows, and we started selling milk. I think he was gone more than when he was working for someone else. He hauled a lot of hay, so Jimmy was gone a lot also, driving the truck for him.

He got a hay baler and started mowing and bailing hay on the side. Milking the cows took way more time than I had, but we sold milk for several years.

The kids, gardening, canning, sewing, quilting, laundry, housework, and school took much of my time. Summertime was not a break; it was a time for working on something. We had plenty of time to play, but quiet time was hard to come by.

I was thankful for the opportunity to learn different skills that would help me later on, but sometimes, I just needed a little time to myself. So, I was thankful that part of each day was our time to do whatever we wanted.

Ma had read the Bible to us all our lives, but I needed some time to read in the quiet for myself. I went to church any time I got the opportunity, especially since I was saved.

I wanted to please the Lord, but I found that I failed Him a lot, so from the time I was fourteen, there was a place in the woods by our house where I often went to pray and study God's Word, especially on Saturdays. In every prayer, I asked God to send me a way to get to church on Sunday. I could go if I had a way, but by that time, my parents did not usually find the time to go.

If I asked, God seemed always to send someone by to take me to church. If I forgot, well, I usually didn't get to go. Maybe God was teaching me the need to ask Him for help. Going to church gave me strength and joy for the week. So, I needed to find a way to get there. Sometimes, Uncle Matt would take me, but only if he was going to town anyway. Once in a great while, he would even go with me.

I remembered the earlier years as we had gone to many revivals at Paint Rock and to the Pentecostal church in Paris for most of my early childhood. My aunt Alene lived next door to it for a while, so I tried to stay with her on Saturday nights, and Ma's brother, Uncle Boyd, lived across the street. Mama went much of the time.

Bro. Loyal Jones was pastor, and his wife was my first Sunday school teacher. I learned a lot from her. God was dealing with me, and I just couldn't be there enough.

That church was always full, and the Spirit of God flowed freely. The music was awesome! Aunt Sarah made it even better with her tambourine and her daughters Lorna and Clyda, along with many others played different instruments. The singing could probably be heard for miles. I have many happy memories of that little Pentecostal church in Paris.

I went to a few other churches as a young child and am so thankful for them.

When I was nine, life changed for us. The pastor from Bethel Baptist Church, Brother Lester Barnes, came to visit and offered to come to get anyone who didn't have a way and wanted to come to church.

Well, it took me all of one second to ask if I could go. My parents didn't say no. So, Brother Barnes came every Sunday at first, then as we were allowed, he came on Sunday and Wednesday evenings also. He surpassed the duties of a pastor. I didn't pick this church; God did.

Uncle Holland's daughter, Vera, and her family went to church at Bethel. Her children and I would grow up together in Bethel Missionary Baptist Church. Vera made every effort to keep all her children in church and close to God. She was a blessing and encouragement to all of us. Her daughter, Sheila, gave me this picture of Bethel Church.

Bethel Missionary Baptist Church

It was taken a few years before Bro. Barnes became pastor, and before I started attending. However, I grew up with many of these children.

Brother Barnes made almost weekly visits to invite and witness to the families of the children that came alone.

The people there were awesome. They worked together and prayed for one another, witnessing to many.

I will never forget him bringing all the kids up to the front of the church each Sunday morning and giving us a chance to quote our memory verse for that week. He tried to instill in us a real desire to study and obey God's Word.

I also could never forget the first Sunday school class I attended there; it was taught by Sister Anita Mars.

Bro. Barnes and our Sunday school teachers encouraged us and taught us to love and obey God first and foremost, but also to love and obey our parents. I learned to love my family in a way I did not know before. The love of God is truly amazing!

Each week, Brother Barnes would go pick up as many kids as he could fit in his car for Sunday school and church. He wasn't the only one. His car was getting very full.

Before long, others were doing the same thing; many children wanted to come, but their parents would not bring them.

One who later came to pick us up was Granvel Fairbanks. He only had a pickup, but it had tall sideboards. He was a willing servant and it seemed to work just find. Many times, it was full.

We had lots of fun. One young lady gave her heart to Jesus, in the back of that truck, on the way home from a revival service. I couldn't wait to get to church and hated to leave and was thankful for the Sunday school books to study at home, and for those who made such an effort to take us.

Brother Barnes had often gone to visit my parents and invite them to church. Thanks to his witnessing to them, I was so blessed when they started taking me to church. Mama first started going with me. Then later Daddy started going.

I gave my heart to Jesus and was saved at nine years old while kneeling at the front seat of Bethel Baptist Church in Paris, on one Sunday night.

God had been tugging on my heart since I was seven when my cousins Lorna and Clyda took me to church and prayed with and for me. I just didn't understand how to let go and let God save me.

Soon after they started, Daddy and Jimmy both made a profession of faith during a revival service.

Brother Barnes baptized all three of us in a few weeks along with about ten others. The joy and relief I felt is unexplainable.

It was awesome going to church with my family. And it was great knowing the love of Jesus. Several of my cousins were often there too. Many of Uncle Loren's family came for a long time. This was an awesome church.

However, after a few years, my parents stopped going. I had to find a way again. The church finally had a bus that would pick us up, so Brother Fairbanks would not have to use his truck.

We were thankful for the bus; however, the bus driver didn't want to come the whole way to my house. I didn't understand. I had to have a way to get almost two miles to the highway. It was too far to walk alone.

When I was a very young child, Ma had read the Bible to me often and encouraged me to believe in and obey the Good Book. It finally came to light when I was saved.

I worried that she might not be saved because she didn't go to church. But she prayed and worshipped God more than we did at church. And I knew she prayed for me. She didn't like riding in cars.

I wanted my family to go with me, and to know God's love as I did, but they seemed to be too busy or something, so from the time I was fourteen, there was a special place in the woods near our house, where I often went to pray.

As I went to my altar in the woods, I prayed for them and my grandparents. I was almost fifteen and knew so little.

One day, as I was praying at my alter and studying my Bible, God put a poem of sorts, in my heart. These words just came to me. I started writing them down. Somehow, it gave me comfort as I was writing.

God's Love for Us

The place I love to go is church.

We go to worship God, and

praise Him for His wonderful love

He shows us through His Word.

He gave His Son to die for us

on the cross of Calvary

That we might live and never die

throughout eternity.

His love for us is beyond compare

but people really don't seem to care

Some even take God's name in vain.

Oh, how can we treat our Lord this way?

It was our sins, not Christ's sins

that nailed his hands and feet.

For us, His side was pierced,

He's done so much for me

No greater love was ever known,

No truer love was ever shown

than that of Christ who died for sinners,

so those who trust Him would not perish.

Through Windows of Time   *(God's Grace in Midst of the Storms)*

Because my Savior loves me so,

I want to serve Him while here below

By telling others of his saving grace,

and how they can escape an awful place.

We, as God's children, should do all we can,

to show others the way who are living in sin

Lord, help us to warn them, remind us to pray

To live right before them - and serve you each day.

June 1967 - Charlotte G. Krigbaum

Chapter 73

The Watch and The Horse

Since we had built a house on their land, about a quarter mile north of their house, up a steep hill, still within walking distance, we went to see Ma and Pa every day.

I was older by then and so were they. Wanting to repay them for their kindness, I often went after school to see what I could do to help them, remembering the many sacrifices they had made for us; like the stamps that Ma had collected that she used to get bed sheets and pillowcases, dishes, or other things they needed.

Well, she never really bought for herself. She would sometimes use her stamps to order sheets or something.

My memories went back to when I was about seven maybe. Ma had said she didn't need anything at that time, so she instead, ordered a complete set of play dishes for me. She got a service setting of eight big plates, small plates, cups, glasses, pots, baking pans, and silver ware.

"This is a big set because I know you will want to share with any of the other children who come around. You must take very good care of them and they will last a long time."

When they arrived in the mail, I wanted to cry. When I opened the box, Pa saw what I had and got up and left the room without a word. I was more than excited with my new dishes. It was not even Christmas or my birthday!

About two hours later Pa came back into the house and I was still playing with the dishes. "Looks like you're going to need a place to put all those. I made this for you to keep them in." He had made me a little shelf to put my dishes on. "We can put it on the wall in the back room. You can't take care of them without a good place to keep them."

Ma and Pa always gave to others. Like I said before, to try to out give them was like trying to outgive God. But I wanted to do something for them; so, I would, once a month, take everything out of her cabinet and wash all the shelves and re-organize them, in addition to helping her with the housework and combing her hair.

She was teaching me to keep house, so it was really for me. Ironing the pillowcases was my regular job, but by this time I could iron shirts and pants. The sheets were still hers. I loved to help her wash the chairs, stove or anything else, and never thought anything about pay. She kept a clean kitchen, so it wasn't hard. Working in the garden with them was work, but also joy.

Again, Ma wanted to pay me for my work. She tried to give me money, I wouldn't take it. She surprised me with a wristwatch. It had cost six dollars!

I was so proud of that watch! She wasn't playing favorites. She loved all her grandkids and she let me know that. "It's just that you are the one here helping me so much and I think you need a watch since you're going to high school. Your parents don't have the money. Most of the older children have watches."

I really did need one because it was difficult getting to class on time, but how did she know? Ma seemed to know everything. I wore it all the time, wondering how I ever made it without a watch.

We were milking cows for a milk company; with twenty cows to milk twice a day. Once in a while they were nearby at milking time, but usually we needed to take the horses to get them from the back forty acres.

We had two horses that my brother and I rode to bring the cows to the barn. One was a small brown horse; the other was white with one glass eye.

For whatever reason, I always rode the white one. She obeyed and rode well, for a while. As long as we didn't take too long, she was happy; however, if she was ready, she was going to the barn, whether the cows were coming or not. Then it was a fight to get her to bring the cows in. "This should be a man's job; by the time we get them there, I'm too tired to milk cows," I grumbled.

She didn't try to buck me off; she would try to find a tree branch that was too low for me to go under. One day she was determined she was going to the barn; I was determined we were going to bring the cows first. I was proud of myself. We had brought the cows up and I had out witted her! Cows were in the corral; I was almost to the gate.

She had probably thought about it the whole way. She didn't get mad, she just got even. One tree with a branch that she could barely get under, and I didn't think about what she was about to do.

With no warning, she side- stepped and took me under that tree, causing me to either need to jump off or try to hang over the side. Afraid she would step on me if I jumped off, I grabbed the saddle horn with my left hand and leaned totally onto the side of the saddle. The branch was so close that a limb on it took my watch off my wrist and threw it somewhere. If my leg had been any bigger it would have badly injured it, but I was small for my age and didn't get hurt much.

I took the horse on to the barn, or she took me, and I went back to find my watch. Mom said I could find it tomorrow; the milking needed to be done. We milked by hand. I could usually milk three cows, but that night I only milked two as I thought of how much I hated that horse and how much I loved my watch.

"Can I go look for my watch now?" Jim milked two or three and Mom and Dad did the rest.

They allowed me to go look for my watch. I looked everywhere! "Surely it can't be far!" The leaves were deep so I dug through them. We looked until it got dark and then had to go to the house.

Mom and Dad tried the next day; they asked any possible question that might help. I looked every day for weeks, as I cried and cried, trying to find a way to tell Ma that I had lost it.

Finally, after several days, I knew she had noticed I wasn't wearing it, so I told her what happened. "I'm so sorry, Ma! I didn't mean to lose it! It was that stupid horse!"

She was understanding and felt bad for me because she knew that I wore it all the time, and that I needed it. "At least you weren't hurt, that's the main thing. I worry about you kids on those horses."

Dad thought about that, I guess; because, a few months later he gave up the milking business, got rid of the cows; all except old Pet, the Jersey that would come up to the door to be milked, twice a day. By that time Ma and Pa had stopped milking. We supplied them with milk since some of us were there every day.

I think I mentioned Sunday was a day to relax and rest which usually included going to church for some of us, music at someone's house. Usually, it was at Pa's.

Monday remained wash day, my whole childhood. Tuesday was ironing day. Wednesday, Thursday and Friday were open for canning, cleaning or anything that was needed.

Sometime during the day on Friday, for much of my life, Ma took her hair down and washed and combed if until it was shiny smooth. It was so long that she could sit on it, way below her waist. She often allowed Alene, Lathy, Wanda or sometimes me to comb it for her. It got to be a bit much for her in later years.

We would braid it and then put it up with hair pins so it would hold for a week. It had been years since she had cut her hair. I never did find my watch that I lost because of that horse. It was hard to tell Ma about that one, but it was gone, I had to.

Chapter 74

My Little Sister

At fourteen I was not ready for the many changes ahead, but life is what it is.

Thomas was only two years old when my little sister was born on Pa's birthday, December 11, 1966.

I guess Mama rocked them both while I was at school. Either way, in this family, babies get rocked to sleep a lot.

I was blessed with three brothers and two sisters. God blessed me with a baby sister. Her name was Sandra. She was a precious jewel.

The first day I kept her, she was three days old. Mama had to go to the laundry mat because she was not able to deal with the wringer washer. Daddy went to do the lifting and help her with everything, so Ma came to help me with Sandra. I was thankful that she was there, as she walked me through everything from feeding and burping to diapers, most of all holding and cuddling. Babies need to feel loved and secure. I had a lot to learn. Ma and Mama would try to teach me something new every day.

Ma said that patience was one of the most important things for anyone to learn. "We must work together and help one another. That is what families do," she would say. Ma let me do everything but was there if I needed help. She was forever the teacher.

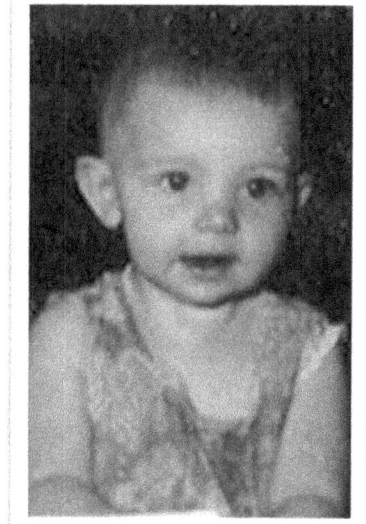

I loved to rock Sandra and sing to her until she went to sleep, every day and night, while Mama rocked Thomas. I doubt she ever just laid down to go to sleep.

She was my baby when I held her. She would sometimes, lay in her bed and drink her bottle if I was too busy. I rocked her because I wanted to. I got more comfort from it than she did, maybe because I remembered Ma rocking me for many years, way beyond what was needed. I was older than ten years old before I stopped letting her hold me. I always felt safe in her arms.

One day Daddy found some baby raccoons out behind the barn, whose mother had been killed by some dogs. He brought them home for me to try to raise.

We found a doll bottle with a rubber nipple that I finally got them to drink from. We found places for all of them except one. It took to the bottle well. Sometimes I would bring the raccoon into the house to feed her and I would give Sandra a bottle in her bed, at the same time.

As she watched the raccoon lay on its back and hold its bottle with all four feet, she started holding hers with both hands and feet.

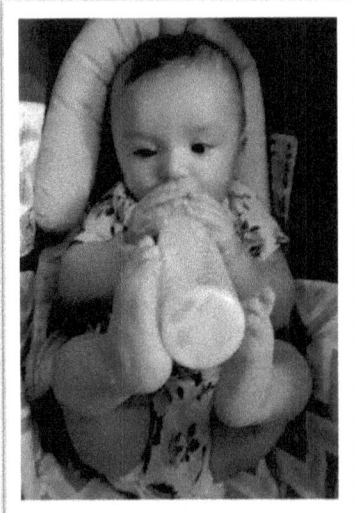

It was so sweet that I called my raccoon Angel. They were fun to watch together. But I only brought it inside when Mama was too busy to watch Sandra, and I had to feed it. We all enjoyed the raccoon, taking her for walks in the woods. We would need to let her go when she was older, so she would need to be used to the woods.

Sandra was the joy of most of my days and she kept us all entertained. I was so thankful for her. She filled my days with joy and exercise. I loved my baby sister and could not imagine my life without children.

As time passed the phone lines came that way and most of us got phones hanging on the wall. That was a real blessing. It changed our world. We knew who was going to Ma's. For whatever reason, I don't remember them ever being alone much. I have often wondered if they needed more alone time.

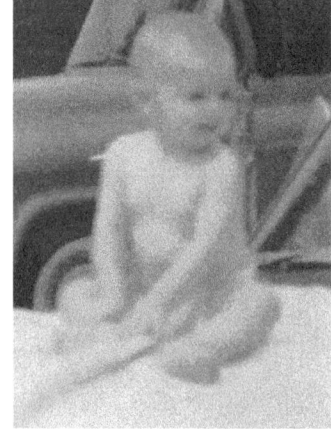

Thomas was only two years older than Sandra, so he wasn't sharing Mama willingly. Therefore, I had Sandra most of the time when school was out.

There was just something about a baby that made life worth living. I got tired and it was hard to get my homework done at times but having a baby sister helped me learn how to care for my own someday, I hoped.

Chapter 75
Dorothea

Mama's family lived so far away that she only saw them a few times a year. When either of them came, it was celebration time. Usually, a large group came together to spend a few days.

It was interesting making pallets in every part of the house and in the cars or on the porch. There was always room for one more. The two families blended together as one.

You might find a game of horseshoes or marbles, maybe homemade ice cream on a hot summer day. But almost always somebody played music at some part of their stay. None of them played, but they loved to listen.

My Grandma Stella would sing, Shake Hands with Mother Again. I can still hear her voice when I think about it. (If I could be living when Jesus come, and know the day and the hour, I'd like to be standing by Mother's tomb, when Jesus comes in his power. I'd like to say Mother this is your child, who wept when you went away. And now my dear Mother it gives me great joy to see you again today.)

Never have I seen or heard this song anywhere else. I only know the words because, in my mind, I hear her singing it. As a young child I would go behind the house and cry when she left, because it would be a long time before we saw them again.

Just when I thought my life was full at fifteen, Mama's brother, Uncle Hoyt had two children he needed someone to watch while he worked.

His mom, my grandma Stella could take care of one. She would keep the youngest, Ellen, but both were just too much for her. So, he brought Thea, the oldest one to me. She was almost three at the time and very active. He asked me if I could keep her until he could find a way to care for her.

School was out for the summer, so I said yes, without even asking Mama. I don't know if he had talked to her.

She reminded me, after he left, that Thea was my responsibility. She said she would watch her later, while I was in school. And I was not to neglect my other duties. I thought, what is one more child?

Uncle Hoyt would pay me to care for Thea. He knew I would keep her without any pay, but he insisted. It would help buy food and other things. With my part of that, I bought a big, large print Family Bible. I don't remember from where. I loved the pictures that told stories by themselves. It cost $30.00 and they allowed me to make $5.00 payments.

Uncle Hoyt always tried to come on weekends to be with Thea. This was a win-win for me. He would usually take us to church on Sunday mornings.

Mama would not let me take Thea to church unless Hoyt took us. So, it was more than a blessing when he came. I hated leaving her any time. She was such a sweet girl. Mama was trying to protect her, I'm sure. She would keep her while I went to church.

If it was late and he didn't want to wake us, and if he didn't have Ellen with him, he would sleep in his car at the gate on Saturday night; then come to the house in the morning before breakfast. Although, I don't know why because, we always waited and watched for him.

He could see Ellen every day, but occasionally, he would bring her with him so she and Thea could play together.

Thea was so precious! I bought some material and made her a cute little dress that wrapped around the back. I made Sandra some dresses also, but Thea was my responsibility.

I could not understand why Mama would not go to church with us. But as I think back. She didn't have a driver's license or a car, at the time. She would let the older children go with me if they chose.

I couldn't understand why any of them would not want to go to church. Maybe the challenge of getting there made it more important. I am thankful to those who made an effort to take us.

I went with a lot of other kids. My brothers and sister would go sometimes. When my brother Jimmy learned to drive by driving in the hay field, on rare occasions he could drive us to the highway to meet whoever was picking us up.

Uncle Hoyt loved taking his babies to church and he was a blessing to all of us.

Thomas was two at that time. You can't watch one without the other and Thomas wasn't giving up his place as the baby. He was a little younger than Thea but they played together well, and were always thinking and getting into something. What one didn't think of, the other did. Surprises were often.

I had no problem having three babies. Of course, Thomas always wanted Mama. That was a blessing in disguise. I thought that having twins or triplets would be the greatest blessing anyone could ever have.

Thea and Thomas played together a lot and with no real problems. They shared toys pretty well and I felt as if this was the way life was to be. I was busy, and so was Mama, but we had lots of good times with the children.

Daddy had found this little car somewhere. Thomas could ride it all over the yard. I was amazed at it myself. The kids loved it and they shared it well, as long as Thomas knew it was his.

Even though gardening and many other things could not be neglected, we would need to do many things, and life seemed very busy, but the kids just brought joy during the rough times.

Sandra was my baby sister, and I loved her a lot, but I loved Thea also. I felt bad for her because she needed a mother that she didn't have at the time. I wanted to make her feel secure. As far as I was concerned, she was mine.

It seemed I lived and thought childishly and for the moment. At that point in my life, I had no idea of the pain of losing a child. I never even thought of the possibility. I was just enjoying my life with them. They made me feel needed and loved. Thomas was excited about his new car with peddles.

Chapter 76
Nothing Lasts Forever

I quit school that next year but promised myself that I would eventually, complete high school, if by correspondence only. It was going to take more than I could make babysitting, but I wanted to have children someday and was not about to have any one of my children want to quit school because I did. So, I would graduate or die trying. However, for now, my life was very full.

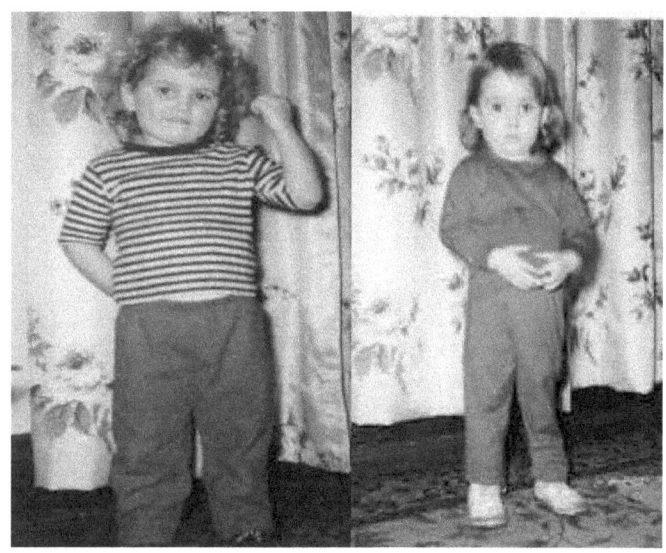

Then suddenly, it happened. I was seventeen and I'd had Thea for almost two years; with no warning, Hoyt and his new wife came to our house. He brought Ellen with him and said he had come to get Thea and told us he had just got married and was moving his new family to Illinois.

Wow! I wanted him to be happy, of course. However, I could never describe the pain I felt that day. How could he do that to me? Thea was his child and I know he must have missed her a lot. I had not even thought of the pain he must have felt. There was nothing I could do. I was losing my first baby!

Uncle Hoyt was happy to have Thea back. I understood that and was happy for him, however, my heart was bleeding, and no one understood. She wasn't mine, but I loved her so much that I felt as if she was.

In no way was I prepared for that day. I tried to smile and be happy for them. It just wasn't happening on the inside.

Dorothea looked happy but confused as they left. She loved her daddy, but she loved us also.

I wondered if she would miss me as much as I was already missing her. God had allowed me to practice my parenting skills for a reason. I wondered what He had in mind for me.

I loved her too much to deal with losing her, yet I had to pull myself together to take good care of my baby sister and brother, while Mama was working.

I needed some time with Ma. She was my comfort source and always knew what to say and how to make life livable. However, she would miss her too, and didn't even get to tell her bye. It would be worse than I could have expected, because he was moving to another state instead of another town. I had no warning, or I would have taken Thea to see Ma that morning. She loved her too.

Ma was sad but glad she would get to be with her dad and sister. Among the many words of wisdom, "Just go get the Good Book and let us read for a little while," was her answer. That seemed to help a lot. Ma always made life a little more bearable.

Sandra was a real joy, and it was not her fault. I got comfort from her, quickly realizing that my workload had been cut in half. Wow! The Bible says, "In everything give thanks."

I was thankful for a little more time to study my correspondence Bible course, and that it was much easier to keep the two babies safe than it was three. Thomas missed Thea but had fun with his new car.

What was God preparing me for? As Sandra grew, she was always sweet, but she had a mind of her own. She wanted to be older than she was, and she wanted to be at Ma's as much as I did.

Chapter 77

Growing Up is Hard

Things changed for Mama also. When Sandra was about a year or so old, she went to work at the pants factory. She also got her driver's license and a car so she could drive to work. That changed things for all of us.

Mama was working all the time. In the summer, I was to have supper ready, and the housework done, with whatever help I could get. Being responsible for kids was not as easy as I thought.

There was Laura and Delmar who were old enough to help with lots of things. Laura would watch the little ones while I did the cooking. That was more helpful than I realized at the time.

Delmar was kind and loving to them also and his personality was amazing. He would try to do anything he was asked to do.

Jimmy was usually helping Daddy or Matt when he was not in school. When he was there; if he wasn't fixing something, he was tearing something apart to see how it worked. Most of the time, he had screws or something left over. But it seemed he could fix about anything.

After I quit school, Mama paid me the same to care for the other children, as Hoyt had been paying me to care for Thea. Soon after Mom went to work, Sandra started calling me Mama. I loved hearing her and I sure loved my baby sister.

Laura would help with dishes or anything else if I would let her, but I usually did it myself, because I could get it done faster. Now, that I think about it, I don't think that was fair to her. She needed to grow up too. She helped with the other children. Maybe I was sometimes too busy to notice.

All I knew was that my days were full. She was five years younger than me, and I suppose tried to help more than I realized. There was just never a dull moment.

Having responsibility for my baby sister and brother made me feel as if I was grown up, the older ones not so much. They didn't want to take orders from a sister. I can't say that I blame them. But life is what it is. I did the best I knew how, though I'm sure it was not always right.

Sandra loved to go to Ma's and if she asked to go, I had to watch her closely or she would go by herself in a brief second.

It was hard to get her to wait for me. She could be playing innocently in the yard, one minute, and be gone the next. If I told her not to do something, she had to do it anyway or find out why, and sometimes the hard way.

She kept my mind busy. But she brought the joy back into my heart that losing Thea had taken away. I would have been lost without her.

Thomas was a mama's boy, with no doubt. I loved him but he always wanted Mama if she was anywhere to be found. I could hold him or do anything with him in the daytime, but, when Mama got home, he wanted nothing to do with me. Mama rocked him to sleep every night; no matter how tired she was, while I rocked Sandra. We had to have two rocking chairs.

And if we went to Ma's, she was always holding or rocking one of them. Most all the little ones went straight to her as they entered her house. It was no different than I had done. Ma loved the babies, and they all knew it.

I loved all the babies that I took care of but losing Thea made me realize that I would always have to part with them. I was glad my little sister would not have to leave.

Sandra and Thomas filled that empty spot in my heart, and Thea was happy to be back with her sister and her daddy.

I spent a lot of time reading to Sandra or playing with her when I could get her to sit still. It was not easy because, whatever the boys wanted to play, she wanted to be a participant, thinking she was bigger and better than any of them.

It was hot in the summer, and we didn't have anything but a box fan. Trying to keep her away from that fan became a real chore. When I was busy with something, she would sneak around behind the fan and try to touch the blades.

One day she managed to get behind it and laughed as she shoved her hand into the fan. Her laugh quickly turned to crying. It cut her finger badly. It was so bad that the end of her finger fell back and I had no phone, I saw that no bone was touched so I closed the cut and I bandaged it the best that I could. I guess I did ok because it healed quickly.

Mama didn't even take the bandage off to look at it. She said just leave it tight. I doubt she knew how bad it was. I always wanted to protect her, probably too much, especially after the fan episode. Sometimes it seemed she could out-think me. If I said no, she was going to try to get to whatever it was, at any cost.

Often, I thought about what I would have done with the three of them. God was teaching and yet protecting.

I hoped to someday have my own babies that would not be taken away. I guess I didn't realize that they grow up. Babies were so much fun but a lot of work trying to keep them safe.

Things were changing for all of us, and children didn't get easier as they got older, just different. Thomas was usually doing whatever the older boys were when they were not in school. It would not be long before he would start school also. He didn't want to be treated like a baby anymore.

Quilting with Ma or Mama had been a lot of fun since I was very young. They tried to teach us what we would need to know by the time we grew up.

Mama taught me to sew on her sewing machine that her dad bought for her. She made all our clothes except for Daddy's pants, which was funny since Mama worked in a pants factory.

I found that I loved to make lots of things. Sewing was fun and helpful and we never bought clothes that we could make.

I finally learned to make my clothes. The first thing I made was a baby quilt and I found sewing on the sewing machine to be fun.

I remembered back when Ma bought me a dress and a long coat for school. They were so special to me because I knew she had sacrificed a lot to get them.

The ones my mom made looked just as good, but the color in the feed sack material didn't last as long. I enjoyed helping or watching Mama sew on her electric machine. It was much easier than the treadle machine that Ma had.

I will always remember my last year of school when I took home economics in my last two years. It was a real treat. Mrs. Shirley Lesley was our teacher. She made a real difference in many of our lives, giving us a reason to learn as she tried to teach us responsibility and safety in cooking, sewing, caring for babies, or whatever life would bring us. We would be adults before we were ready.

I loved to sew. For this dress, I got to use new material. It was yellow with white flowers, though, it doesn't show in the picture. It had a strip down the front with lace on each side. I had fun making it and I was thankful for my teacher, who was so patient with us. Mama bought the material for this one.

My parents knew that I was getting older, and life would soon change for me. They must have realized it more than I did, because, I had no idea that life could change so fast.

I thought it would be like this forever. We got up with the chickens and went to bed with music. Daddy played and sang every night and we listened to records as we went to sleep. I also loved when he played the fiddle. He seemed to be able to play any instrument that he picked up, within minutes. We had musicals almost every week.

Most of Daddy's family played something and the kids were encouraged to sing or play whatever they wanted. Any instrument was available to all.

Pa always played his fiddle. Occasionally, if there was another fiddle, he would call a square dance. That was a lot of fun to watch.

More families together meant more babies to watch. But we all helped each other and enjoyed the music. Ma always reminded us to take good care of the little ones. I praise God for her.

It was fun to have so many cousins of all ages together while growing up. The older ones, like Linda and Connie, helped watch after the little ones. That was our responsibility. We accepted it with pride. We all played together, no matter the age.

Chapter 78

Bad Year with The Flu

One year Ma was so sick with the flu. Wanda had come to take her turn caring for her. She had been sick so long that her hair was bothering her so Wanda got the scissors and cut it off short. It was shocking to see it at first, but we got used to it and so did Ma. She never allowed it to grow out again.

One of the worst years was probably around 1967 or 68, I was sixteen, I think. It seemed that the whole family became sick with a major flu virus. Mama could almost always keep going, no matter how sick she was, but this year she was down as well as Dad and some of the children.

Since we lived closest to them, we were trying to take care of Ma and Pa also. It seemed everyone was sick. If any wasn't sick, we didn't want to expose them. I walked up and down that steep hill between houses almost every day.

At seventy-four, Ma and Pa were in good health, but we figured they had earned a rest, so we took turns going down to help them out. Alene and Lathy lived about a mile away, so they usually took their turn, helping with laundry, cooking, cleaning, or whatever was needed.

One week was almost too much for me. No one was left to care for Ma and Pa but me for a few days. I learned to appreciate nurses and aides that week. I would make some kind of soup or something they could eat, at our house, and then take some down for Ma, Pa and Matt. They might or might not eat it; if not, I would make something else and try to get them to drink liquids.

The doctor had been there and might have to come back, but with no phones, we just did the best we could.

Alene and Lathy were sick also and were not able to walk the mile to care for them and no one was able to go and get them.

One evening I went down to help and realized that I needed to stay. I was praying that someone else would come. None of us had phones and no one knew how sick they were.

Beginning to feel uncertain as to whether I was glad to be the one well or not, I hated to leave them. "Ma, do you need anything else? I may need to go check on the others, to check the fire and get them something cold to drink, at least. I'll try to come back in a little while."

Ma and Pa were so much worse than everyone else. I was really scared they might not make it and hoped the doctor would come back soon.

She managed a weak, "Don't worry about us, just try not to get sick yourself. You need some rest and it will be dark soon."

She was right about the dark and I was hoping she wouldn't notice how much that scared me. We had wolves that came up after dark and black bears that came up to the house periodically. Frankly, I was scared stiff to go home after dark! But, what choice did I have?

That was not going to be a good night; I tried to prepare myself for it all evening. Neither family could be left without help all night.

What was I going to do? Why was I the one not sick? "I'm sorry, Lord. Thank you that I am well. Would you make the others well also? This is too much for one person."

That night proved to be a long night for all of us, fever was very high at both houses. I liked to think that I was grown, but I was just a kid! No matter, they would do it for me, and do a better job, so I tried to quit complaining to myself and pull up some bravery. I was going to need it.

Trying to sleep about an hour or two, at each house if I could, all through the night, I went either up or down that hill. Going down the hill, I ran and prayed every step of the way, trying not to appear scared when I got there.

In the early part of the night, I could hear the wolves howling; they seemed closer than I would like. A bear had been seen there not long before. My imagination was running wild and it was so dark that I could hardly see at all. Ma was too sick to notice my white face and lack of breathing.

"I can't do this! Yes, I can, just take one trip at a time and pray." I argued with myself. It was about 2:00 am.

My alarm went off. I woke up, helped Ma and Pa with whatever they needed, checked their fever, gathered up all the courage I could muster, and started up the hill to do what I could.

Fever was a real problem, aspirin, cold water, cold cloths; anything I could think of, telling myself, "Only one more time after this and it will be light outside." Running as much as possible, it still was a steep hill and making it to the house alive and unharmed was my goal. I wondered why I couldn't drive the car.

Mom was feeling better when I got there. Dad's fever was going down also. Too bad we didn't have a phone; I could have stayed at Ma's. Mom was up, doing for the children. "You get some sleep. You'll need to go back in a couple of hours. Was their fever still high? I could try to go if you want me to."

"No, Mama; I will go. Their fever was still high, and I hated to leave them, but was worried about the rest of you. You get well." The fact is that it took everything I could do to refuse her offer. I was scared stiff. The big bear that we had seen, just a few weeks earlier, was out there somewhere and had not long before, come all the way to our house and stood up on its hind paws, leaning on the bedroom window. However, Ma was really sick. I would do what I had to do.

Daddy said he was long gone. My dad didn't lie, I knew that, but he didn't know everything either. If I could just make it to their house one more time, it would be daylight when I woke up again. Two trips accomplished; I'm still alive with one to go.

Since Mom was up and about, I helped her with the children a little, then headed back down the hill. I could get the trip over with instead of worrying about it.

Mama said that I needed to get some sleep. She could handle things up there for the rest of the night.

The last trip was the hardest, but quickest. It was almost totally dark. I ran anyway, hoping I didn't fall over something, especially an animal. Just before I reached their yard a wolf howled just a short distance away. My fast turned into faster. "I am not going back out there tonight!" I said as I opened the door.

Pa was awake. "You're back awful soon. Did you go home? Are they feeling better?"

"Yes, Mama is feeling better, so I came back here for the rest of the night. It sure is dark out there tonight and I'm glad I don't have to go back. Can I get either of you anything, are you feeling better?"

"A little, I thought I might try to chunk up the fire. I just feel very weak and useless, but I needed to get up.

That was a good sign to me that he might be getting better. "I'll check the fire, Pa. You rest. We'll get through this night. It will make us appreciate sleep more. First let me get you some fresh water."

I knew he was still very ill, because he said, "ok", and went back to bed. We made it through the next day and then Alene came down to help. The next night was much better; Alene stayed with Ma and Pa after that, until everyone was well again. Aunt Alene to the rescue again. I thanked God for her. It would have been much harder without her.

Within a few weeks things were back to normal and Pa and Ma were outworking again. We did have a lot of catching up to do, especially with washing clothes and bedding. God had blessed our family one more time.

I learned a lot that week. There is really nothing we can't do if God wants us to. He will make a way where there seems to be no way.

The Bible says that in everything we should give thanks. We were thankful it had been during the winter, so we didn't have so much work that didn't get done in the gardens and fields. God brought all of us through a really bad year with the flu. For which we were truly thankful. God is good.

I was getting older but not ready for the many changes that were coming. Life is so uncertain and changes so fast. I just needed to know how to listen when he called.

Chapter 79

My Repeated Dream

As a teenager, I did a lot of thinking as I sewed or did housework. I dreamed of being a mother like Ma was a grandmother to me.

Mama had six children. I was the oldest, so I didn't have as much special time with her as I would have liked, though, I knew she loved me, and I loved her and the babies.

For years, I must have been restless because, at night I kept having the same dream, over and over. I dreamed that I was married; yet I don't remember my husband's face. It was all about his two precious little girls. One was about three and the other maybe two.

We married so that I could take care of them because he had to leave. Soon after we married, he went off to work or war somewhere and left the girls with me. I never saw him again, which was strangely un-disturbing.

I had two little girls that were mine. They didn't really know me, at first, so I spent much of my time trying to get them to love and trust me and know that I loved them and would always be there for them. I wanted to be sure to keep them safe and happy. They seemed sad at first, but kind and respectful. They accepted me but missed their daddy as they awaited his return.

It was hard trying to reassure them that their daddy loved them and would be back when he could. I knew he loved them and wanted to make sure they were taken care of properly. It seemed that I always woke up just before he got home.

It was such a good dream that I didn't want to wake up, sometimes. I loved them and wanted so badly to be their mother.

Why this exact dream came to me so often and for so many nights and years, I guess I will never know. I missed Thea, maybe. It always seemed so real that I would sometimes look for them when I first awoke. It would take a minute to realize that I was dreaming again.

I missed those girls that I never actually had. To this day, I can still see those two beautiful little girls with the long blond hair that I loved to brush as we started our days. They were my stepdaughters. I was their mother.

This was only a dream and I tried to get it out of my mind, but it just would not leave. I wasn't sure where it was coming from, but I was beginning to pray and ask God to teach me to be a good mother for the children He would surely someday send me.

After taking care of my siblings and Dorothea, I realized that it was not an easy chore, but I had so much love to give and wanted to be a good mother someday.

Chapter 80

My First Job

When I was seventeen, my parents told me that I could apply for a job if I wanted to. Being surprised, the idea took a little getting used to. Sandra was my baby, as far as I knew, and I would miss her if I went to work. She had somewhat filled a small part of the void that Thea had left in my heart. She also kept me active.

It was then that I began to realize how Mama must have felt, having to leave her children every day. I had to think about it for a while. Then one day, I decided to try. I would be eighteen in about six months.

I went that next week and applied for a job at the pants factory where Mama worked. For whatever reason, they hired me. I was working by the next Monday. Life is full of surprises. Aunt Alene lived near us and would take care of the little ones and the older ones were in school.

One of the hardest things about getting a job was knowing that I would not be there to help Ma with laundry and other things. I felt guilty, somehow, but I knew Alene and Lathy were there for her. I guess I just really missed her. She had always been my stronghold, but I realized I could not remain a child forever. I just treasured any time I got with her.

In a few months, my mom often introduced me to her friends as her old maid daughter. She had been married at fourteen. She didn't always even tell them my name. I knew that she loved me and was proud of me, however, I didn't always see it. Maybe, she was trying to lighten my anxieties in the workplace.

This job paid $1.60 per hour. That would mean over $50 a week. With that much money, I could buy us a dinette set and living room furniture. It took all Mama and Daddy could make just to provide the necessary things.

The bench that they had made was ok, but it would be nice to have chairs with backs. I wanted to do my part, so I bought some furniture and began making payments. Good old credit building, lol!

I was proud that I could get credit, but as I think back on it, my dad was the one they trusted. He trusted people and they trusted him. He always said a man was only as good as his word.

Anyway, I would make payments until they were all paid for. Oh well, it was nice to have the new chairs to sit on so, I was glad.

Life was different for me. I enjoyed sewing and the fact that I had a job. But I couldn't wait to get home to Sandra. I wondered if Mama felt the same way. It had never occurred to me that she might miss being home with her children. I thought she wanted to work.

Thinking back over the years of growing up, there have been many special times that we all enjoyed with Mama. I found myself thinking of them as I worked. It made the day go faster. She had always been a very hard worker and there was nothing she couldn't do. I was glad to finally get to enjoy time with her instead of watching children while she did other things. The one-on-one time was great.

No matter what we were asked to do, it was best to try. We got in trouble for saying, "I can't," about anything. Her words were, "Can't never could do anything, but I'll try usually gets the job done."

One of my favorite memories of her was waiting for Daddy to get home from work, so we could eat supper together. If we could find the time, after a long day's work in the factory, garden or something else, we would take songbooks outside and sing together, until he got home from work.

Mama taught us one very special song that we found in one of the books. It became one of my favorites! Funny thing is, when we sang it in church one night, I didn't even recognize the song. I had been so glad they had chosen it and then I couldn't sing it with them!

As I learned to read music and learned to play it on the piano, I just didn't like it. When I sang that song, after that, I wanted to play it by ear. I liked Momma's version much better, and never played it by note anymore. And I could not sing it at church with them. It just didn't work for me.

It had not occurred to me that she may have just made up the tune for us because we wanted to learn it. Or maybe that was how she had learned it.

Wow! My mother had musical talent that we never recognized. She did love to sing and did in church some, but she didn't go often. Most of the time she preferred to listen to Daddy play his guitar and sing. She usually, was busy cooking or something else, maybe even making ice cream, a special treat that we often enjoyed in the summer.

Music in our house was daily! I loved to sing with Daddy in the evenings. It seemed that music was the time to relax and release all the toils and trials of the day. One of my favorite songs that Daddy sang was Yellow Rose of Texas.

In later years he would call me Yellow Rose, as a CB handle. We would talk every morning. Somehow it made me feel special that he still wanted to check on his oldest girl, to make sure she was ok.

I am ever so thankful for the music in our family and for that old CB radio that kept us in touch.

I missed what I thought was my baby, Sandra, while I worked, but she seemed to be doing just fine without me. I felt good about being able to have a job and could do things for her that I never had before. I was always glad to get back home to her.

It seemed she missed me for a while, then she got used to my being gone. Between Aunt Alene and Ma, I guess she stayed busy and happy. I soon realized that Aunt Alene took much better care of her than I ever could have. She had wisdom of years I suppose.

Life would have been so empty without either of them. I didn't have any idea how life could change in such a short period of time, and I seemed to have much to learn. My life would never be the same.

Any time with Ma was treasured more than ever after my going to work, and I felt bad because I was not there to help her.

It had felt good to feel important and needed, however I soon realized that Alene and others were always there for her. It was a family who helped one another. Someone was always at their house. I have to wonder if Ma and Pa would have enjoyed more time alone.

No one picked cotton anymore because the combine had taken it over. Daddy hauled a lot of hay, and we all did what we could in the truck patches and gardens. It seemed that everything was changing, and life had never been so busy.

Chapter 81

My Unexpected Move

It was almost my eighteenth birthday and I was scared and knew nothing about life. I just felt that it would soon be time that my parents would expect me to move out and do the best I could.

Our house was small. I slept on the couch since Sandra had outgrown her baby bed. It was either that or in a bed with two sisters.

It made me feel proud to have helped with something. It felt good to sleep on the couch that I had purchased. The alone time was good also.

We had three small bedrooms and six children. Three children to a room, which was no big thing, it didn't take much room to sleep. Maybe the alone time was good for me.

Three boys slept in one bed, but I was seventeen and needed my space to think. However, I had to wait till everyone else was in bed to go to sleep. The record player was in the living room. I could change the records as I chose. We listened to it every night as we went to sleep. Either my parents or I would turn it off when the last one on the stack played.

I was working and told myself that in a year or two I might need to consider my own life a little. With no idea of what to even think about, I was in no hurry, just dreaming again, or so I thought.

Although, I stayed busy at home or at Ma's when I wasn't working, my work more than likely put more work on other parts of our family, especially with the gardens and other things.

I missed helping Ma with her washing. She had taught me to use the wringer washer. She always washed on Mondays and ironed on Tuesdays. I knew that Aunt Alene and Lathy would help her as they always had. We had each taken turns to help Ma over the years, but I missed my time with her. Wash day was sometimes like quilting day; it was family day.

Ma always ironed, even her sheets. I usually got to iron her pillowcases if I was there on Tuesdays, but as a teenager, she had taught me how to iron the sheets, not that we ever did at home, but Ma wanted her bed clean, fresh and with no wrinkles. It was fun times and I missed that time with her when I went to work.

Ironing sheets didn't happen at our house. We were doing good to iron the things we wore after Mama and I both went to work. To be honest, fewer things at our house got ironed from then on.

The gardens and truck patches of corn and beans were always ready for Mama and me when we got home from work in the summer. Everyone picked and canned as they found the time.

I was glad it was about over for the year, so we could spend more time on other things. I found that just because you have a job doesn't mean the work does itself at home. But I was tired and glad to see the seasons change. I would just love to have a few days to do nothing after work.

That was a funny thought; there are always children, cooking, and housework. Laundry day had changed to Saturday for us, so that day was taken. I found myself thankful that Alene or Lathy were helping Ma on Mondays. However, I truly missed my days of washing clothes with Ma in the washing machine that had taught me to be careful.

Study time was precious. Bible study got interrupted often. I could not wait to get to church each week. It was a day of total peace.

On my eighteenth birthday, I went to church and Sunday school, as usual, on the church bus.

God, being the awesome God that He is, was walking before me and opened a door that I did not know existed.

Totally unexpectedly, He brought a wonderful lady to church that morning. Her name was Betty Scrudder.

She was a Jr. High School teacher and as I began to realize, a devoted Christian. She said Happy Birthday and started talking to me. It was so easy to talk to her that I began talking when I usually would not have said much.

Before I knew what was happening, I told her that I was eighteen and planning to look for a place to live in town as soon as I could afford it. I wanted to be able to get to church without having to ask for a ride because I still didn't have a car or a driver's license. I needed to walk to church. I could get a ride to work.

We talked for a while after church, and she told me that she was looking for a roommate and asked if I would be interested in sharing the rent and expenses with her in a trailer.

I thought about it, and the fact that I was still paying for furniture. We went over what it would cost per month, and then I saw that it might work. I would soon be done with my payments.

I was glad God had allowed me to buy them for my family. It gave me a feeling of love and satisfaction because they had always taken good care of me. I was glad I got a chance to do something for them.

Betty had some furniture, and there was an extra bed in the trailer already. As I soon found out, it had a feather mattress! It was awesome!

The temptation was too great. I decided to try it, thinking that I could always go back home if it didn't work out or if Sandra missed me or I missed her too much.

To my parent's surprise, Betty brought me home after church that day and met them. I told them she was looking for a roommate to share expenses with and that I wanted to move in with her. I would get a ride to work from someone. Her trailer was right on the highway, near town.

As I nervously awaited their response, to my surprise, they just accepted what I told them with no questions or argument. It was like they expected it. I didn't know how to feel. I was happy, excited, and scared, all at the same time.

I expected them to mention the furniture, but they didn't. They would have tried to help pay for it, but it was my responsibility. I would do it. I'm sure they thought about it.

And then there was Ma and Pa; how could I move off and leave them? They had always been there for me. I thought they really needed me. There was always so much to do on that farm. But it was a big family and growing. Others would be there for them.

I am not sure why I even could think of such a thing because, they were always the ones doing for others. All those gardens and fields were for all of us; anyone who needed or wanted any of it, family, friends, or strangers, were welcomed to anything they wanted.

I wanted Betty to meet Ma, and I had to go tell her I was moving, or maybe ask her if she was ok with it. It was hard to tell her anything without wanting her advice. I told her I would come to visit as often as possible, knowing I didn't have a car.

To my surprise, she was ok with it. She just wanted me to be safe and happy. Her response was, "Just always read and do as the Good Book Says, and you'll be alright."

I could hardly believe this myself; all my life, I had wanted Mama and Daddy to live close enough to Ma so I could see her every day. Now, on my own accord, I was moving away from her with a stranger. What was I thinking? But somehow, it just felt right.

I went home and gathered some of my belongings and clothes and left with Betty that day. Life as I knew it was past, and a new adventure was coming.

I moved into her spare room that very day. I had never met this lady before, but everything about her said that Jesus was everything to her. I would have a way to church every service.

She had just moved there and started teaching at County Line School and had just joined Bethel Church. From that day on, it was like we were sisters and very best friends.

We became prayer partners and went to every service and other church services for miles around, especially any time there was a revival or special service. I would never have to miss church again, nor would my family if I could get them to go. God is so good!

Oh, at first, it was hard. I knew life had to go on, and I had to grow up. I found myself crying one day because I realized that with freedom came responsibility and no one to protect me. I had to make all of my own decisions, right or wrong. Mama had said that if I made my bed hard, I would just have to lay in it.

They would advise me but no longer tell me what to do. That was a scary thing. If I make mistakes, there is no one to blame but me. I didn't trust myself.

Betty and I would go pick up my siblings every service that they would agree to go. That had been my only hesitation about moving. I loved my baby sister so much and I missed the others also, but we all finally had a way to get to church every service! Sometimes, when we took the kids home, she would take me to visit Ma, but we couldn't stay as long as I would have liked.

When I moved out, I had left my bride doll and would get it later. Laura was older and thought it needed a haircut. When I came to visit one day, I found her clear plastic slipper in the yard and went to find my doll.

It wasn't the same doll anymore, so I gave it to Laura. I don't think she ever got a bride doll. Maybe Mama thought I should give her mine. She was right; I should, and finally did.

Things happened, and of course, life was not all peaches and cream. But if I needed anything, I knew who to go to. God would never leave or forsake me if I obeyed Him. It was my job to plant or water, but it was God's place to give the increase. I felt Him with me.

I had found a joy that I had never experienced, but I sure missed my family time, especially my baby sister. I even asked Mama if I could take her with me when I moved. I knew the answer, but I would see her often.

Betty was the perfect prayer partner. Her answer was to pray about everything, great or small. She was that strong Christian influence that I had needed for years. God will always provide if we ask him. In some ways, she reminded me of things Ma had said.

Several months later, the church started a visitation program. We went out by twos once a week. It was exciting meeting new people and offering children rides to church if their parents couldn't come.

Sometimes, I would take a turn watching the children so their mothers could go. Either way, I felt useful. The church grew, but I grew also. I had never dreamed of the chance to be and do what I was doing. My joy was overflowing, and I thanked God every day. God had much for me to do.

Soon, I was teaching Bible School and Sunday school. My life would never be the same. I understood how much other children needed a way to church. The blessings would have been unbelievable if I hadn't experienced them myself. Praying with Betty every night, sometimes for hours, really gave me peace and a greater desire to serve the Lord. He gave me what I didn't know I needed.

Before we prayed each evening, we went over our written prayer lists, naming each one and adding to them. Always fraying for both our families. Praising God for the prayers He had and would answer.

There were times when one or both of us had special burdens that were heavy, people with serious problems. Some nights, we prayed and cried and pleaded with God until way after midnight; praying until we felt a peace that God had heard us.

One of the things we both needed to pray about was moving closer to town. We had lived in the trailer for several months. I still didn't have a car. Some of my co-workers picked me up for work every day. What I really missed was my time with Ma. There just didn't seem to be enough time, and I still didn't have a car.

We found a perfect house near the pants factory where I worked. I could walk to work. That was money saved because I did not have to pay for a ride. God is always looking out for us. In His time, He provides for our needs.

It was a perfect house with two bedrooms, a living room, and a kitchen with a screened-in back porch. We had to purchase furniture, but that was ok. My other payments were paid off. I knew we could get more. Betty bought a living room suit, and I bought a dinette set for our big kitchen. Betty already had bedroom furniture, and I was able to purchase my first, very own bedroom suit.

I even got a desk that I was soon going to need for my correspondence school; my joy was overflowing. I was finally going to finish high school. Betty was such an encouragement to me.

We prayed for my parents to give their hearts totally to God and find the love for God that would bring them and their children to church. I wanted Mama to know the joy that I had come to know.

It was amazing that, on the nights that we stayed up so late praying, getting less than four or five hours of sleep, I felt as if I had slept all night and was refreshed and ready for a good day. I was not tired. God is Good! No time with our Lord is wasted.

Bible School was the highlight of my summer. Betty and I would pick up children for miles around, bringing in as many as we could fit into her car.

There were no seatbelts in the cars then, I guess because it seemed we stacked them three high at times. What a joy! I loved taking children to church, which otherwise might never have had an opportunity to hear about God's love.

My heart cried for some of the children who had so little, sometimes, so little love. The children invited children. We picked up what we could, while others picked up as many as they could. God would make a way. We could not refuse anyone. Betty and I often took several of them home with us for lunch after church on Sunday.

Always getting attached, those children became my life. I tried but didn't always get to bring Sandra and Laura, or the boys home with me. Mama would take them home on the times that she came because she worked during the week and wanted her children with her on Sundays. I was glad when Mama finally started coming to church more.

She was saved and baptized within that year and would never miss a service after that. I guess you could say she hit the ground running. She became very active in church and studied her Bible every day.

This was the mother I had long been praying for. I wondered what it would be like for the other children now that she was saved. She was a hard worker at anything she did. I was looking forward to seeing her work in church.

Before long, she was teaching Sunday School and bringing her children and any others that she could to church with her. Her car was as full as Betty's. It was time to praise the Lord again.

She would not stop there. In later years, she would carry on as Betty and others had done for her children. She would take many children to church for as long as she could. Many would be saved because of my mother. Her kids, Sunday school kids, were taught to sing, I Have Decided to Follow Jesus.

Some might even think it was funny that she was doing for other children what some had done for hers. Mama was glad that I had found such a friend and life. Betty had been good for her, also.

Being older than me, Mama probably thought Betty would be taking care of me, but what she did was treat me as her equal.

We shared everything; expenses, cooking, housework, and everything else equally, except I didn't have a car. That worked out because we went everywhere together, anyway.

The greatest joy of our summer was Vacation Bible School. It was my first year to teach Bible School and I felt truly blessed. I took my vacation that week. Sometimes, we had over a hundred children in Bible School. I loved all my students, even those who were a little challenging.

Our lives were very full of work and church, but I missed my time with Ma and hoped she knew that I was thinking about her all the time. Every opportunity that I got to go see her was priceless. I would be glad if I could get a car and driver's license so I could go see her more often.

She had always been there for all of us. It was hard for me to go weeks at a time, sometimes not seeing her. I felt that I needed to do whatever I could for her. I loved her so much more than I ever thought possible and longed for more time with her, but God is Good. He would make a way in His time and in His way. All I could do was pray for her and go to see her whenever I had the opportunity. I was sure she was often praying for me.

Author's Biography
Charlotte Krigbaum Tucker Rowlett

Charlotte Krigbaum was the oldest of six children and grew upon a farm in Logan County. Born in 1952 to Dale and Peggy (Hicks) Krigbaum, she was raised near Paris, Arkansas during the transition time from the horse and wagon days to riding in cars and trucks.

She spent many hours trying to help her grandparents on the farm, to find that they were the ones helping her, encouraging her to use whatever talents God had given her. She wished to write in order to share their memories and stories with her children. They lived a simple country life, poor, but never knew it.

I am Charlotte. we lived near Paris but were in the Magazine school district, so we got to ride the school bus at least an hour both ways. One of the ways we passed the time was by singing. My cousin, Brenda, had a beautiful voice and knew lots of songs, so we sang as much as the driver would allow.

I had some really great teachers who taught us that everyone had talents, not all the same, but we should be the best that we could be at whatever talent we had. I never did find mine, so I tried lots of things. Writing is a passion that I can't seem to ignore.

Growing up near my grandma and grandpa was a real blessing. They helped all of us more than we knew. They had such an impact on my life that I wanted to write a book about them and the way they seemed to be able to cope with anything that happened, and carry on with a smile. I always hoped that when I grew up, I could be like my grandmother, Laura (Graham) Krigbaum.

I fall really short of that; however, I did learn a lot from her which has sustained me in many situations and hardships that would also help me in raising my own children. I feel blessed beyond measure to have had so many years with her.

As the Bible teaches, the trial of our faith is a very important part of life. God is able to handle anything we have to deal with in His way and in His time. He knows what we need before we do or think to ask.

Ma seemed to have all the answers, and I am still looking, as I enjoy my grandchildren. I know she prayed for me.

As a mother of seven and a grandmother, I have found myself many times thinking, what would Ma do in this situation? I found that I needed a lot more time in the Good Book (Bible) and a lot more prayer time to raise my children.

It was in the still of the nights that I got more out of reading and prayer time. It seemed that the more I sacrificed my sleep, the more strength God gave me for the next day.

My daddy's large family often worked together and played music together. It has remained an important part of my life.

I owned a music store for some time, hoping to keep my children interested in music and passing it on to their children. It wasn't so much about the music as it was just enjoying time together and helping one another whenever needed, as Ma and Pa had encouraged all of us to do.

In 2014, I published a condensed version of this book; however, there is too much left out of it, so I want to go back and add so many things I left out. To do that, I must put it in two books. This is only a part of the story. The second book is being edited and hopefully will be done soon.

www.ingramcontent.com/pod-product-compliance
Lightning Source LLC
Chambersburg PA
CBHW051346110526
44591CB00025B/2927